Innovation, Entrepreneurship, and Technological Change

Innovation, Entrepreneurship, and Technological Change

Albert N. Link

Donald S. Siegel

OXFORD
UNIVERSITY PRESS

*This book has been printed digitally and produced in a standard specification
in order to ensure its continuing availability*

OXFORD
UNIVERSITY PRESS

Great Clarendon Street, Oxford OX2 6DP
United Kingdom

Oxford University Press is a department of the University of Oxford.
It furthers the University's objective of excellence in research, scholarship,
and education by publishing worldwide. Oxford is a registered trade mark of
Oxford University Press in the UK and in certain other countries

© Oxford University Press 2007

The moral rights of the author have been asserted

First published 2007
Reprinted 2012

British Library Cataloguing in Publication Data
Data available

Library of Congress Cataloging in Publication Data
Data available

ISBN 978-0-19-926883-2

For Carol and Sandra

☐ ACKNOWLEDGEMENTS

This book has benefited from the advice and assistance of many individuals. Our academic friends, and numerous economists and management scholars with whom we interact professionally, provided useful comments on various aspects of this project. We thank specifically Philippe Aghion, Leanne Atwater, David Audretsch, Richard Disney, Maryann Feldman, Mike Gallaher, John Haltiwanger, Jonathan Haskel, Susan Helper, Adam Jaffe, John Jankowski, Boyan Jovanovic, Catherine Morrison Paul, Jeff Petrusa, Philip Phan, Bruno van Pottelsberghe, Kjell Salvanes, Robert Sauer, John Scott, David Waldman, Charles Wessner, Paul Westhead, and Mike Wright for encouragement and for insightful suggestions.

We are also grateful for the comments that we received on previous versions of research presented in this book from the seminar participants at Wake Forest University, Purdue, Arizona, Arizona State, Universite Libre de Bruxelles, CERGI-EI, UC-Riverside, University of Illinois at Chicago, University of Sussex, University of London–Royal Holloway College, University of Nottingham, University of Lancaster, University of Leicester, Rensselaer Polytechnic Institute, NBER, New York University, Max Planck Institute, Stevens Institute of Technology, CEPR, Norwegian School of Economics and Business Administration, Conference on Comparative Analysis of Enterprise Data (CAED), EARIE, Strategic Management Society Meetings, International Schumpeter Society Conference, the Academy of Management Meetings, National Research Council, and the Technology Transfer Society Conference.

The financial support of the Alfred P. Sloan Foundation, through the NBER Project on Industrial Technology and Productivity; the Kauffman Foundation; and the National Science Foundation is gratefully acknowledged. Various aspects of our own research discussed herein were graciously funded by these organizations.

We are also deeply indebted to the many administrators, scientists, managers, and entrepreneurs who agreed to be interviewed in our qualitative studies and those conducted by other authors.

Finally, and most importantly, we thank our loving wives, Carol and Sandra, and our wonderful children, Jamie and Kevin, and William, Joshua, Shira, and Ben, for providing the warmth and emotional sustenance that made this project possible. We dedicate this book to them.

☐ CONTENTS

LIST OF FIGURES   viii
LIST OF TABLES   ix

1 Innovation, entrepreneurship, and technological change: an overview   1

2 The entrepreneur as innovator   14

3 Fundamental concepts of innovation and technological change   27

4 R&D and firm performance   36

5 The economics of R&D and economic growth   74

6 Innovation in the service sector   86

7 Technological spillovers and general purpose technologies   97

8 University technology transfer   108

9 University research parks   138

10 Government as entrepreneur and innovator   149

11 Innovation, entrepreneurship, and technological change: a research
   agenda   171

REFERENCES   180
INDEX   206

☐ LIST OF FIGURES

3.1 Labor-saving, capital-saving, and neutral technological change, output held constant   29

6.1 Model of innovation relevant to the manufacturing sector   91

6.2 Model of innovation relevant to the service sector   93

10.1 Spillover gap between social and private rates of return to R&D   153

10.2 A public good model of R&D spending   166

☐ LIST OF TABLES

2.1 Summary of the entrepreneur as innovator from an historical perspective   26

4.1 International R&D expenditures for selected countries, by source of funds, 2002–4   38

4.2 International R&D expenditures for selected countries, by performer, 2002–4   39

4.3 Alternative definitions of R&D   42

4.4 Firm-level empirical studies of the relationship between R&D and productivity growth   48

4.5 Empirical studies of the relationship between research partnerships and firm performance   53

4.6 Event studies of technology investment activities   58

4.7 Studies of the relationship between information technology and firm performance   59

4.8 Empirical studies of the impact of R&D and information technology on wages and labor composition   66

5.1 Estimates of the rate of technological change, post-World War II studies of the US economy   75

5.2 Comparison of old growth theory and new growth theory   81

5.3 Potential sources of technological/knowledge spillovers   82

5.4 Industry and aggregate-level empirical studies of the relationship between information technology and productivity growth   83

6.1 Public good characteristics of the elements of innovation in the manufacturing sector   92

8.1 Quantitative and qualitative research on the effectiveness of licensing of university-based inventions   122

8.2 Quantitative and qualitative research on university-based entrepreneurial activity   123

9.1 Selected empirical studies of university research parks   144

10.1 Empirical studies of the economic impact of public investments in technology infrastructure   160

10.2 Empirical studies of the social need for public investments in technology infrastructure   163

10.3 Taxonomy of public–private partnerships   164

10.4 Public–private partnerships: the National Cooperative Research Act of 1984   165

10.5 Recent studies of the effects of research partnerships on economic performance   168

1 Innovation, entrepreneurship, and technological change: an overview

1.1. Introduction

There is growing interest in the managerial and policy implications of innovation and entrepreneurship. This is a natural result of the shift toward a knowledge economy, as well as a substantial increase in public investment in institutions (e.g. universities) and programs (e.g. the Small Business Innovation Research (SBIR) Program) designed to stimulate such activities.

A concomitant trend has been the rise of research partnerships involving firms, universities, nonprofit organizations, and government agencies. Examples of research partnerships are research joint ventures (RJVs), strategic alliances and networks involving high-technology organizations, industry consortia (e.g. SEMATECH), cooperative research and development agreements (CRADAs) involving federal laboratories and firms, engineering research centers (ERCs) and industry–university cooperative research centers (IUCRCs) sponsored by the US National Science Foundation (NSF), federally funded research and development centers (FFRDCs), science/research parks and high-technology incubators (many of which are located at universities), and licensing and sponsored research agreements involving universities, government laboratories, and firms, and university-based start-ups.

Some of this growth in research partnerships can be attributed to at least three public policy initiatives:

- an increase in the incidence of public–private partnerships
- relaxation of antitrust enforcement related to collaborative research, and
- promotion of the transfer of technology from universities to firms.

The end result is a complex web of institutions and agents engaged in innovation and entrepreneurship.

Understanding the antecedents and consequences of innovation and entrepreneurship is critical because technological change has been shown to be related to improvements in economic performance at the firm, industry, and national level (Link and Siegel 2003). At the regional level, there has also been a substantial increase in activities to promote technology-based economic development. Universities are increasingly being viewed by policy-makers as engines of regional economic growth via the commercialization of intellectual property through technology transfer. The primary commercial mechanisms for technology transfer are licensing agreements, RJVs, and university-based start-ups.

Our book will provide a comprehensive and integrative overview of the burgeoning literature on innovation, entrepreneurship, and technological change. This literature is highly interdisciplinary and heterogeneous. Many authors have examined the *institutions* that have emerged to facilitate innovation and entrepreneurship, such as firms, universities, science/research parks, incubators, industrial laboratories, university technology transfer offices (TTOs), and IUCRCs. Other authors have focused more directly on innovative and entrepreneurial *agents*, such as industry and academic scientists or entrepreneurs in firms or universities. While most of these studies have been based on econometric methods, others employ qualitative methods and field-based interviews.

A key objective of this book is to synthesize key research findings from management and economics on these topics in a user-friendly format for broad consumption by scholars and students in economics, sociology, organizational theory, strategy, and entrepreneurship. To accomplish this goal, we:

- precisely define key concepts
- present an organized framework for analyzing innovation, entrepreneurship, and technological change
- provide interpretative historical examples
- compare and contrast different theoretical frameworks
- provide user-friendly interpretation of quantitative and qualitative findings, and
- emphasize international comparisons of innovation infrastructure and technology policy.

Innovation, entrepreneurship, and technological change are not sequential concepts; each is a process that builds upon, as well as affects, the other two. The title of this book is not intended to suggest that innovation leads to entrepreneurial activity, and entrepreneurial activity leads to technological change. Many scholars have envisioned a variation of the so-called linear model, but such a model is not descriptive of reality. Rather, the title refers to the three processes with which this book relates. These three concepts are interrelated over time meaning that one affects all others as: Innovation ↔ Entrepreneurship ↔ Technological Change ↔ Innovation.

This book discusses innovation, entrepreneurship, and technological change as interrelated concepts, although the focus of any particular chapter, especially the early chapters in which certain fundamental concepts are discussed, is likely only to be on one of the concepts. And, as interrelated concepts, we discuss them from three interrelated perspectives: an economic, managerial, and public policy perspective. Finally, to the extent possible, our discussions are segmented to emphasize the agents and institutions that are involved. By agents we mean the micro unit to which a concept is related, generally the individual; by institutions we mean a more aggregate unit to which the same concept is related, generally a firm, a university, or a public agency.

1.2. **Some basic concepts**

Several basic concepts are pervasive throughout this book. Here, we only briefly introduce and define these concepts; each is discussed in greater detail in the appropriate chapter(s).

The first concept is entrepreneurship. As we write in Chapter 2: 'throughout intellectual history as we know it, the entrepreneur has worn many faces and played many roles' (Hébert and Link 1988: 152). Hébert and Link have defined the entrepreneur as: '... someone who specializes in taking responsibility for and making judgmental decisions that affect the location, the form, and the use of goods, resources, or institutions' (1988: 155). Thus, broadly speaking, entrepreneurship refers to perception of opportunity and the ability to act on that perception. In this book we focus exclusively on the business and public policy implications of entrepreneurship.

The second concept is innovation. Following Bozeman and Link (1983: 4): 'Invention is the creation of something new. An invention becomes an innovation when it is put in use.'

When innovation is conceptualized in a static sense, as just above, an innovation put in use is a new technology. When the innovation is the final marketable result, it is called a product innovation; when the innovation is applied in subsequent production processes, it is called a process innovation.

More interesting for our purposes is a dynamic view of innovation, that is, of the process whereby an invention becomes an innovation—the so-called innovation process. Viewed in this context, there is a distinct role for entrepreneurship. When innovation is viewed as a process, the role of public policy also becomes clearer, namely the role becomes one of enhancing or speeding up the innovation process.

As with entrepreneurship and innovation, the concepts of technology and technological change are varied. In a narrow sense, as suggested above, technology refers to a specific physical or tangible tool—an innovation. In a broader sense, technology refers to intangible tools such as technological ethic or organizational technology; technological change describes an entire social process. We will discuss technological change as it specifically related to productivity and economic growth.

In Section 1.3 we discuss innovation, entrepreneurship, and technological change from the historical perspective of the development of the US biotechnology industry. This focused discussion is intended to be introductory material to illustrate, through example, how these three concepts are interrelated.

1.3. **An introductory illustration: the development and commercialization of biotechnologies**

The development and commercialization of biotechnology in the United States represents a phenomenon that illustrates the interrelationship among the concepts of innovation, entrepreneurship, and technological change.[1] This illustration sets the stage for subsequent chapters in the sense that the topics covered relate to innovation, entrepreneurship, and technological change.[2]

The discussion below emphasizes that the historical process of the development and commercialization of biotechnology is not one that began with an innovation (and the relevant innovations were generally funded by the US government; this fact anticipates that the government often acts as an entrepreneur as we discuss in a subsequent chapter), was exploited by entrepreneurs (individual scientists and their universities), and subsequently brought about technological change and attendant economic growth (regional growth as well as national growth). One could view this process as a linear progression, but it would be a view that we eschew. Rather, as we describe below, the development and commercialization of biotechnologies integrates these three concepts in an evolutionary way.

1.3.1. BACKGROUND INFORMATION: DEFINING BIOTECHNOLOGY

A number of alternative, yet similar, definitions of biotechnology appear in the academic, as opposed to the scientific, literature. Several of these definitions are excerpted below to illustrate the evolving nature of the underlying technology; these alternative definitions are discussed for completeness rather than as motivation to posit one definition over another.

According to the US Department of Commerce (2003: 3):

...biotechnology [is] the application of molecular and cellular processes to solve problems, conduct research, and create goods and services.

The hallmark of biotechnology, according to the US Department of Commerce (2003: 7) is:

...cellular and genetic techniques that manipulate cellular and subcellular building blocks for applications in various scientific fields and industries such as medicine, animal health, agriculture, marine life, and environmental management.

More simply, the North Carolina Biotechnology Center defines biotechnology as:[3]

A collection of technologies that use living cells and/or biological molecules to solve problems and make useful products.

This definition is similar to the definition posited by Toole (2003: 176):

At the broadest level, biotechnology refers to the use of micro-organisms to make or modify a product or process.

Finally, Audretsch (2001: 3) defined biotechnology as:

...techniques and technologies that apply the principles of genetics, immunology and molecular, cellular and structural biology to the discovery and development of novel products.

It is important to emphasize that it is not the products and processes associated with biotechnology that are its defining characteristics, but rather, biotechnology is defined with regard to the techniques or fundamental technologies used to develop products and processes. According to Paugh and Lafrance (1997: 21), for example:

...biotechnology is not defined by its products but by the technologies used to make those products. Biotechnology refers to a set of enabling technologies by a broad array of companies in their research, development, and manufacturing activities.

Cells contain genetic material, DNA, that acts like a blueprint for the function and structure of the cell. Through biotechnology, the genetic blueprint can be isolated, copied, and rearranged at the molecular level to alter or manipulate the function and structure of the cell (Paugh and Lafrance 1997).

In all likelihood, these and like definitions of biotechnology will be modified over time as the biotechnology industry, as we now know it, matures and as the underlying technologies become embedded within the production processes of other industries. For example, molecular and cellular biology will increasingly be integrated with chemical and computer technology as the process of research and development (R&D) becomes further automated. And definitions that are based on the techniques and technologies currently in use will evolve as new techniques and technologies are developed and put into place.

1.3.2. DEFINING THE US BIOTECHNOLOGY INDUSTRY

Definitions aside, the term biotechnology industry remains somewhat misleading to academics, although the term is casually and widely used by public policymakers as well as the popular press. One possible reason for this lack of definitional clarity about the bounds or dimensions of the industry is that there is in the United States, for example, as well as in other industrialized nations, no single group of homogeneous firms or organizations that clearly defines such an industry (Toole 2003). In the United States, firms that are involved in the technology that resulted from advances in bioscience, namely biotechnology, are not classified separately for industrial census purposes. One reason for this classification void is that the application areas of biotechnology are relatively new and they are themselves evolving. And another reason is that the scope of application of that technology across traditionally defined industries is vast and constantly changing. Accordingly, a number of scholars have argued that one should not think of a biotechnology industry in the traditional sense of products and products produced by similar techniques, but rather in terms of an agglomeration of scientific and product collaborations (Liebeskind et al. 1996; Oliver 2001, 2004; Weisenfeld et al. 2001; Zucker et al. 2002).

The US Department of Commerce (2003) recently surveyed a large number of US firms that identified themselves as biotech organizations. These organizations operate in a variety of traditionally defined industries, thus illustrating the heterogeneous nature of the application of the underlying technologies. The application industries, along with the 2002 percentage (rounded) of respondents in each, are basic industries and materials (4.3%), chemical manufacturers (4.4%), information and electronics (4.3%), machinery manufacture (0.6%), medical substances and devices (32.6%), various services (R&D, testing, diagnostic, etc.) (40.9%), and 13.0 percent of the respondents could not identify a specific application industry.

Prevezer (1998), among others, conceptualized the so-called biotechnology industry in terms of the applications that the sector develops:

- therapeutics sector—developing therapeutic application (drugs)
- diagnostic sector—creates diagnostic applications
- chemicals sector—makes pesticides, insecticides, and new chemicals
- agriculture sector—develops seed, plant, and animal applications

- food and cosmetic sector—formulates enzyme applications
- environmental sector—deals with waste products, and
- energy sector—seeking biomass energy sources.

Although somewhat imprecise, and ill-defined from a strict economics definition of an industry as discussed below, the number of new so-called biotech firms has increased over the past two decades in all industrial nations, albeit erratically, over time in a given nation as well as over time across nations. As opposed to defining the biotechnology industry in terms of application industries or areas, one possible alternative is to think about the biotechnology industry in terms of the sectors from which those organizations involved in the overall value added process come. Thus, one could think of the biotechnology industry as having three distinct segments. The first segment includes universities and research institutes where the underlying bioscience base upon which the technology is created; the second segment includes dedicated biotechnology firms (DBFs) which rely on the science base and, building upon it, develop new technological procedures and techniques; and the third segment includes user firms which apply the technological procedures of DBFs to application areas, and these firms are often referred to as biotechnology commercializing firms (BCFs).[4]

According to Lehman (2003), using Ernst & Young proprietary data from 2002, the top five states in the United States in terms of the number (in parentheses) of biotechnology firms—DBFs plus BCFs—were (in 2002): California (410), Massachusetts (210), Maryland (95), North Carolina (87), and Pennsylvania (71).

1.3.3. HISTORICAL BACKGROUND ABOUT BIOSCIENCE AND BIOTECHNOLOGY[5]

Science, in a broad sense, is the search for knowledge, and that search is based on observed facts and truths. Thus, science begins with known starting conditions and searches for unknown end results (Nightingale 1998). Technology, in contrast, is the application of new and unapplied knowledge, learned through science, to known practical problems. Technological change is the rate at which new and unapplied knowledge is diffused and put into use in the economy. Thus, and this distinction is important for understanding the biotechnology industry, bioscience is the search for new knowledge in the biological sciences, and biotechnology is the application of bioscience to new products and processes. This distinction parallels the Bozeman and Link (1983) distinctions among invention and innovation and technology mentioned above and discussed in subsequent chapters.

The biotechnology industry began with breakthroughs in the biosciences.[6]

- In 1953, Watson and Crick discovered the double helix structure of DNA.
- In 1957, Kornberg revealed how DNA is replicated through the discovery of the enzyme DNA polymerase I.
- In 1973, Cohen and Boyer developed the recombinant DNA (r-DNA) technique.
- In 1975, the first monoclonal antibodies were discovered.

It is important to point out that the above four chronological events are the precursor events to the development of the underlying bioscience. While they are, indeed, events that occurred in the United States at US universities, the resulting knowledge has public good characteristics that thus represented at that time and now the building blocks for worldwide applications.

The scientists involved in these events were entrepreneurs. They not only perceived an opportunity but also they acted upon it and their actions resulted in a discovery and a patented invention. Subsequently, others perceived the importance of these discoveries and patented inventions and acted upon that knowledge to create related products and processes—innovations. The application of those products and processes brought about technological change and firm performance, and in turn it affected overall economic growth. It should also be emphasized that the fundamental inventions of these scientists was aided by public funds through research grants. The entrepreneur as innovator is the topic of Chapter 2.

The four dated bioscience breakthroughs bulleted above were used—perceived and acted upon—very quickly by DBFs to develop biotechnologies, and, not surprisingly, these DBFs located near the bioscience breakthroughs in San Francisco and nearby Silicon Valley and in Cambridge, MA.

- In 1976, Genentech (a DBF) was founded in San Francisco by venture capitalist Robert Swanson of Kleiner Perkins and professor Herbert Boyer of the University of California at San Francisco.[7] The goal of the new company was to use bioscience to synthesize human insulin. This was accomplished in 1978.
- In 1978, Biogen (a DBF) was founded in Cambridge, MA, by Harvard professor Walter Gilbert, among others including MIT professor Phillip Sharpe.
- In 1979, Genentech developed the first synthetic human growth hormone, somatropin.
- In 1980, based on the Nobel Prize winning research of Gilbert in sequencing nucleotides, Biogen agreed to allow pharmaceutical company Schering-Plough (a BCF) to license beta interferon.

- In 1982, the Food and Drug Administration (FDA) approved the Genentech–Eli Lilly (a pharmaceutical company and a BCF, as well as a competitor of Schering-Plough) product, Humulin, for commercial use.

There are at least two generalizations that come from these parallel pioneering bioscience and biotechnology histories of innovative activity and related entrepreneurial activities. First, unique, specialized knowledge—tacit knowledge which requires face-to-face interaction as opposed to codified knowledge—is prerequisite or a necessary condition for the creation of a DBF.[8] Genentech in San Francisco and Biogen in Cambridge, MA, were formed on the basis of tacit bioscience knowledge from the University of California at San Francisco and from Harvard University and MIT, respectively; this knowledge was transferred through scientists.[9] Second, DBFs rely on strategic alliances with established companies—pharmaceutical BCFs in these early instances—to bridge the intellectual gap between science and technology, and then technology and commercialized products.[10]

Knowledge per se is a pure public good. Knowledge per se has the characteristic of being a nonexcludable good, meaning that others cannot be prevented from accessing it. Knowledge per se also has the characteristic of being a nonrivalrous good, meaning that one can benefit from the knowledge without reducing the ability of others to use it. That said, codified knowledge is closer to being a pure public good than is tacit knowledge. The application of tacit knowledge is partially excludable; it is a complement to, in the case of biotechnology, bioscience.

1.3.4. BIOTECHNOLOGY CLUSTERS

According to Porter (1998: 78–9), clusters are:

...geographic concentrations of interconnected companies and institutions in a particular field....A cluster's boundaries are defined by the linkages and complementarities across industries and institutions that are most important to competition....Clusters rarely conform to standard industrial classification systems, which fail to capture many important actors and relationships in competition....Clusters promote both competition and cooperation....Clusters represent a kind of new spatial organization form in between arm's-length markets on the one hand and hierarchies, or vertical integration, on the other. A cluster, then, is an alternative way of organizing a value chain.

On the basis of the historical activity surrounding the San Francisco and Cambridge phenomena, it follows that DBFs would spin-off from universities heavily involved in the biosciences and employing key scientists, and these entrepreneurial biotechnology firms would be within clusters of each other and of pharmaceutical firms or other application firms.

The San Diego biotechnology area developed similarly to the San Francisco and Cambridge areas. The Salk Institute was founded in 1955, followed by the Scripps Research Institute in 1960 and the University of California at San Diego (UCSD) in 1964. The Burnham Institute was founded in 1976 by William H. Fishman and his wife Lillian Fishman. Fishman spent his research career at Tufts University School of Medicine. The Foundation originally focused on cancer research but today its focus is much broader. Hybritech was founded in 1978 and was San Diego's first DBF; it was acquired by Eli Lilly in 1986. Hybritech became the anchor firm in the San Diego area (Porter 2001*a*, 2001*b*).[11]

Aside from these three regional cases, Zucker and Darby and their colleagues (1997, 1998)—as well as others such as Audretsch and Stephan (1996)—using US data have demonstrated empirically that the timing and location of new DBFs can be explained in large part by the presence of bioscience scientists in a particular location at a particular point in time.

Why do biotechnology firms cluster?[12] From a theoretical perspective, there are both demand and supply forces at work that result in the clustering of DBFs, as well as the clustering of larger application firms with whom the DBFs have a strategic alliance relationship. On the demand side, within a cluster there are sophisticated users for the bioscience-based biotechnology of the DBFs.[13] And, search costs for users of the technology are minimized. Of course, there are disadvantages associated with clustering, namely greater competition for the developed technologies.

On the supply side, there are within clusters more skilled and specialized labor, although there is also more competition for that pool of labor. And, clusters provide a greater opportunity for knowledge—tacit knowledge in particular—spillovers. The theory of agglomeration economics emphasizes this latter point (Swann 1998).[14,15] According to Beaudry and Breschi (2003: 326):[16]

...transmission of technological knowledge works better within spatial boundaries because this type of knowledge has a tacit and uncodified nature and thus flows through networks of interpersonal communications.

1.3.5. SUMMARY OBSERVATIONS

This brief historical trace of the development of the US biotechnology industry illustrates the interrelationships among innovation, entrepreneurship, and technological change. Through the industry's evolution, university scientists have taken on both the role of entrepreneur as well as innovator, and given their innovations firms have been born and have themselves acted entrepreneurially to contribute to technological change and economic growth.

1.4. **Overview of the book**

In Chapter 2 we discuss, from an intellectual history perspective, the entrepreneur as innovator. Our discussion draws on the writings of early philosophers and economists, Joseph Schumpeter in particular, who have molded the concept of the entrepreneur and have helped to define what he or she (hereafter, he) does as relates to innovation. Our emphasis on this historical treatment of the entrepreneur follows from two premises. The first premise is that the entrepreneur, or entrepreneurship, is a term or concept that elicits a wide range of interpretations. Thus, through the historical trace in this chapter were attempt to bound the person or concept. The second premise follows in part from the first; contemporary teachings about entrepreneurship are for the most part void of an understanding and appreciation of the intellectual history related to the person or concept. When an historical grounding is present, or at least referenced—and both are rare—contemporary scholars begin with Schumpeter's writings yet generally fail to place those writings in any perspective.

In Chapter 3, we introduce some fundamental concepts on the relationships among innovation, entrepreneurship, and technological change. These relationships are critical for understanding the economic underpinnings of studies about R&D, an input into the innovation process, and firm performance (Chapter 4) and about R&D and economic growth (Chapter 5). In Chapter 3, we present models of technological change that have become the cornerstone of what has become known as the economics of R&D and the fields of innovation and technology policy. In later chapters, we build on these models to emphasize the interrelationship among innovation, entrepreneurship, and technological change.

Our focus in Chapters 4 and 5 is on the extant empirical literature as is our emphasis throughout the book. We contend that academics often overlook the evolution of prior scholarship for one reason or another. Thus, we devote a significant portion of these chapters to a review of the literature with a specific emphasis on levels of analysis—individuals, universities, firms, industries, and economies.

In Chapter 6, we analyze innovation in the service sector and compare and contrast innovative activity in the manufacturing sector to that of the service sector. In many industrialized nations the service sector is the largest sector, and in most industrialized nations it has in recent years been the fastest growing. For the most part, economists have ignored the empirical study of innovation as it relates to the service sector possibly because data are less available and economic models are posited in terms of a well defined and measurable output.

In Chapter 7, we illustrate the importance of technological spillovers in an economy through two examples of general purpose technologies (GPTs), the

Internet and nanotechnology. While this chapter traces the evolution of these two particular GPTs, it nevertheless segues into subsequent discussions about technology transfer, especially from universities (Chapters 8 and 9) and about the government as entrepreneur and innovator (Chapter 10).

In Chapter 8, our emphasis shifts toward university-based technology transfer and the related role of universities as critical institutions, along with their faculty who are critical agents, within the innovation, entrepreneurship, technological change paradigm. Through an extensive review of the literature we illustrate the role and importance of university technology transfer in these three paradigm activities.

Related to the role of universities is a burgeoning element of that institution, namely science/research parks (hereafter research parks). Extant knowledge about the role of university research parks is discussed in Chapter 9, as is the related empirical literature.

The topic of Chapter 10 is the government as entrepreneur and innovator. Our emphasis is on the government as a provider of technology infrastructure. We illustrate in this chapter how technology infrastructure relates to earlier models of economic and productivity growth, and we offer an economic rationale for public sector support of innovation and a rationale for the government acting as an entrepreneur.

Finally, we offer a concluding statement in Chapter 11.

NOTES

1. This section draws from Link (2005a).
2. We thank Maryann Feldman for suggesting biotechnology as an integrating example for the book.
3. See, http://www.ncbiotech.org/biotech101/glossary.cfm#b
4. The term corresponding to DBFs in many European and Asian countries is new technology-based firms (NTBFs) (Lehrer and Asakawa 2004).
5. Public support of the biosciences is important but not within the boundaries of this illustrative example. For a detailed discussion of so-called public–private partnership policies, see Link (2006b). It should be noted, however, that much of the path breaking bioscience research was funded by the National Institutes of Health and the National Cancer Institute, and in 1980 the US Supreme Court in *Diamond* v. *Chakrabarty* approved the principle of patenting genetically engineered life forms; in that year, Cohen and Boyer received a patent for gene cloning.
6. This historical timeline comes from http://www.ncbiotech.org/biotech101/timeline.cfm and from Orsenigo (1989).
7. According to Prevezer (2001: 26): 'The ethos of the early biotechnology firms such as Genetech…was one of openness and informality, encouraging an academic atmosphere in the hope of attracting high caliber research scientists and encouraging them to maintain their scientific links. …'

8. According to Powell et al. (2002: 291): 'The importance of tacit knowledge, face-to-face contact, and the ability to learn and manage across multiple projects are critical reasons for the continuing importance of geographical propinquity in biotech.'

9. Using US survey data, Audretsch and Stephan (1999a, 1999b) showed that about 50 percent of the founders of new biotechnology firms, DBFs, were from universities and about one-third of them retained their university affiliation after the firm was established.

10. According to Sharp (1991), early-on established pharmaceutical firms did not comprehend the vast applications of biotechnology and accordingly did not establish in-house R&D areas. By the mid-1980s, as market potential was realized, pharmaceutical companies developed in-house expertise—absorptive capacity (Cohen and Leventhal 1989)— and either formed strategic research alliances with DBFs or merged with them. Cooke (2001) demonstrates the importance of the DBF-to-BCF relationship in the UK.

11. Agrawal and Cockburn (2003) also emphasized the importance of anchor tenants for stimulating regional economic growth, in all industries not just in biotechnology. Anchor tenants because of their size and scope of research activities can more readily absorb university research and stimulate local industrial technology development.

12. Marshall (1920: 271–2) noted: 'When an industry has chosen a locality for itself it is likely to stay there long, so great are the advantages which people following the same skilled trade get from near neighborhood to one another ... And presently subsidiary trade grows up in the neighborhood.'

13. Orsenigo (2001) claims that Italy failed to develop biotechnology clusters due to an absence of research activity in firms with whom DBFs could collaborate. This is an important finding for those involved in technology-based economic growth.

14. See also, Audretsch (1998), Audretsch and Feldman (1996, 1999), Breschi and Lissoin (2001), Jaffe (1989), and Jaffe, Trajtenberg, and Henderson (1993) for empirical support of this agglomeration effect.

15. Swann, Prevezer, and Stout (1998) argued that incumbent firms in a cluster of similar firms will grow faster than new entrants because the incumbent firms are better placed to take advantage of knowledge spillovers.

16. Henderson (1986) and Krugman (1991) emphasized conceptually and empirically the importance of location, per se. Arthur (1989) and David (1985) emphasized conceptually the related importance of network externalities. David (1985) also argued in general, but this argument applies particularly well to biotechnology clusters, that chance or historical events (e.g. scientists with a breakthrough discovery) can lock a technology (e.g. an industry in the case of biotechnology) on a particular path of development. See also, Porter (1998). Clustering gives positive feedback to continue the path dependency of the particular technology. This idea has, according to Arrow (2000), its origins in the early writings of Veblen and Cournot. It also can be traced to the evolutionary economic concepts of Nelson and Winter (1982).

2 The entrepreneur as innovator

2.1. Introduction

One role of an entrepreneur is as an innovator, an association made popular by Joseph Schumpeter. As Schumpeter's view has come to dominate the field, the earlier history of the concept—particularly that part which linked entrepreneurship and innovation—has become increasingly obscured and forgotten.[1] This chapter attempts to set forth a chronological trace of the entrepreneur as innovator in an effort to present the relevant intellectual history as well as to presage Schumpeter's contributions so as to enrich the analytical nexus between entrepreneurship and innovation.[2] Following Hébert and Link (2006), we categorically group theories of entrepreneurship as supply-side or demand-side, and for each we discuss the contributions of the early writers on this topic.

2.2. Supply-side theories of entrepreneurship

A supply-side theory of entrepreneurship emphasizes the role of the entrepreneur in production and distribution of goods and services for which there is an independently determined demand. Such theories essentially address the question: Given the pattern of demand for existing goods and services, what role does the entrepreneur play in the market place? The earliest inquiries into the subject tended to focus on this question.

2.2.1. RICHARD CANTILLON (1680–1734)

The term *entrepreneur* is a word of French origin that does not appear often in the prehistory of economics. Its common, though imprecise, use in the eighteenth century is corroborated by an entry in Savary's *Dictionnaire Universel de Commerce* (1723) in which *entrepreneur* is defined as one who undertakes a project; a manufacturer; and a master builder. An earlier form of the word, *entrepredeur*, appears as early as the fourteenth century (Hoselitz 1960). Throughout the sixteenth and seventeenth centuries the most frequent usage of the term connoted a government contractor, usually of military fortifications or public works.

The first significant writer to make frequent and obtrusive use of the term in a semblance of its modern form was Cantillon, an eighteenth-century businessman and financier. Cantillon's *Essai* is a watershed in the history of entrepreneurship because it establishes the entrepreneur as a central figure in the marketplace. Describing the nascent market economy of eighteenth-century Europe, Cantillon established the entrepreneur as the intermediary between landowners and hirelings. Landowners—the fashion leaders of society—established patterns of consumption in conformance with their individual tastes and preferences. They, in turn, relegated production of goods and services to entrepreneurs, who bore the risks associated with market judgments about production and distribution. Although Cantillon's entrepreneurs did not engage in the 'creative destruction' of demand that Schumpeter described (ultimately demand is set by the landowners), they nevertheless innovate in other ways befitting their intermediary status. For example, as they became aware that consumers are willing to pay a little extra in order to buy in small quantities rather than stockpile large quantities, they managed the circulation of goods accordingly.

Another way that Cantillon's entrepreneur can innovate is by arbitrage. An arbitrageur can create time and place utility by moving goods from low-valued use to high-valued use. Noting the opportunities for profit that existed between the countryside and Paris, Cantillon (1931: 150–2) maintained that as long as they can cover their transportation costs, entrepreneurs 'will buy at a low price the products of the villages and will transport them to the Capital to be sold there at a higher price'. These two examples show that in contrast to Schumpeter (discussed below), Cantillon's innovative entrepreneur worked basically on the supply side of the market.

2.2.2. ABBE NICHOLAS BAUDEAU (1730–92)

Another writer who developed a theory of entrepreneurship that anticipated future developments was Baudeau, a clergyman. A member of the French school of economists that has come to be known as the Physiocrats,[3] Baudeau believed in the primacy of agriculture. In depicting the agricultural entrepreneur as a risk bearer, he echoed Cantillon. But Baudeau established even more overtly than Cantillon the concept of the entrepreneur as innovator, one who invents and applies new techniques or ideas in order to reduce his costs and thereby raise his profit.

Consider the nature of risk faced by the agricultural entrepreneur. The rent he pays to the landlord is the surplus of farm revenue over necessary costs of production, including some payment for his own services. For the tenant farmer, rent is a cost determined in advance of production. The Physiocrats favored stabilizing these costs as much as possible through long-term leases, while wage rates were usually fixed at or near subsistence levels. Thus, the farmer operating with a long-term lease faced certain fixed costs, but uncertain harvests and hence uncertain sales prices. Note the powerful suggestion that it is the role of the entrepreneur to devise legal/contractual/administrative arrangements that improve market efficiency or lower market risk.

In his analysis of entrepreneurship, Baudeau emphasized and explored the significance of ability. He underscored the importance of intelligence, the entrepreneur's ability to collect and process knowledge and information. Intelligence—knowledge and the ability to act—also gives the entrepreneur a measure of control, so that he is not a mere pawn to the capitalist. Hence, Baudeau (1910: 46) described the entrepreneur as an active agent: 'Such is the goal of the grand productive enterprises; first to increase the harvest by two, three, four, ten times if possible; secondly to reduce the amount of labor employed and so reduce costs by a half, a third, a fourth, or a tenth, whatever possible.'

Baudeau's theory of entrepreneurship presupposes that economic events fall into two categories, those that are subject to human control and those that are not. To the extent that the entrepreneur confronts events under his control, his success depends on knowledge and ability, which he may use in all manner of 'creative' ways to try to reduce risk. To the extent that he confronts events beyond his control, however, he places himself at risk that is not likely to yield to innovative measures.

2.2.3. JEREMY BENTHAM (1748–1832)

British classical economists paid little attention to the role of the entrepreneur in a market economy, choosing to elevate the capitalist to the top of the economic hierarchy. Bentham, whose ties with France and its intellectual tradition were much stronger than those of his contemporaries, was an exception. The contrast between Bentham and Smith on the subject of the entrepreneur is most evident in their debate over usury laws. Smith and Bentham agreed on the premise that the regime most favorable to the development of inventive faculties was that of economic liberalism. But, unlike Smith, Bentham (1952) defended usurers and projectors as useful agents. Both helped to advance the cause of inventive genius, each in his own way. It is something of a puzzle that Smith would, on the one hand, recognize innovation as a professional activity while, on the other hand, ignore its importance in a different context. In his denunciation of usury, Smith failed to acknowledge the importance of the innovator. Bentham aptly pointed this out in his *Defence of Usury* (1787), the first publication that brought him fame as an economist. There Bentham detailed how laws against usury limit the overall quantity of capital loaned and borrowed and how such laws keep away foreign money from domestic capital markets. Both these effects tend to throttle the activities of successful entrepreneurs. Although Bentham used the customary term projector, he was quite precise in his definition of this term as any person who, in the pursuit of wealth, strikes out into any new channel, especially into any channel of invention. He argued that interest rate ceilings tend to discriminate against entrepreneurs of new projects, because, by their novelty, such projects are more risky than those already proven profitable by experience. Moreover, legal restrictions of this sort are powerless to distinguish bad projects from good ones.

In pleading the cause of the projectors, Bentham, the inventor of the Panopticon, was to some extent pleading his own case. Panopticon was the name Bentham gave to his idea of a model prison. The concept involved both an architectural and an institutional innovation. Bentham's ideal prison was circular. All the cells were arranged concentrically around a central pavilion, which contained an inspector, or at most a small number of inspectors. From his central position the inspector(s) could see at a glance everything that was going on, yet he was rendered invisible by a system of blinds. In this way, too, outside visitors could inspect the prisoners, as well as the prison's administration, without being seen. According to Bentham, this constant scrutiny of the prisoners would deprive them of the power, and even the will, to do evil. Bentham was never able to attract enough backers to make his model prison a reality, but his basic concept was tried in other countries. What is more pertinent to our story than Bentham's plan of prison reform is the administrative innovation that he attached to it: the principle of contract management. This principle relies on the proper structuring of economic incentives and the dynamic activities of the entrepreneur to achieve the desired result of economic efficiency.

To Bentham, true reform would obtain in prisons only if the administrative plan simultaneously protected convicts against the harshness of their warders and society against the wastefulness of administrators. The choice, as he saw it, was between contract management and trust management. The differences have been summarized by Halevy (1955: 84):

Contract-management is management by a man who treats with the government, and takes charge of the convicts at so much a head and applies their time and industry to his personal profit, as does a master with his apprentices. Trust management is management by a single individual or by a committee, who keep up the establishment at the public expense, and pay into the treasury the products of the convicts' work.

In Bentham's judgment, trust management did not provide the proper junction of interest and duty on the part of the entrepreneur. Its success therefore depends on public interest as a motivating factor. Bentham, like his proclaimed mentor, Smith, had much more confidence in individual self-interest as the spur to human action. The beauty of contract management was that it brought about an artificial identity of interests between the public on the one hand and the entrepreneur on the other. The entrepreneur in this case was an independent contractor who purchased, through competitive bid, the right to run the prison, thereby also acquiring title to whatever profits might be earned by the application of convict labor. Such an entrepreneur manager could maximize his long-term gains by preserving the health and productivity of his worker-convicts. In this manner public interest became entwined with private interest.

In 1787, Bentham completed the idea of contract management by a new administrative arrangement: he thought that life insurance offered an excellent means of joining the interest of one man to the preservation of a number of men. He, therefore, proposed that after consulting the appropriate mortality tables, the entrepreneur (e.g. prison manager) should be given a fixed sum of money for each convict due to die that year in prison, on condition that at the end of the year he must pay back the same sum for each convict who had actually died in prison. The difference would be profit for the entrepreneur, who would thereby have an economic incentive to lower the average mortality rate in his prison (Bentham 1962: 53).

Aside from the fact that Bentham was virtually alone among British classical economists in his repeated emphasis on the entrepreneur as an agent of economic progress, it is noteworthy that his administrative arrangement of contract management recast the entrepreneur in the position of government contractor, that is, a franchisee who undertakes financial risk in order to obtain an uncertain profit. Bentham also explicitly tied his notion of entrepreneur-contractor to the act of innovation. He defended contract management as the proper form of prison administration on the ground that it is a progressive innovation and should therefore be rewarded accordingly, no less than an inventor is rewarded for his invention (Bentham 1962: 47).

2.2.4. J. H. von THÜNEN (1785–1850)

Thünen is best known in the history of economics for his contributions to location theory, but in the second volume of *The Isolated State* (1850) he set forth an explanation of profit that clearly distinguished the function and reward of the entrepreneur from that of the capitalist. Thünen identified entrepreneurial gain as profit minus (*a*) interest on invested capital, (*b*) insurance against business losses, and (*c*) the wages of management. For Thünen, this residual is a return to entrepreneurial risk. In the subsequent framework established by Knight, entrepreneur risk is uninsurable, insofar as Thünen (1960: 246) declared: 'there exists no insurance company that will cover all and every risk connected with a business. A part of the risk must always be accepted by the entrepreneur.'

Contemporary economics relies on the concept of opportunity costs to measure entrepreneurial risk (Kanbur 1980). Thünen (1960: 247) seemed to have had the same argument in mind when he wrote:

He who has enough means to pay to get some knowledge and education for public service has a choice to become either a civil servant or, if equally suited for both kinds of jobs, to become an industrial entrepreneur. If he takes the first job, he is guaranteed subsistence for life; if he chooses the latter, an unfortunate economic situation may take all his property, and then his fate becomes that of a worker for daily wages. Under such unequal expectations for the future what could motivate him to become an entrepreneur if the probability of gain were not much greater than that of loss?

Thünen clearly appreciated the difference between management and entrepreneurship. He maintained that the effort of an entrepreneur working on his own account was different from that of a paid substitute (manager), even if each has the same knowledge and ability. The entrepreneur takes on the anxiety and agitation that accompanies his business gamble; he spends many sleepless nights preoccupied with the single thought of how to avoid catastrophe, whereas the paid substitute, if he has worked well during the day and finds himself tired in the evening, can sleep soundly, secure in the knowledge of having performed his duty. Anyone who has nursed along a new enterprise knows precisely of what Thünen speaks.

What is especially interesting about Thünen's treatment is how he turns the discussion from the trials of the entrepreneur into a kind of crucible theory of the development of entrepreneurial talent. The sleepless nights of the entrepreneur are not unproductive; it is then that the entrepreneur makes his plans and arrives at solutions for avoiding business failure. Adversity in the business world thereby becomes a training ground for the entrepreneur. As Thünen put it (1960: 248):

Necessity is the mother of invention; and so the entrepreneur through his troubles will become an inventor and explorer in his field. So, as the invention of a new and useful machine rightly gets the surplus which its application provides in comparison with an older machine, and this surplus is the compensation for his invention, in the same way what the entrepreneur brings about by greater mental effort in comparison with the paid manager is compensation for his industry, diligence, and ingenuity.

What makes this a significant step forward in the theory of entrepreneurship is the fact that Thünen successfully joined the separate strands of entrepreneurial theory that, on the one hand, characterized the entrepreneur as risk bearer (e.g. Cantillon), and, on the other hand, portrayed him as innovator (e.g. Baudeau and Bentham). Economic analysis having come this far by 1850, we may well question whether Schumpeter took a step backward in the next century by excluding risk bearing from the nature of entrepreneurship, confining its meaning instead solely to innovative activity.

Thünen was quite explicit about the fact that there are two elements in entrepreneurial income: a return to entrepreneurial risk and a return to ingenuity. Labeling the sum of these two as business profit, Thünen (1960: 249) established a cleavage between the respective roles of capitalist and entrepreneur:

Capital will give results, and is in the strict sense of the term capital, only if used productively; on the degree of this usefulness depends the rate of interest at which we lend capital. Productive use presupposes an industrial enterprise and an entrepreneur. The enterprise gives the entrepreneur a net yield after compensating for all expenses and costs. This net yield has two parts, business profits and capital use.

2.3. **Demand-side theories of entrepreneurship**

A demand-side theory of entrepreneurship emphasizes the role of the entrepreneur in changing the nature of demand for existing goods and services by introducing new goods and services or new combinations of existing goods and services. Such theories essentially address the question: Given the pattern of supply for existing goods and services, what role does the entrepreneur play in the marketplace?

2.3.1. GUSTAV SCHMOLLER (1838–1917)

Economic thought in the late nineteenth and early twentieth centuries developed differently in Germany than it did in England, or throughout the rest of Europe. This was due in part to the influence on economic method of the German Historical School. The historicists believed that in order to understand man's economic behavior and the institutions that constrain it, economics must describe human motives and behavioral tendencies in psychologically realistic terms. Schmoller represented the second generation of German historicists. He amassed mountains of historical data in order to analyze actual economic behavior. From his examination of these data he discovered a unique central factor in all economic activity—the enterprising spirit, the *Unternehmer*, or entrepreneur. Schmoller's entrepreneur was a creative organizer and manager whose role was innovation and the initiation of new projects (Zrinyi 1962). He combined factors of production to yield either new products or new methods of production. Schmoller's entrepreneur possessed imagination and daring. More significantly, Schmoller began to direct attention to the role of the entrepreneur on the demand side of economic activity.

2.3.2. WERNER SOMBART (1863–1941) AND MAX WEBER (1864–1920)

Schmoller's ideas were extended by third-generation German historicists, Sombart and Weber. Sombart introduced a new leader who animates the entire economic system by creative innovations. This entrepreneur combined the powers of organization described by Schmoller with a personality and ability to elicit maximum productivity from individuals engaged in the productive process. Whether he is a financier, manufacturer, or trader, Sombart portrayed the entrepreneur as a profit maximizer.

The German historicists characterized the entrepreneurial process as a breaking away from the old methods of production and the creation of new ones. This disequilibrating process was particularly emphasized by Weber. He sought to explain how a social system, as compared to an individual enterprise, could evolve from one stable form (perhaps under an authoritarian structure) to another type of system. Historically, he identified such changes with a charismatic leader, or entrepreneur-like person (Carlin 1956).

As if to heighten the dynamic nature of his entrepreneurial construct, Weber (1930: 67) began his analysis of change with a stationary state situation:

We may . . . visualize an economic process which merely reproduces itself at constant rates; a given population, not changing in either numbers or age distribution. . . . The tasks (wants) of households are given and do not change. The ways of production and usances of commerce are optimal from the standpoint of the firm's interest and with respect to existing horizons and possibilities, hence do not change either, unless some datum changes or some chance event intrudes upon this world.

In such a stationary society there is nothing that requires the activity traditionally associated with the entrepreneur. 'No other than ordinary routine work has to be done in this stationary society,' declared Weber (1930: 67), 'either by workmen or managers.' Yet, inevitably, change occurs. Weber (1930: 68) described a likely scenario:

Now at some time this leisureliness was suddenly destroyed, and often entirely without any essential change in form of organization. . . . What happened was, on the contrary, often no more than this: Some young men from one of the putting-out families went out into the country, carefully chose weavers from his employ, greatly increased the rigor of his supervision of their work, and thus turned them from peasants into laborers...he would begin to change his marketing methods...he began to introduce the principle of low prices and large turnover. There was repeated what everywhere and always is the result of such a process of rationalization: those who would not follow suit had to go out of business. The idyllic state collapsed under the pressure of a bitter competitive struggle....

Competition, in other words, is driven by an entrepreneur type. The critical characteristics of Weber's successful entrepreneur are his religious imperatives, which make up what is called the Protestant ethic. Consequently, in the final analysis Weber's theory of social and economic change is as much sociology as economics.

2.3.3. JOSEPH SCHUMPETER (1883–1950)

Schumpeter was schooled by the Austrian economists of the Vienna Circle but was heavily influenced by Weber. He set out to develop a theory of economic development in which the entrepreneur plays a central role. By applying new combinations of factors of production, Schumpeter's entrepreneur becomes the motive force of economic change. He is thereby responsible for the rise and decay of capitalism. The talented few who carry out innovations by devising new technologies, discovering new products, and developing new markets account for the short and long cycles of economic life. Schumpeter viewed economic development as a dynamic process, a disturbing of the status quo. He viewed economic development not as a mere adjunct to the central body of orthodox economic theory, but as the basis for reinterpreting a vital process that had been crowded out of mainstream economic analysis by the static, general equilibrium approach. The entrepreneur is a key figure for Schumpeter because, quite simply, he is the *persona causa* of economic development.

Schumpeter combined ideas from many earlier writers, but the demand-side emphasis that marked the Germanic tradition dominated his treatment of entrepreneurship. His entrepreneur is a disequilibrating force. For Schumpeter the concept of equilibrium that dominated twentieth-century economics served as a mere point of departure. The phrase he coined to describe this equilibrium state was the circular flow of economic life. Its chief characteristic is that economic life proceeds routinely on the basis of past experience; there are no forces evident for any change of the status quo. Schumpeter (1934: 42–3) described the nature of production and distribution in the circular flow in the following way:

[I]n every period only products which were produced in the previous period are consumed, and...only products which will be consumed in the following period are produced. Therefore workers and landlords always exchange their productive services for present consumption goods only, whether the former are employed directly or only indirectly in the production of consumption goods. There is no necessity for them to exchange their services of labor and land for future goods or for promises of future consumption goods or to apply for any 'advances' of present consumption goods. It is simply a matter of exchange, and not of credit transactions. The element of time plays no part. All products are only products and nothing more. For the individual firm it is a matter of complete indifference whether it produces means of production or consumption goods. In both cases the product is paid for immediately and at its full value.

Within this system, the production function is invariant, although factor substitution is possible within the limits of known technological horizons. The only real function that must be performed in this state is '. . . that of combining the two original factors of production, and this function is performed in every period mechanically as it were, of its own accord, without requiring a personal element distinguishable from superintendence and similar things' (Schumpeter 1934: 45). In this artificial situation, the entrepreneur is a nonentity. 'If we choose to call the manager or owner of a business "entrepreneur"', wrote Schumpeter (1934: 45–6), then he would be an entrepreneur 'without special function and without income of a special kind.'

For Schumpeter, the circular flow is a mere foil. The relevant problem, he wrote in *Capitalism, Socialism and Democracy* (1950: 84), is not how capitalism administers existing structures, but how it creates and destroys them. This process—what Schumpeter called creative destruction—is the essence of economic development. In other words, development is a disturbance of the circular flow. It occurs in industrial and commercial life, not in consumption. It is a process defined by the carrying out of new combinations in production. It is accomplished by the entrepreneur.

Schumpeter reduced his theory to three elemental and corresponding pairs of opposites: (*a*) the circular flow (i.e. tendency toward equilibrium) on the one hand versus a change in economic routine or data on the other; (*b*) statics versus dynamics; (*c*) entrepreneurship versus management. The first pair consists of two real processes; the second, two theoretical apparatuses; the third, two distinct types of conduct. The theory maintained that the essential function of the entrepreneur is distinct from that of capitalist, landowner, laborer, or inventor. According to Schumpeter, the entrepreneur may be any and all of these things, but if he is, it is by coincidence rather than by nature of function. Nor is the entrepreneurial function, in principle, connected with the possession of wealth, even though he held that 'the accidental fact of the possession of wealth constitutes a practical advantage' (Schumpeter 1934: 101). Moreover, entrepreneurs do not form a social class, in the technical sense, although in a capitalist society they come to be esteemed for their ability.

Schumpeter admitted that the essential function of the entrepreneur is almost always mingled with other functions, such as management. But management, he asserted, does not elicit the truly distinctive role of the entrepreneur. 'The function of superintendence in itself, constitutes no essential economic distinction', he declared (1934: 20). The function of making decisions is another matter, however. In Schumpeter's theory, the dynamic entrepreneur is the person who innovates, who makes new combinations in production.

Schumpeter described innovation in several ways. Initially, he spelled out the kinds of new combinations that underlie economic development. They encompass the following: (*a*) creation of a new good or new quality of good; (*b*) creation of a new method of production; (*c*) the opening of a new market; (*d*) the capture of a new source of supply; (*e*) evolvement of a new organization of industry (e.g. creation or destruction of a monopoly). Over time, of course, the force of these new combinations dissipates, as the new becomes part of the old (circular flow). But this does not change the essence of the entrepreneurial function. According to Schumpeter (1934: 78), 'everyone is an entrepreneur only when he actually "carries out new combinations", and loses that character as soon as he has built up his business, when he settles down to running it as other people run their businesses'.

Alternatively, Schumpeter (1939: 62) defined innovation by means of the production function. The production function, he said, 'describes the way in which quantity of product varies if quantities of factors vary. If, instead of quantities of factors, we vary the form of the function, we have an innovation.' Mere cost-reducing adaptations of knowledge lead only to new supply schedules of existing goods, however, so this kind of innovation must involve a new commodity, or one of higher quality. However, Schumpeter recognized that the knowledge supporting the innovation need not be new. On the contrary, it may be existing knowledge that has not been utilized before. According to Schumpeter (1928: 378):

[T]here never has been anytime when the store of scientific knowledge has yielded all it could in the way of industrial improvement, and, on the other hand, it is not the knowledge that matters, but the successful solution of the task *sui generis* of putting an untried method into practice—there may be, and often is, no scientific novelty involved at all, and even if it be involved, this does not make any difference to the nature of the process.

In Schumpeter's theory, successful innovation requires an act of will, not of intellect. It depends, therefore, on leadership, not intelligence, and, as noted above, it should not be confused with invention. On this last point, Schumpeter (1934: 88–9) was explicit:

To carry any improvement into effect is a task entirely different from the inventing of it, and a task, moreover, requiring entirely different kinds of aptitudes. Although entrepreneurs of course may be inventors just as they may be capitalists, they are inventors not by nature of their function but by coincidence and vice versa. Besides, the innovations which it is the function of entrepreneurs to carry out need not necessarily be any inventions at all.

The leadership that constitutes innovation in the Schumpeterian system is disparate, not homogeneous. An aptitude for leadership stems in part from the use of knowledge, and knowledge has aspects of a public good. People of action who perceive and react to knowledge do so in various ways; each internalizes the public good in potentially a different way. The leader distances himself from the manager by virtue of his aptitude. According to Schumpeter (1928: 380), different aptitudes for the routine work of static management results merely in differential success at what all managers do, whereas different leadership aptitudes mean that 'some are able to undertake uncertainties incident to what has not been done before; [indeed] ... to overcome these difficulties incident to change of practice is the function of the entrepreneur'.

Schumpeter's influence on the theory of economic development has been enormous, in part because of the simplicity and power of his theory, and in part because that theory extends rather than replaces many ideas from earlier writers. The simplicity and power of Schumpeter's theory is summed up in his own words: 'The carrying out of new combinations we call "enterprise"; the individual whose function it is to carry them out we call "entrepreneurs"' (Schumpeter 1934: 74).[4]

2.4. **Conclusions**

Schumpeter is generally credited with establishing the entrepreneur as innovator and disassociating the entrepreneur from the risk-taker. A brief survey of the historical roots of entrepreneurship, however, reveals that despite the early and persistent connection made between risk and entrepreneurship by writers of the eighteenth and nineteenth centuries, the implicit, if not explicit, link between innovation and the entrepreneur was never far from mind. These ideas and concepts are summarized in Table 2.1. Early treatments, however, tended to examine the entrepreneurial function from the supply side. Schumpeter switched emphasis to the demand side. Moreover, he made the entrepreneur the pivotal figure not only in the analysis of static market phenomena but in a sweeping theory of historical change.

Broadly speaking, entrepreneurship refers to perception of opportunity and the ability to act on that perception. With respect to innovation, perception of opportunity refers, according to Schumpeter, to the creation of new goods, the creation of new methods of production, the opening of new markets, capture of new sources of supply, and the evolvement of new organizations of industry.

Table 2.1. Summary of the entrepreneur as innovator from an historical perspective

Author(s)	Characterization of the entrepreneur as innovator
Cantillon	Entrepreneur, an intermediary between landowners and hirelings is innovative by coordinating production and distribution
Baudeau	Entrepreneur is innovative by inventing and applying new techniques to reduce costs and increase profits
Bentham	Entrepreneur is innovative in the role of an administrative manager through adoptive new administrative arrangements
Thünen	Entrepreneur is innovative by ensuring against business losses through ingenuity
Schmoller	Entrepreneur is innovative as an organizer and manager by introducing new projects
Sombart and Weber	Entrepreneur is innovative by influencing organizations to change from one stationary state to another
Schumpeter	Entrepreneur is innovative when, in response to new information, he creates new goods or goods of a higher quality, or creates a new method of production, or opens new markets, or captures new sources of supply, or is involved in a new organization of industry

And, the related entrepreneurial action refers to the new combination of resources that bring about these opportunities.

Shane (2003: 20) emphasized about Schumpeter's entrepreneur that:

...the existence of entrepreneurial opportunity [and hence innovative activity] involves the introduction of new information...

Entrepreneurial opportunity is the innovative reaction to and use of new information that brings about, or at least precipitates, creative destruction.

In contrast, Kirzner (1979, 1985) has argued that the entrepreneur reacts to existing information, not new information, in ways that others have not. It is the Kirznerian entrepreneur's new reaction that is his defining characteristic. Such a defining characteristic defines the entrepreneur as perceptive, but not necessarily innovative.

⬜ NOTES

1. Gallaher, Link, and Petrusa (2006) note that contemporary treatments of the subject tend to view the entrepreneur-as-innovator entirely as a Schumpeterian figure.
2. This chapter draws from Hébert and Link (1988, 2006).
3. After Cantillon's death, economic analysis in France was dominated by a group of writers who called themselves *Les Economistes*. As the term economist became more general in use, however, historians began to refer to this particular group of French writers as 'The Physiocrats' (the term *physiocracy* means role of nature). Its leader was Quesnay.
4. Paradoxically, the role of the entrepreneur in standard microeconomic theory remains virtually nonexistent. Baumol (2006) offers some insights into why this omission persists.

3 Fundamental concepts of innovation and technological change

3.1. Introduction

In this chapter, we conceptualize technology as the physical representation of knowledge.[1] This starting point provides a useful foundation for understanding technological change and specifically investments in innovation as a determinant of technological change. Any useful device is, in part, proof of the knowledge-based or informational assumptions that resulted in its creation. The information embodied in a technology varies accordingly to its source, its type, and its application. For example, one source of information is science, although scientific knowledge is rarely sufficient for the more particular needs entailed in constructing, literally, a technological device. It could be useful in this regard to think of science as focusing on the understanding of knowledge and technology as focusing on the application of knowledge.

Other sources of knowledge include information from controlled and random experimentation, information that philosophers refer to as ordinary knowledge, and finally, information of the kind that falls under the rubrics of creativity, perceptiveness, and inspiration. Regarding perceptiveness, Machlup (1980: 179) argued that formal education is only one form of knowledge. He asserted that knowledge is also gained experientially and is gathered and processed at different rates by each individual. The following statement reflects Machlup's notion of perception quite clearly:

Some alert and quick-minded persons, by keeping their eyes and ears open for new facts and theories, discoveries and opportunities, perceive what normal people of lesser alertness and perceptiveness, would fail to notice. Hence new knowledge is available at little or no cost to those who are on the lookout, full of curiosity, and bright enough not to miss their chances.

This informational view of technology implies that technology per se is an output that arises from a formal, rational, purposively undertaken process. Such an idea—the production of technology—highlights the role of knowledge and research produces knowledge in the generation of technology—as well as the role of entrepreneurship in terms of perception and action. And the concept of research underscores the myriad sources available from which knowledge can be acquired. Technologies can thus be distinguished, albeit imperfectly, by the amount of embedded information. More concretely, R&D activities and related investments—wherever they are based—play a large role in creating and characterizing new technologies.

As previously stated, it is useful to think of an invention as the creation of a new technology. Innovation, then, is the first application of the invention—the technology—in production. Scherer's study (1965) of the Watt–Boulton steam-engine venture supports this relationship between invention and innovation in the process of technological change. Because innovation or application implies the beginning of a diffusion process, these conceptualizations parallel the Schumpeterian idea that there are phases in the process of technological change: invention, innovation, diffusion, and imitation.

Schumpeter's contribution to the history of economic thought on innovation, entrepreneurship, and technological change and economic growth in the early and mid-1900s has significantly influenced how many economists and other scholars and researchers approach the broader topic of technological change and economic performance. According to Schumpeter (1939: 62), as discussed in Chapter 2, innovation can meaningfully be defined in terms of a production function, and, in a sense, as a factor shifting the production function:

[The production function] describes the way in which quantity of product varies if quantities of factors vary. If, instead of quantities of factors, we vary the form of the function, we have an innovation.

Schumpeter noted that mere cost reducing applications of knowledge lead only to new supply schedules of existing goods. Therefore, this kind of innovation must involve a new commodity or one of a higher quality—a product innovation.

More than two decades after these writings of Schumpeter, Usher (1954) independently rediscovered these same concepts. He posited that technology is the result of an innovation, and an innovation is the result of an invention. An invention, of course, results as the emergence of new things requiring an act of insight going beyond the normal exercise of technical or professional skills.

3.2. Factor-saving classification schemes

Economists have evaluated the effect of technological change on production in terms of changes in the amount of capital (K) and labor (L) used in production. This aspect of firm performance will be further discussed in subsequent

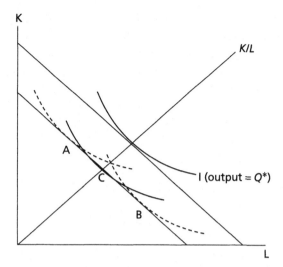

Figure 3.1. Labor-saving, capital-saving, and neutral technological change, output held constant

chapters. To simplify the analysis and exposition, we assume that K and L are the only two factors of production. We recognize that intermediate materials and services, and even money are also utilized in producing goods and services. The simplest classification scheme assumes that technological change alters the input mix for a given level of output. For a given level of output and input price ratio, a labor-saving technological change results in a higher capital-to-labor ratio; a capital-saving technological change results in a lower capital-to-labor ratio; and a neutral technological change results in an unchanged capital-to-labor ratio.

Consider isoquant I in Figure 3.1, which corresponds to a given level of output, Q^*. A labor-saving technological change is illustrated as isoquant I shifting inward to point A, where the capital-to-labor ratio is higher than along the ray K/L. Similarly, a capital-saving technological change is illustrated as isoquant I shifting inward to point B where the capital-to-labor ratio is lower than along ray K/L. A neutral technological change results in an inward shift of isoquant I to point C. At point C, Q^* is produced with an unchanged ratio of capital-to-labor but with proportionally less of each input.

This factor-saving conceptualization of technological change implicitly assumes that technology leads to cost-reducing changes in the production process, rather than to new or improved quality products. This distinction between cost-reduction and product improvement is important for understanding the nature of technological change within a production function framework, and it is emphasized again in Chapter 4. Very simply, this factor-saving conceptualization highlights the distinction between a process innovation and a product innovation. This notion also highlights one difference between economic and management scholars who study technological change. Economists have long emphasized cost reduction, perhaps, and this is somewhat speculative, because it is the dual of profit maximization and profit maximization is a fundamental theoretical premise of the discipline. Management scholars have emphasized product enhancement, perhaps, and this again is somewhat speculative, because it relates to the behavior assumptions of managers and to their strategy for maximizing shareholder wealth.

The factor-saving classification scheme discussed above is most applicable at the plant, firm, or industry level with a focus on the short run when output levels can meaningfully be thought of as remaining constant. The classification scheme represents an unrealistic starting point for an aggregate taxonomy when output levels will change.

Alternative factor-saving classification schemes dominated the very early technological change literature. These schemes are based not on a constant level of output as illustrated in Figure 3.1, but rather on a constant factor-to-factor or factor-to-output ratio.[2] All of the schemes were set forth within the neoclassical tradition of economics, namely as a production function represented as $Q = f(K, L, t)$.[3]

3.3. Models of technological change

Much of the early literature on the economics of technological change was based on production function models in which the output (Q) of an economic unit (a plant, a firm, or an industry) is represented simply as a function of capital (K) and labor (L):

$$Q = A(t) \, F(K, L) \qquad (3.1)$$

where $A(t)$ is a disembodied time-related shift factor, or, in terms of Figure 3.1, a neutral technological change whereby isoquant I shifts inwardly to point C.

Solow (1957) advanced the concept of an aggregate production function and illustrated it by assuming that the function was Cobb–Douglas in form:

$$Q = A(t) K^{\alpha} L^{\beta} \qquad (3.2)$$

where, assuming perfect competition (in output and input markets) and constant returns to scale, α and β $(\alpha + \beta = 1)$ are the shares of income distributed to capital and labor respectively. Perfect competition means that firms are assumed to be price takers in factor markets and have no market power in its output market.

It follows mathematically from equation (3.2) that the impact of technological change on production can be approximated as a residual growth rate measured in terms of the percentage change in output less the weighted percentage change in capital and labor (where the weights are α and β, respectively). This so-called Solow residual is generally referred to as the percentage change total factor productivity (TFP), or simply total factor productivity growth or productivity growth, and, based on equation (3.2), it is generally denoted as $\dot{A}/A$.[4]

Beginning in the early 1960s, researchers have engaged in empirical analyses to estimate the impact of investments in R&D on productivity growth under the implicit assumption that R&D is an input into innovation and innovation leads to technological change as measured by the growth in TFP. These empirical studies are reviewed in Chapter 4, but the model is presented here and derived more completely in the Appendix to this chapter.

Conceptualizing the general production function in equation (3.1) at the firm level, and introducing the firm's stock of technical capital, T, as a third input, the model becomes:

$$Q = A(t)\, F(K, L, T) \tag{3.3}$$

If the source of the firm's technical capital is its R&D, where R&D is the primary investment flow into the stock of technical capital, then a model relating productivity growth to investments in R&D (RD) takes the form:[5]

$$\frac{\dot{A}}{A} = \lambda + \rho\left(\frac{RD}{Q}\right) \tag{3.4}$$

Empirical estimates of ρ from equation (3.4) have been interpreted from both a pure economic perspective as well as from a public policy perspective as the marginal private rate of return to investments in R&D, as discussed in Chapter 4.

Because equation (3.4) has been estimated so extensively in the economics literature, we derive the equation in the Appendix to this chapter and discuss there certain characteristics of the Cobb–Douglas specification presented in equation (3.2).

3.4. **Conclusions**

Equation (3.4) has been the workhorse model for empirical studies estimating the returns to R&D. These studies are of academic importance because R&D expenditures are an important strategic investment made by firms; they are of public policy importance because estimates of ρ motivate innovation policy, in general, and R&D policy, in particular. From a public policy perspective, estimates of ρ, the marginal private rate of return to R&D, could motivate the public sector to initiate or adopt policies to stimulate additional R&D spending by private sector firms. A firm will invest in R&D to the point where the marginal private rate of return is equal to the marginal private cost. A high marginal private rate of return to R&D, high relative to the marginal rate of return to other investments assuming marginal costs are the same, suggests that society would value additional private dollar investment in R&D more than the firm because of the spillover benefits from the resulting new knowledge. Thus, a high marginal private rate of return could suggest public policies to lower the firm's marginal private cost thereby inducing more R&D which would be in the best interest of society. The R&D tax credit in many industrialized nations is an example of such a public policy—in some nations the tax credit is for R&E, where experimentation (E) expenditures relate to a narrower set of activities than do development (D) expenditures, as also discussed in Chapter 4.

In Chapters 4 and 5, we discuss the economics of R&D with respect to firm performance and economic performance, respectively. Our emphasis in both chapters is on the empirical findings in the academic literatures.

☐ APPENDIX: DERIVATION OF EQUATION (3.4)

Solow's pioneering study (1957) was the first to posit explicitly an aggregate production function. His Divisia or geometric index was formulated from a Cobb–Douglas production function written in terms of capital and labor and was characterized by linear homogeneity and disembodied Hicks neutral technological change. The functional form that Solow worked from was represented above as equation (3.2) and referred to in this Appendix as equation (A3.1):

$$Q = A(t)K^{\alpha}L^{\beta} \qquad \text{(A3.1)}$$

where, assuming perfect competition and constant returns to scale, and where, α and β ($\alpha + \beta = 1$) are the shares of income distributed to capital and labor respectively. It follows that the impact of technological change on production can be approximated as a residual growth rate.

Taking the natural logarithm of both sides of equation (A3.1) yields:

$$\ell n Q = \ell n\, A(t) + \alpha\, \ell n K + \beta\, \ell n L \qquad \text{(A3.2)}$$

Taking the time derivative of both sides of equation (A3.2) and rearranging terms yields:

$$\left\{ \frac{\frac{\partial \ell n A}{\partial t}}{\ell n A} \right\} = \left\{ \frac{\frac{\partial \ell n Q}{\partial t}}{\ell n Q} \right\} - \alpha \left\{ \frac{\frac{\partial \ell n K}{\partial t}}{\ell n K} \right\} - \beta \left\{ \frac{\frac{\partial \ell n L}{\partial t}}{\ell n L} \right\} \qquad \text{(A3.3)}$$

Redefining the left-hand side of equation (A3.3) in terms of the definition of TFP growth yields:

$$\left\{\frac{\frac{\partial TFP}{\partial t}}{TFP}\right\} = \left\{\frac{\frac{\partial A}{\partial t}}{A}\right\} = \frac{\dot{A}}{A}. \tag{A3.4}$$

More descriptively, technological change, denoted in equation (A3.4), and seen from equation (A3.3), as $\dot{A}/A$, represents the percentage change in output per time period t that is not explained by the weighted percentage change in capital and labor, where the weights are α and β, respectively. In other words, $\dot{A}/A$ is an impact indicator.

As Domar (1961: 712) more realistically characterized the results of this model, 'A is a residual. It absorbs, like a sponge, all increases in output not accounted for by the growth of explicitly recognized inputs.' Certainly, if the underlying production function was specified in terms of several inputs, A could mathematically be constructed given each input's relative share, but the interpretation of such a constructed measure would remain the same—a residual.

This Solow residual measure of TFP growth has formed the foundation for an extensive body of empirical literature, which is reviewed in Chapters 4 and 5. Part of this literature includes studies that attempted to correlate investments in technology with $\dot{A}/A$. However, despite its widespread use, the index does not distinguish between pure technological change and changes in efficiency with which properly measured resources, including technology, are used. This shortcoming has motivated many to move to a frontier production function framework. Other shortcomings of the Solow residual are that it picks up the effects of suboptimal capacity utilization, returns to scale, mismeasurement of inputs and output, and imperfect competition.

For completeness of exposition, the Cobb–Douglas production function in equation (A3.1) has several unique features. Technological change is simultaneously Hicks neutral, Harrod neutral, and Solow neutral (Link and Siegel 2003).

If $A(t) = e^{\lambda t}$ in equation (A3.1), with λ being a parameter reflecting the rate of disembodied technological change, then, following Stoneman (1983), technological change is Hicks neutral at rate m:

$$Q = e^{mt}K^a L^{1-a} = (Ke^{mt})^a (Le^{mt})^{1-a}; \quad \lambda = m \tag{A3.5}$$

and Harrod neutral at rate m:

$$Q = e^{m(1-a)t}K^a L^{1-a} = K^a(Le^{mt})^{1-a}; \quad \lambda = m(1-a) \tag{A3.6}$$

and Solow neutral at rate m:

$$Q = e^{mat}K^a L^{1-a} = (Ke^{mt})^a L^{1-a}; \quad \lambda = ma \tag{A3.7}$$

The explicit assumption of neutrality is a limitation associated with any TFP index derived from a Cobb–Douglas specification. There is some empirical evidence that technical progress has been labor-saving over time, as was originally hypothesized by Hicks (1932). The pioneering work in this regard traces to Moroney (1972), Binswanger (1974), Binswanger and Ruttan (1978), and Cain and Patterson (1981).

Moroney (1972) found strong evidence for 1949 to 1962 that technological change was not Hicks neutral with US manufacturing industries. In 11 of 20 two-digit SIC industries studies, the bias was labor-saving. Cain and Patterson (1981) reached a similar finding using historical US manufacturing data over the period 1850–1919. Binswanger (1974) and Binswanger and Ruttan (1978) reported that technological changes in US agriculture between 1912 and 1968 were biased. These changes were fertilizer-using and labor-saving, accompanied by a decrease and increase respectively in those factors' prices. Subsequent research, using microeconomic data-sets and more advanced econometric techniques, validates these foundation conclusions.

Returning to the explicit derivation of equation (3.4) from the chapter, researchers introduced the stock of technical capital, T, as an explicit third input into the underlying production function as was shown in the chapter as equation (3.3) and referred to in this Appendix as:

$$Q = A(t)\, F(K, L, T) \tag{A3.8}$$

In terms of equation (A3.8) being represented as Cobb–Douglas:

$$Q = Ae^{\lambda t} K^{\alpha} L^{\beta} T^{\gamma} \tag{A3.9}$$

where λ is a disembodied rate of growth parameter and again α, β, and γ are relative shares. Constant returns to scale are assumed with respect to K and L, but not with respect to T $(\alpha + \beta + \gamma) = (1 + \gamma) > 1$ for $\gamma > 0$.

Using logarithmic transformations and differentiating with respect to t yields:

$$\left\{ \frac{\frac{\partial Q}{\partial t}}{Q} \right\} = \lambda + \alpha \left\{ \frac{\frac{\partial K}{\partial t}}{K} \right\} + \beta \left\{ \frac{\frac{\partial L}{\partial t}}{L} \right\} + \gamma \left\{ \frac{\frac{\partial T}{\partial t}}{T} \right\} \tag{A3.10}$$

Residually measured productivity growth is defined, as above, as:

$$\frac{\acute{A}}{A} = \left\{ \frac{\frac{\partial Q}{\partial t}}{Q} \right\} - \alpha \left\{ \frac{\frac{\partial K}{\partial t}}{K} \right\} - \beta \left\{ \frac{\frac{\partial L}{\partial t}}{L} \right\} = \lambda + \gamma \left\{ \frac{\frac{\partial T}{\partial t}}{T} \right\} \tag{A3.11}$$

In equations (A3.9) and (A3.11), the parameter γ both the relative share of T and the output elasticity of T:

$$\gamma = \left(\frac{\partial Q}{\partial T} \right) \left(\frac{T}{Q} \right) \tag{A3.12}$$

Substituting the right-hand side of equation (A3.12) into equation (A3.11), and rearranging terms, yields:

$$\frac{\acute{A}}{A} = \lambda + \rho \left(\frac{\acute{T}}{Q} \right) \tag{A3.13}$$

where $\acute{T} = (\partial T/\partial t)$ and for $\rho = (\partial Q/\partial T)$. From equation (A3.13), ρ is the marginal product of technical capital and $\acute{T}$ is the decision-making unit's (e.g. firm's in most cases) net private investment in the stock of technical capital. It was generally assumed in the early empirical work, that the stock of R&D-based technical capital does not depreciate, or if it does depreciate it does so very slowly. Thus $\acute{T}$ is reasonably approximated by the flow of self-financed R&D expenditures in a given period, RD, as:

$$\frac{\acute{A}}{A} = \lambda + \rho\left(\frac{RD}{Q}\right) \tag{A3.14}$$

and ρ is interpreted as the marginal private rate of return to R&D.

As an aside, Link (1978) demonstrated mathematically, based on the theoretical research of Kamien and Schwartz (1969, 1971), that R&D enters the production function through capital augmentation and labor augmentation. Thus:

$$Q = H(B_K K, B_L L) \tag{A3.15}$$

where B_K and B_L are factor augmenting coefficients and where each is functionally related to R&D allocated toward K augmentation and L augmentation, respectively.

☐ NOTES

1. This chapter draws from Link (1987) and Link and Siegel (2003).
2. A mathematical treatment of alternative factor-saving classification schemes is in Link and Siegel (2003).
3. The function $f(K, L, t)$ is assumed to be linearly homogeneous and twice differentiable: $f_K, f_L > 0$ and $f_{KK}, f_{LL} < 0$.
4. $\acute{A}$ denotes the time rate of change in TFP and thus $\acute{A}/A$ denotes the percentage rate of change in TFP.
5. See Link and Siegel (2003) and the Appendix to this chapter for the derivation of equation (3.4) based on the assumption that F($\cdot$) is Cobb–Douglas in form.

4 R&D and firm performance

4.1. Introduction

As discussed in Chapter 3 with specific reference to equation (3.4), R&D activity, or more precisely investments in R&D, is positively related to TFP or productivity growth. Stated differently, empirical studies, based on estimation of variants of equation (3.4), have consistently found that there is a positive statistical relationship between numerous proxies for innovation (e.g. R&D employment, R&D expenditures, and patents) and indicators of performance (e.g. accounting profits, stock prices, and productivity). This statistical finding appears to hold both over various levels of aggregation (plant, firm, industry, and country levels) and over alternative econometric specifications (production, cost, and profit function) (Griliches 1998).

In this chapter, we expand upon this statistical finding in two ways. First, we discuss the nature of R&D activity. Next, we review, in detail, the extant literature on R&D and firm performance. These extensions are critical because many of the studies in the literature demonstrate that the impact of R&D on firm performance depends on the type of R&D that is conducted or the source of R&D funding. That is, it is critical to analyze the various components of R&D, in order to accurately assess firm-level returns to R&D, as well as the impact of innovative activity on society.

4.2. Dimensions of R&D

Investments in R&D are a key leading indicator of advancements in science and technology. These advancements result in technological change (new products and processes and ultimately, the creation of new sectors), which leads to improvements in economic growth and standards of living. Finally, in a knowledge-based economy, R&D is increasingly an integral part of business and corporate-level strategy as firms seek to enhance production differentiation through product innovation and development and/or enhance efficiency through process innovation. Thus, R&D is an important input directly related to firms' growth and competitiveness strategies as well as to a nation's global competitiveness.

There are three fundamental dimensions to R&D. The first dimension relates to the source of funding of R&D (who finances the R&D), the second to the performance of R&D (who conducts the R&D), and the third to the character of use of R&D (whether the undertaking is of a basic, applied, or development nature). These three fundamental dimensions are not mutually exclusive.

Table 4.1 shows the sources of funding of R&D for selected countries. In every country listed in the table with the exception of the Russian Federation, the majority of R&D is financed by industry. Nearly 75 percent of total R&D is financed by industry in Japan and South Korea, about 65 percent in Germany and the United States, and only 30 percent in the Russian Federation.

R&D is performed within the context of what has become known as the national innovation system (Nelson 1993). Nelson defines a national innovation system as a set of institutions whose interactions determine the innovative performance of national firms. Metcalfe (1995: 212) defines a national innovation system as:

… that set of distinct institutions which jointly and individually contribute to the development and diffusion of new technologies and which provides the framework within which governments form and implement policies to influence the innovation process. As such, it is a system of interconnected institutions to create, store, and transfer the knowledge, skills, and artifacts which define the new technologies.

The importance of the concept of a national innovation system is that it emphasizes the linkages among the players involved in innovative activity, as well as the innovation process. Traditional analysis of technology policy has typically focused on inputs (e.g. R&D expenditure or employment) and outputs (e.g. patents) and not on linkages or the innovation process as a dynamic process.

The venue for the performance of R&D within a national innovation system is the research laboratory. Many scholars have set forth alternative definitions of a national innovation system. According to Crow and Bozeman (1998: 42), for example, the US national innovation system may be thought of as 'the complex network of agents, policies, and institutions supporting the process of technical advance in an economy'.

Table 4.2 shows that in every nation, industry is the largest performer of R&D. In every nation except Canada, the percentage of R&D performed in industry is approximately 65 percent; in Canada it is just over 50 percent. In Canada, however, about 38 percent of R&D is performed in the higher education sector (colleges and universities), whereas in the other countries this percentage is only between 10 and 20 percent.

Vannevar Bush is credited for first using the term basic research. In his 1945 report to US President Roosevelt, *Science—the Endless Frontier*, Bush used the term and defined it to mean research conducted without thought of practical

Table 4.1. International R&D expenditures for selected countries, by source of funds, 2002–4

Country	Total	Source of R&D funds					Performers (% distribution)
		Industry	Government	Higher education	Private nonprofit	Abroad	
Japan (2002, billions of yen)	15,551,513	11,486,713	2,830,142	1,004,191	171,032	59,435	100.0
Germany (2003, millions of euros)	54,310	35,910	16,910	0	230	1,260	100.0
France (2002, millions of euros)	34,527	17,990	13,244	242	295	2,756	100.0
Italy (2003, millions of euros)	NA	NA	NA	NA	NA	NA	na
United Kingdom (2002, millions of pounds)	19,568	9,138	5,268	196	963	4,003	100.0
Canada (2004, millions of Canadian dollars)	24,487	11,314	8,672	1,781	787	1,933	100.0
Russian Federation (2003, billions of rubles)	169,862	52,257	101,252	807	278	15,268	100.0
South Korea (2003, billions of won)	19,068,682	14,113,599	4,548,933	256,825	70,467	78,858	100.0
United States (2003, millions of US dollars)	284,584	179,615	88,778	7,944	8,247	NA	100.0

NA = assumed negligible or not available; na = not applicable.
Source: Science and Engineering Indicators 2006 (National Science Board 2006).

Table 4.2. International R&D expenditures for selected countries, by performer, 2002–4

Country and R&D performer	Total
Japan (2002, billions of yen)	15,551,513
Industry	11,576,842
Government	1,483,209
Higher education	2,158,797
Private nonprofit	332,665
Percent distribution, sources	100
Germany (2003, millions of euros)	54,310
Industry	37,910
Government	7,300
Higher education	9,100
Private nonprofit	NA
Percent distribution, sources	100
France (2002, millions of euros)	34,527
Industry	21,839
Government	5,709
Higher education	6,512
Private nonprofit	468
Percent distribution, sources	100
Italy (2003, millions of euros)	NA
Industry	7,102
Government	2,507
Higher education	NA
Private nonprofit	NA
Percent distribution, sources	NA
United Kingdom (2002, millions of pounds)	19,568
Industry	13,110
Government	1,752
Higher education	4,416
Private nonprofit	290
Percent distribution, sources	100
Canada (2004, millions of Canadian dollars)	24,487
Industry	12,534
Government	2,564
Higher education	9,319
Private nonprofit	70
Percent distribution, sources	100
Russian Federation (2003, billions of rubles)	169,862
Industry	116,248
Government	42,945
Higher education	10,298
Private nonprofit	372
Percent distribution, sources	100
South Korea (2003, billions of won)	19,068,682
Industry	14,509,663
Government	2,401,051
Higher education	1,932,663
Private nonprofit	225,304
Percent distribution, sources	100
United States (2003, millions of US dollars)	284,584
Industry	196,112
Government	25,747
Higher education	47,683
Private nonprofit	15,042
Percent distribution, sources	100

NA = assumed negligible or not available; na = not applicable.
Source: Science and Engineering Indicators 2006 (National Science Board 2006).

ends. Since that time, policymakers have been concerned about definitions that appropriately characterize the various aspects of scientific inquiry that broadly fall under the label of R&D and that relate to the linear model that Bush proffered, as discussed below.

Definitions are important to international and national statistical organizations, like the broadly supported Organisation for Economic Co-operation and Development (OECD) and NSF in the United States, because such agencies collect expenditure data on R&D and on other science and technology indicators. For those data to reflect accurately investments in technological advancement, to be comparable over time within a nation, and to have a degree of comparability across nations, there must be a set of reporting definitions that remain consistent over time.

The classification scheme used by the NSF for reporting purposes was developed for its first industrial survey in 1953–4, as documented in Link's history (1996b) of the classification scheme. While minor definitional changes were made in the instrument in the early years of the survey, namely to modify the category originally referred to as basic or fundamental research to simply basic research, the concepts of basic research, applied research, and development have remained much as was implicitly contained in Bush's 1945 so-called linear model: *Basic Research → Applied Research → Development.*

The objective of basic research is to gain more comprehensive knowledge or understanding of the subject under study, without specific applications in mind. Basic research is defined as research that advances scientific knowledge but does not have specific immediate commercial objectives, although the research may be in fields of present or potential commercial interest. Much of the scientific research that takes place at universities is basic research.

Applied research is aimed at gaining the knowledge or understanding to meet a specific recognized need. Applied research includes investigations oriented to discovering new scientific knowledge that has specific commercial objectives with respect to products, processes, or services.

Development is the systematic use of the knowledge or understanding gained from research directed toward the production of useful materials, devices, systems, or methods, including the design and development of prototypes and processes. In the United States, about 60 percent of total R&D is development, with just over 21 percent of R&D being allocated to applied research and about 19 percent to basic research.

Different sectors contribute disproportionately to the US funding and performance of these R&D component categories. Applied research and development activities are primarily funded by industry and performed by industry. Basic research, however, is primarily funded by the federal government and generally performed in universities and colleges.

4.3. **Alternative definitions of R&D**

Three different definitions of R&D, from three alternative sources, are presented in Table 4.3 to illustrate similarities and differences in the description of that activity. NSF identifies basic research, applied research, and development as the three distinct types of activities classified for reporting purposes under the rubric of R&D as previously discussed. All three activities require either the creation of new knowledge or a novel application of existing knowledge. Once a production process is established, activities associated with any further development of that process are not considered as R&D. Furthermore, NSF omits all social science research from its definition of R&D activities, as also shown in Table 4.3.

The Frascati Manual, which guides the collection of R&D data throughout the European Union (EU), classifies R&D activities into three similar categories: basic research, applied research, and experimental development, and all activities classified as R&D must be in the pursuit of new knowledge or the discovery of new applications for existing knowledge, product, or process. The Frascati Manual's definition lists relatively fewer disqualifying criteria for R&D activities (see Table 4.3).

Finally, the US 1981 R&E tax credit definition uses the term 'qualified research' to identify activities aimed at creating new information or products and new applications of existing knowledge as applied to existing products. The Act also addresses the issue of modification or adaptation, omitted by the other two institutional definitions. The Act states that modification or adaptation of existing products to meet a client's needs is not considered R&D (see Table 4.3).

4.4. **R&D and firm performance**

A critical issue for managers and public policymakers is the nature of the relationship between investment in R&D and corporate performance. From a managerial perspective, corporate executives seek to understand how investments in and the adoptions of new technology can be used to achieve and sustain a competitive advantage. Achieving and sustaining a competitive advantage is a central theme of corporate strategy and a primary responsibility of top-level managers. This fundamental issue has public policy ramifications because, from a national perspective, firms aggregate to industries and industries aggregate to the economy as a whole. And, from a holistic perspective, new technologies spillover to firms in myriad industries either in the form of technology itself or as embodies in equipment used throughout the supply chain.

Table 4.3. Alternative definitions of R&D

US NSF	EU Frascati	US R&E Tax credit bill
The following are included in the definition of R&D:		
Basic research: Pursue new knowledge whether or not the search has reference to a specific application. Limited to federal, university, and nonprofit organizations.	*Basic research* is work done to acquire new knowledge, without any particular application or use in view.	Research that is undertaken to discover information technical in nature and holds applications useful in developing a new or improved business component of the taxpayer.
Applied research: Apply existing knowledge to problems involved in creating a new product or process.	*Applied research* is original investigation to acquire new knowledge directed toward a practical objective or a single product, operation, method, or system.	Research that seeks a new or improved function performance, reliability, or quality.
Development: Apply existing knowledge to problems involved in improving an existing product or process.	Experimental development is systematic work, drawing on existing knowledge aimed at producing new, or to improving substantially, existing products.	Not specified.
The following are not included in the definition of R&D:		
Not specified.	Not specified.	Adaptation of existing business components to fit a particular customer's requirements.
R&D from acquired firms prior to acquisition.	Not specified.	Not specified.
Amortization above actual cost of property and equipment related to firm R&D.	Not specified.	Not specified.
Test and evaluation once a prototype becomes a production model.	Not specified.	Research after commercial production of the business component.
Routine product testing.	Routine product testing.	Market research, testing, or development (including advertising or promotions).
Consumer, market, and opinion R&D; advertising new products or processes.	General purpose data collection.	Routine data collection.
Geological and geophysical exploration activities.	Analysis of soils and atmosphere.	Not specified.
Quality and quantity control.	Not specified.	Routine or ordinary testing or inspection for quality control.
Troubleshooting for breakdowns in production.	Scientific and technical information assistance.	Scientific and technical information assistance.
Social sciences, etc.: any research in the social sciences, arts, or humanities.	Social sciences, etc.: any research in the social sciences, arts, or humanities.	Social sciences, etc.: any research in the social sciences, arts, or humanities.
Not specified.	Feasibility studies (e.g. a study of the viability of a petrochemical complex in a certain region).	Efficiency survey.
Management and organization R&D.	Administration and other supporting activities.	Activity relating to management function or technique.

Sources: NIST (2005) and Gallaher, Link, and Petrusa (2006).

4.4.1. RESOURCES AND CAPABILITIES

The theoretical paradigm that dominates the economic and strategic management and economics literature is the resource based view of the firm (RBV), first introduced by Wernerfelt (1984) and subsequently refined by Barney (1991). The RBV perspective, which built upon earlier work by Penrose (1959), posits that firms are bundles of heterogeneous resources and capabilities, and those resources and capabilities are imperfectly mobile. Barney (1991), for example, asserted that if these resources and capabilities are valuable, rare, inimitable and nonsubstitutable, they constitute a source of sustainable competitive advantage.

Teece, Pisano, and Shuen (1997) extended the RBV framework to dynamic markets, hence the origin of the popular term dynamic capabilities within the strategic management literature. The dynamic capabilities perspective explains how some firms achieve a competitive advantage within industries characterized by unpredictable and rapid environmental changes. A firm's search for new sources of competitive advantage is typically viewed as being evolutionary and path dependent, meaning that technologies, and the institutions associated with them are self-reinforcing. Once a technology is established, it and its variations progressively dominate the market often at the social expense of improved technologies.

The RBV framework, albeit now the dominant paradigm in management and in some areas of economics, appears to be in contrast with the paradigm that preceded it, namely Porter's theory (1980, 1985) of competitive advantage. Porter's arguments are, to a large extent, a popularization of the so-called Harvard School ideas of industrial organization (IO), namely the structure–conduct–performance (S–C–P) paradigm originally set forth by Mason (1939) and Bain (1959). The S–C–P framework is based on the premise that an industry's performance depends on the conduct or behavior of buyers and sellers, and the conduct of buyers and sellers in turn depends on the structure of the industry in which they interact. An implication of the framework is that firms in consolidated industries can persistently earn excess profit by engaging in predatory behavior, such as creating or raising entry barriers, and, in general, exploiting their market power. Porter extended this framework by emphasizing the importance of the external environment of the firm in their formulation of strategy.

In apparent contrast to this emphasis on external forces, the RBV framework emphasizes internal forces and their impact on firm performance. The RBV framework is an extension of the so-called Chicago School of IO. The views of Demsetz (1973) and others asserted that the ability of firms to persistently earn excess profit is not due to their ability to exploit their market power, but rather because they are internally highly efficient or innovative. Chicago School economists have argued that the firm's possession of unique or appropriable assets or resources is important to its persistent competitive advantage.

Cockburn, Henderson, and Stern (2000) asserted that Porter's environmental perspective on corporate strategy and the RBV framework were not in contrast, but rather have complementary elements. While Porter's model is based on the notion that a corporate strategy of differentiation, in conjunction with desirable external industry conditions, can enable firms to achieve and possibly sustain a competitive advantage, proponents of the RBV framework focus on the firm's internal capabilities.

Not surprisingly, RBV research has evolved to focus on own self-financed investments in technological resources and capabilities as critical determinants of competitive advantage. For many large firms, R&D activity consists of internally funded and internally performed R&D projects, as well as internally funded and externally performed—in collaboration with other firms—R&D ventures. While both economics and management scholars have devoted much attention to evaluating the returns to internally performed R&D, relatively more attention has been shown by those in management to examining the antecedents and consequences of collaboration—technology alliances, networks, and partnerships involving other firms and organizations—as venues for the performance of R&D.

In discussing dynamic capabilities, Eisenhardt and Martin (2000) noted the importance of a technological gatekeeper in an organization. A technological gatekeeper is an individual, or perhaps a group of individuals, who engages in interacting with scientists in other organizations. Fostering such relationships generates two potential resource benefits to the firm. The first benefit is specific knowledge about others' innovations and technologies that could ultimately be appropriated, and the second benefit is general knowledge that could enhance the firm's workforce.

Powell, Koput, and Smith-Doerr (1996) and Henderson and Cockburn (1994) found, as had Link and Rees (1990), that such external relationships with scientists in other organizations helped firms in biotechnology and pharmaceuticals, respectively, increase their internal R&D efficiency. Both groups of authors interpreted these findings as indicative of the fact that scientific collaboration resulted in an enhancement in organizational capabilities. Such capabilities are critical in these industries because both sectors have been experiencing rapid technological change.

4.4.2. FRAMEWORK FOR ANALYSIS, MEASUREMENT ISSUES, AND EMPIRICAL EVIDENCE

Many academics have assessed the relationship between R&D and firm performance using the production function framework introduced in Chapter 3.[1]

$$Q = A(t) F(K, L, T) \qquad (4.1)$$

where Q represents output, $A(t)$ a disembodied shift factor, K capital, L labor, and T the stock of technical capital. Mathematically it follows, under the assumption that $F(\cdot)$ is Cobb–Douglas in nature and under the assumption that R&D (RD) is the primary investment flow into the stock of technical capital, that:

$$\acute{A}/A = \lambda + \rho\,(RD/Q) \qquad (4.2)$$

where, $\acute{A}/A$ is TFP growth and ρ is the return to investments in R&D. Griliches and Lichtenberg (1984) have referred to versions of equation (4.2) the R&D capital stock model.

Before reviewing the literature in which econometric versions of equation (4.2) have been estimated, it is important to emphasize several hallmark studies related to the formulation of the model itself and to the interpretation of an estimated value of ρ.

First, equation (4.2) is narrowly conceived because the firm's stock of technical knowledge, T, could come from alternative sources, not only from internally funded R&D. Following Charles River Associates (1981) and Tassey (1982), there are at least three general sources from which the firm could acquire technical knowledge. There is, of course, the firm itself through its own internally funded investments in R&D, as reflected in equation (4.2). And, the firm could itself invest in R&D and undertake that activity internally or in collaboration with other firms. The firm could purchase technologies from other firms thereby gaining applications of those firms' R&D (e.g. technologically advanced equipment in general or, for a specific example, specialized information technology (IT)). The firm could also acquire technical knowledge from the government, from federal laboratories in particular, or through the conduct of contracted R&D funded by the government. This later point, in particular the role of government in innovation, is discussed in Chapter 10.

Second, Scherer (1982) demonstrated that the estimation of ρ could be a conservative estimate of the private return to R&D because the R&D stock of technical knowledge depreciates over time.

And third, Schankerman (1981) argued that the effects of previous R&D activity are already included in measures of the stock of K and L, thus because of double counting ρ is really a measure of the excess rate of return—in excess of normal remuneration of conventional factors of production—to R&D.

Two approaches to estimating the contribution of R&D to firm performance as measured by TFP growth are commonly used. The first approach is to directly estimate the production function parameters from a version of equation (4.1), including some proxy for the level of R&D investment as an argument of the production function. The second approach is to estimate a reduced-form version of the R&D capital stock model, such as equation (4.2). In the review of the empirical literature that follows, the application of the first method is referred to as the production function approach, and the application of the second method is referred to as the R&D intensity approach.

A number of measurement issues surround the estimation of equation (4.2). These issues relate, in part, to the measurement of TFP growth and they are not specific to the framework for analysis. First, management scholars have typically been more interested than economists in other proxies for firm performance, such as those related to accounting profit and stock prices. Furthermore, it is notoriously difficult to derive accurate measures of TFP. This is especially the case when TFP measures are calculated from publicly available data-sets (e.g. Compustat (the United States), Datastream (UK), and Onesource (UK)). In fact, it is probably inappropriate to estimate TFP using such data—although it has been frequently done as reviewed in Link and Siegel (2003)—because reliable and comprehensive information on capital and intermediate materials are not typically reported on financial statements and thus are not contained in such data-sets.

Second, the accuracy of a TFP measure depends on the accuracy of input and output price deflators because inputs and output must be computed in constant dollars in order to construct real inputs and output measures. Mismeasurement of prices is caused primarily by incomplete adjustment for quality change. Siegel (1994) reported that the Bureau of Labor Statistics' (BLS) producer price index, the most commonly used indicator of the rate of inflation in the United States, misses, on average, about 40 percent of quality changes. The official policy of the BLS is that prices are adjusted for improvements in quality that are reflected in changes in cost or when new products are incorporated in the price index. This adjustment means that costless improvements in quality, due to technological change, are not reflected in the price measure.

Third, measurement errors are problematic in high-technology industries, and other sectors of the economy that make substantial investments in R&D and IT because such investments could improve the quality of inputs and output. Unfortunately, many quality improvements are not incorporated in price indexes. Thus, a quality bias could distort conventional estimates of the marginal productivity of investments in technology, which are typically based on the assumption that prices are measured without error.

And fourth, many large firms have plants in technologically diverse industries, with substantial variation in price changes. However, such plants must be grouped, at the corporate level, into a single industry classification to match with public domain data. As Lichtenberg and Siegel (1991) demonstrated, the use of a single set of inputs and output deflators to construct estimates of the real inputs and output of firms can introduce a substantial amount of measurement error into the calculation of TFP measures.

Selected firm-level studies of the R&D to productivity growth relationship are discussed below. Generally, firm-level estimates of productivity derived from establishment-level data overcome some of these problems (Griliches 1986; Lichtenberg and Siegel 1991).

There is a vast and important—important especially for public policy purposes—literature that analyzes the relationship between R&D and productivity growth. Table 4.4 summarizes the findings from selected firm-level studies.

On the basis of an analysis of US chemicals firms, Minasian (1969) reported that R&D has a positive and significant impact on productivity growth. He estimated the private rate of return to R&D to be 54 percent. Griliches (1980a, 1980b) extended his analysis to a much large sample of US manufacturing firms operating during a more recent period. He separated the R&D financed by the firm from the total R&D conducted by the firm, of which the federal government funded a portion, and he reports an overall lower estimated rate of return. Mansfield (1980) and Link (1981a, 1981b) reached a similar conclusion, but they also extended the scope of analysis by disaggregating self-financed R&D by character of use: basic research, applied research, and development. As reported by Odagiri (1983), Griliches and Mairesse (1983), and Griliches and Mairesse (1986), evidence from France and Japan during similar time periods was remarkably similar with the US findings.

A natural extension of the R&D capital stock model, whether based on the production function model or the R&D intensity reduced-form model, is to assess whether the returns to research vary by the character of use of R&D. Greater availability of comprehensive micro data-sets and greater acceptance of researcher-conducted firm surveys enabled versions of equation (4.2) to be estimated where the R&D variable is disaggregated both by character of use, by source of funding—self-financed R&D versus federally financed R&D—and by activity—R&D directed toward new products versus R&D directed to new processes. Other distinctions that have been analyzed by researchers include domestic versus foreign R&D and internal versus external R&D, where the latter refers to research that is contracted to other organizations.

Mansfield (1980), Link (1981a, 1981b), Griliches (1986), and Lichtenberg and Siegel (1991) found strong evidence that basic research generates a substantial productivity premium for firms. Furthermore, in their studies, each of the researchers decisively rejected the hypothesis that the returns to basic research are the same as those that accrue to the firm from its applied research or development investments. Link (1982a) found that the returns to process innovation are higher than the returns to product innovation, based on US data. Scherer (1982, 1983) and Terleckyj (1982) verified Link's finding at the US industry level, as did Medda, Piga, and Siegel (2005) for Italian firms.

Another result reported in several firm-level studies (Griliches 1986; Lichtenberg and Siegel 1991; Link 1981a, 1981b) is that self-financed R&D

Table 4.4. Firm-level empirical studies of the relationship between R&D and productivity growth

Author(s)/Year	Specification	Country	Characteristics of the study/key results
Minasian (1969)	Production function	United States	Small sample, 17 firms, estimated rate of return of 54%
Griliches (1980a, 1980b)	Production function	United States	Large sample, based on linking NSF annual survey of R&D to CM; estimated rate of return of 27% for total R&D and 36.5% for company financed R&D
Link (1980)	Production function	United States	Rate of return to R&D among chemical firms increases with the size of the chemical firm to a point, then remains constant
Mansfield (1980)	R&D intensity	United States	Estimated rate of return of 28% for self-funded R&D; high productivity premium associated with basic research
Link (1981a)	R&D intensity	United States	Positive and statistically significant relationship between R&D and output; estimated rate of return of 0%
Link (1981b)	R&D intensity	United States	High productivity premium associated with basic research
Schankerman (1981)	Production function	United States	First study to address 'double counting' of physical and knowledge capital when assessing the returns to R&D; estimated rate of return of 49%
Link (1982a)	R&D intensity	United States	Higher returns to process innovation than product innovation
Link (1982b)	Production function	United States	Small impact from federal R&D on productivity growth of firms; rate of return low
Link (1982c)	Production function	United States	R&D directed to meeting environmental regulations has no measurable impact on productivity growth of chemical firms
Odagiri (1983)	R&D intensity	Japan	Large sample (N = 370) of Japanese manufacturing firms; estimated rate of return of 11%; highest returns in the chemicals, drug, and electric equipment industries
Griliches and Mairesse (1983)	Production function	United States and France	Panel data econometrics; estimated rate of return of 19%
Link (1983)	Production function	United States	Technology embodied in purchased capital has positive impact on productivity growth of firms purchasing the capital
Clark and Griliches (1984)	R&D intensity	United States	On the basis of the 'PIMS' File-A 'Business-Unit' data-set; estimated rate of return of 20%; no evidence of deterioration in returns to R&D during the 1970s
Griliches and Mairesse (1984)	Production function (levels and first differences)	United States	Panel data econometrics to deal with simultaneity problem between R&D and productivity; estimated rate of return of 42%
Griliches (1986)	Production function and R&D intensity	United States	On the basis of a large US Census-based sample of firms; estimated rate of return of 39%; productivity premium for basic research
Griliches and Mairesse (1986)	Production function (levels and first differences)	United States and Japan	Panel data econometrics to deal with simultaneity problem between R&D and productivity; estimated rate of return of 33%

Study	Approach	Country	Findings
Bernstein and Nadiri (1989a)	Dynamic duality approach (dynamic cost function estimation)	United States	Controls for the 'quasi-fixity' of physical capital by allowing for adjustment costs; estimated rate of return of 33%
Bernstein and Nadiri (1989b)	Dynamic duality approach (dynamic cost function estimation)	United States	Controls for the 'quasi-fixity' of physical capital by allowing for adjustment costs; estimated rate of return of 33%
Lichtenberg and Siegel (1991)	Production function and R&D intensity	United States	Large sample (over 2000 firms); based on linking NSF annual survey of R&D to ASM; estimated rates of return of 13% to total R&D, 35% to self-financed R&D, 134% to basic research; impact of R&D on productivity remained strong during the productivity slowdown during the 1970s
Hall and Mairesse (1995)	Production function (levels and first differences)	France	Impact of R&D on productivity high in the 1980s; correction for double counting important; parametric estimation of production function preferred to the R&D intensity model; estimated rate of return of 33%
Griliches and Regev (1995)	Production function (levels and first differences)	Israel	Rate of return to R&D estimated five times higher than return to investment in physical capital
Crepon, Duguet, and Mairesse (1998)	Production function (levels and first differences)	France	Controls for simultaneity and selectivity (some firms do no R&D) in econometric analysis; estimated rate of return of 33%
Loof and Heshmati (2002)	R&D intensity	Sweden	Controls for simultaneity and selectivity in econometric analysis; estimated rate of return of 13%
Medda, Piga, and Siegel (2003, 2005)	Production function and R&D intensity	Italy	Controls for selectivity in econometric analysis; estimated rate of return of 33%; external R&D has stronger impact on productivity than internal R&D, especially R&D conducted jointly with universities

is a significant determinant of own productivity growth but federally financed R&D investment is not. These results are consistent with industry-level evidence presented in Terleckyj (1974) and Griliches and Lichtenberg (1984). There are at least two related explanations for such a finding. First, it is often the case that federally financed R&D is of a development nature, which will not likely be correlated with productivity growth measured in terms of TFP growth.

Second, federally financed R&D may not have a directly measurable impact on TFP but rather an indirect relationship since it likely increases the efficiency of the firm's own financed R&D (Link 1981a). Leyden, Link, and Bozeman (1989) and Leyden and Link (1991a, 1991b) found that public and private R&D are complements, although Lichtenberg (1984, 1987, 1988) presented empirical evidence that is inconsistent with this hypothesis. David, Hall, and Toole (2000) have reconciled this debate.

Another issue investigated within the R&D capital stock model is whether a firm's internal research projects generate higher internal returns to the firm than external research projects. The latter category includes collaborative research—conducted through RJVs and other research partnerships—as well as contract research with other organizations. Medda, Piga, and Siegel (2003) found that external R&D, especially that R&D conducted jointly with universities, had a stronger impact on productivity than internal R&D among Italian firms, confirming the earlier preliminary finding by Link, Tassey, and Zmud (1983) and Link and Rees (1990). In a similar vein, Link (1981a, 1981b) and Link and Bauer (1989) found that collaborative R&D increases the effectiveness of self-financed internally performed R&D.

As the literature on the relationship between R&D and productivity growth evolved and firm- and plant-level micro data-sets became more readily available, economists and management scholars have developed improved modeling and econometric techniques. These techniques permit researchers to relax some of the assumptions inherent to many of the earlier estimated versions of models.

For example, Bernstein and Nadiri (1989a, 1989b) provided an important extension of the literature in two respects. First, the authors estimated a version of equation (4.2) that is not based on the restrictive assumption that the underlying production process is Cobb–Douglas. Implicit in the assumption of a Cobb–Douglas production function is that factor markets are perfectly competitive and thus a firm will instantaneously adjust its capital and labor. Bernstein and Nadiri relaxed this assumption by incorporating input, capital in particular, adjustment costs in the econometric procedure. This adjustment was critical because some studies (Paul and Siegel 1999) showed that ignoring fixities in capital result in biased estimates of the returns to R&D. The second innovation in the Bernstein and Nadiri studies is the use of a cost function rather than a production function. This is important because cost minimization is regarded as a more viable maintained assumption than profit maximization, which is the maintained assumption in production function analysis.

There are at least two important and related econometric issues regarding the R&D capital stock model: namely, simultaneity between R&D and productivity growth, and a misspecification of the model. The simultaneity issue was first discussed by Baumol and Wolff (1983), who assert that standard reduced form R&D to productivity growth equations does not take account of feedback effects from productivity growth to either the level of R&D or its efficiency. Regarding specification, there is a related body of literature on the determinants of a firm's decision to engage in R&D. Correlated with that decision are firm size, firm diversification, ownership structure of the firm, and other related variables.

To the extent that these variables are correlated with productivity growth, estimates of the rate of return to R&D are likely to be biased. More specifically, a failure to control for the firm-level decision to engage in R&D is potentially problematic, since many companies report zero R&D expenditure. It is interesting to note that most empirical studies of the returns to R&D have been based only on firms that conduct R&D. A failure to take account of the determinants of the decision to engage in innovation might result in underestimation of the returns to R&D for the representative firm.

Crepon, Duguet, and Mairesse (1998) were the first scholars to deal with both of these econometric concerns simultaneously. The empirical results in Crepon, Duguet, and Mairesse (1998) are important because they found that simultaneity appears to interact with selectivity. Their estimates of the private return to R&D were lower with these adjustments than without. Loof and Heshmati (2002) presented similar findings using a sample of Swedish firms. Medda, Piga, and Siegel (2003) confirmed these results, based on a sample of Italian firms.

In sum, several key stylized facts have emerged from the vast empirical literature on the connection between R&D and productivity growth literature. These are:

- The private returns to R&D investments appear to be positive, and statistically significant, across nations and during most time periods, even during the global productivity slowdown of the 1970s and early 1980s.

- Evidence of large private returns to R&D suggests that firms are under investing in R&D from a social perspective. This finding has been used to justify public policies to encourage additional private R&D.

- The private returns to firm-financed R&D appear to be higher than comparable returns to federally financed R&D.

- There appears to be a productivity premium associated with basic research.

- Correcting for simultaneity and sample selection bias appears to reduce the magnitude of estimates of the returns to R&D, but they are still positive and statistically significant.

- Similar patterns emerge from cost-function and production-function based studies of the relationship between R&D and productivity.

4.5. Research partnerships and firm performance

4.5.1. STRATEGIC RESEARCH PARTNERSHIPS

The empirical literature on the relationship between research partnerships and firm performance is essentially an extension of the research on R&D and productivity growth. This is the case because research partnerships involve strategic R&D activity—hence the often used term strategic research partnership (SRP)—and productivity growth is an important aspect of firm performance. Also, the notion of research partnerships follows from the RBV because collaboration is a purposive effort to expand the level of resources and capabilities per se as well as the effectiveness of resources and capabilities.

The RJVs are a subset of SRPs. RJVs are discussed from a public policy perspective in Chapter 10 as an example of the government as entrepreneur and innovation. There is a vast empirical literature on the antecedents and consequences of participation in an RJV, which we review below.

The salient characteristics and results from this empirical literature are presented in Table 4.5. For the purpose of constructing this table, partnerships are defined broadly to include RJVs, strategic alliances and networks, industry consortia, CRADAs, participation in infrastructural organizations (e.g. ERCs, IUCRCs, FFRDCs, science/research parks), relationships between high-technology firms and venture capital funds, licensing and research agreements (involving universities, government laboratories, and firms), university-based entrepreneurial start-ups, and coauthoring between academics and industry scientists. Many of these are public–private partnerships.

The activities included in this definition of a partnership have expanded in recent years due to the rise in university–industry technology transfer (UITT) activities. As described in Siegel, Waldman, and Link (2003), the recent increase in UITT, through a technology transfer office (TTO) and other formal means, led to a concomitant rise in the incidence and complexity of research partnerships involving universities and firms. In recent years, universities have become more receptive to the idea of accepting an equity position in an entrepreneurial start-up, in lieu of up-front licensing revenue.

There have been several data-sets analyzed in such empirical studies. As noted in Hagedoorn, Link, and Vonortas (2000), the three key files used

Table 4.5. Empirical studies of the relationship between research partnerships and firm performance

Author(s)/Year	Partnership(s)	Methodology	Measure of firm performance
Link and Bauer (1989)	US RJVs	Regression analysis	Market share, rate of return to self-financed R&D
Hagedoorn and Schakenraad (1994)	Strategic technology alliances	Structural equation modeling (LISREL)	Patents
Sakakibara (1997a)	Japanese research consortia	Regression analysis	Qualitative measures of project-related firm R&D expenditure
Sakakibara (1997b)	Japanese research consortia	Regression analysis	Contribution of R&D consortia to the establishment of competitive position
Branstetter and Sakakibara (1998)	Japanese research consortia	Regression analysis	Patents
Cockburn and Henderson (1998)	US collaborative relationships involving public and privately financed scientists	Regression analysis	R&D expenditures; important patents
Baum, Calabrese, and Silverman (2000)	Strategic technology alliances in Canadian biotechnology industry	Regression analysis	Revenues, R&D employees, R&D expenditure, and patents
Scott (1996)	US environmental RJVs	Regression analysis	Self-reported and statistical measures of the effects of cooperation on R&D
Link, Teece, and Finan (1996)	US research joint venture (RJV), SEMATECH	Qualitative analysis	Self-reported measures of success
Link (1998a)	US government-sponsored R&D projects, ATP	Qualitative analysis	Effects on research productivity
Vonortas (1999)	US government-sponsored R&D projects, ATP	Qualitative analysis	Effects on research productivity
Link and Scott (1998a)	US government-sponsored R&D projects, ATP	Qualitative analysis	Commercialization results, spillover effects; effects on competitiveness
Lerner (1999)	US government-funded R&D projects, SBIR program	Regression analysis	Growth in employment and sales; ability of firms to attract venture capital funding
Griliches and Regev (1995)	Government-funded R&D projects conducted by Israeli manufacturing firms	Regression analysis	R&D expenditure, TFP
Klette and Moen (1998)	Government-funded R&D projects conducted by Norwegian manufacturing firms	Regression analysis	Private R&D expenditure; ratio of self-financed R&D to sales
Klette and Moen (1999)	Government-funded R&D projects in IT conducted by Norwegian manufacturing firms	Regression analysis	Private R&D expenditure; ratio of self-financed R&D to sales

(Cont.)

Table 4.5. Continued

Author(s)/Year	Partnership(s)	Methodology	Measure of firm performance
Wallsten (2000)	US government-funded R&D projects, SBIR program	Regression analysis	R&D expenditures
Gompers and Lerner (1999)	US firms financed by venture capital firms	Regression analysis	Limited analysis of the financial performance of venture capital funds
Hall, Link, and Scott (2001)	US government-sponsored R&D projects, ATP	Regression analysis	No direct measure of performance except project termination; qualitative measures of how universities and firms interact in research
Adams, Chiang, and Starkey (2001)	US UITT; IUCRCs; ERCs; NSF science and technology centers; industrial laboratories	Regression analysis	Hiring of engineering and science graduates; coauthoring with academics; using faculty members as consultants; patents; R&D expenditure
Gray, Lindblad, and Rudolph (2001)	US UITT; IUCRCs	Regression analysis	Member retention in IUCRC
Santoro and Gopalakrishnan (2001)	US UITT; ERCs; IUCRCs	Regression analysis and qualitative research	Self-reported measures of technology transfer activity involving research centers
Caloghirou, Tsakanikas, and Vonortas (2001)	UITT transfer-RJVs involving universities; European Frameworks Programme	Regression analysis	Self-reported measures of various aspects of R&D performance; ability to achieve synergies in research and proxies for absorptive capacity
Adams, Chiang, and Jensen (2000)	CRADAs involving US federal laboratories and firms	Regression analysis	Patents; R&D expenditure
Jaffe, Fogarty, and Banks (1998)	US federal laboratory, Electro-Physics Branch (EPB) of the NASA Lewis Research Center	Qualitative analysis	Citations of patents; proxies for absorptive capacity
Siegel, Westhead, and Wright (2003a, 2003b)	UK firms located on UK science parks	Regression analysis	Patents; copyrights; new products/services to existing customer base; new products/services in new markets; TFP of research efforts

in these analyses are the Maastricht Economic Research Institute on Innovation and Technology-Cooperative Agreements & Technology Indicators (MERIT-CATI) file, the NSF's CORE (COoperative REsearch) data-set, and the National Cooperative Research Act-Research Joint Venture (NCRA-RJV) data-set.

Numerous authors have also examined specially constructed data-sets, consisting of firms that have received funds from government programs that support technology-based partnerships, such as the Advanced Technology Program (ATP) within the US Department of Commerce's National Institute of Standards and Technology (NIST) and the US SBIR programs (Audretsch, Link, and Scott 2002; Link 1996a, 1998a, 2001; Link and Scott 1998a, 2001; Vonortas 1999). Typically, these authors have linked program-specific information to firm-level surveys of production, R&D, profitability, and stock prices in order to assess the impact of the SRP on firm performance (Lerner 1999, Wallsten 2000).

A portion of the research summarized in Table 4.5 is based on qualitative analysis. In fact, some researchers have designed their own surveys and administered them to firms involved in SRPs (Adams, Chiang, and Starkey 2001; Franklin, Wright, and Lockett 2001; Hertzfeld, Link, and Vonortas 2006; Link and Bauer 1989; Meseri and Maital 2001). Also, researchers have availed themselves of proprietary data-sets, such as files created by the Securities Data Company, Science Citation Index, Recombinant Capital, Corporate Technology Directory, and Venture Economics (Anand and Khanna 2000; Cockburn and Henderson 1998; Lerner and Merges 1998) in efforts to capture, quantitatively, as many of the subtleties associated with collaboration as possible. Several empirical studies of SRPs resulting from UITT are based on the comprehensive survey conducted by the Association of University Technology Managers (AUTM) (Carlsson and Fridh 2002; Friedman and Silberman 2003; Siegel, Waldman, and Link 2003; Thursby and Thursby 2002). Other authors have relied on archival data on patents, licenses, and start-ups at several major universities (Mowery and Ziedonis 2000).

In addition to myriad data sources, authors within this genre of research have defined firm performance in several ways. The more conventional measures are patent activity, short-run movements in stock prices, TFP growth, and R&D activities. Researchers have also examined technology licensing, patents and scholarly article citations, coauthoring behavior, job and new firm survival, new products, and revenue growth. Not surprisingly, management and finance scholars have tended to focus on explaining financial performance and accounting profitability, while economists have typically analyzed the impact of partnerships on various dimensions of R&D behavior—R&D inputs such as expenditures and R&D outputs such as patenting and even TFP growth.

In summary, there are several key stylized facts that emerge from the SRP literature. These are:

- Investment in a SRP is associated with greater firm performance.
- Involvement in a SRP leverages the efficiency of self-financed R&D at both the time of involvement as well as in subsequent periods.

Regarding this second stylized fact, the implicit assumption from which it follows is that the underlying production function is:

$$Q = A(t) F(K, L, B(t)T) \qquad (4.3)$$

where, the augmentation of T is through $B(t)$ and $B(t)$ characterizes the nature and extent to which firms engage in SRPs.

4.5.2. EVENT STUDIES

In recent years, many researchers have used the event study methodology to assess the impact of technology-related activities or events, such as firm involvement in RJVs and strategic technology alliances as well as R&D investment activity, on firm performance measured in terms of a stock price effect. The logic of event studies is that the event, meaning the announcement of a firm's unanticipated investment in a technology-related activity or an unanticipated technological occurrence, provides new information about the potential future profitability of the firm. The more important is the event, the greater the effect is on the firm's stock price.

Event studies have several advantages. First, they focus on an observable market output associated with a firm's technology-related investments. In most cases, a firm will not report such output. Patents are one exception, but not all innovative firms patent. And second, stock prices are an output that cannot be manipulated in the short run by managers, whereas accounting profit can be. Despite the advantages of event studies, they do suffer from several critical limitations. As McWilliams and Siegel (1997) noted, event studies are based on a number of limiting assumptions, and thus the results from event studies may not accurately inform future managerial strategies. One such assumption is that the event being studied is unanticipated, which may or may not be the case. Furthermore, by the nature of stock prices, only publicly traded firms are candidates in event studies, but many closely held firms are equally as innovative. Finally, Shleifer (2000), among others, has expressed skepticism about the efficient markets hypothesis, which provides the theoretical basis for the capital asset pricing model and the associated event study methodology. Thus, short-run movements in stock prices may not be an accurate proxy for the long-run performance of technology-based firms.

The standard event study methodology is based on a regression market index model:

$$R_{it} = a_i + \beta_i R_{mt} + \varepsilon_{it} \qquad (4.4)$$

where R_{it} is the rate of return on the share price of the being-studied firm, firm i, over time period, t, prior to the technological event being studied having occurred; R_{mt} is the rate of return on a portfolio of comparable stocks over period t; a_i is the intercept term; β_i is the slope coefficient which is interpreted as a measure of the systematic risk of the firm; and ε_{it} is the error term.

Given regression estimates of a_i, $\tilde{a}_i$, and of β_i, $\tilde{\beta}_i$, the firm's abnormal stock return (AR) meaning its return above what would normally be predicted from equation (4.4) is a residual defined as:

$$AR_{it} = R_{it} - (\tilde{a}_i + \tilde{\beta}_i R_{mt}) \qquad (4.5)$$

On the basis of versions of equation (4.5), the statistical analysis in an event study asks if the abnormal returns, over a short period of time, hypothesized to be associated with the technology event, are statistically different from zero.

Table 4.6 synthesizes the results from a number of event studies. In summary, there are several key stylized facts that emerge from the event studies of SRPs:

- The announcement of a technology-related event, such as firm involvement in an RJV or technology alliance, enhances shareholder value.
- The results from event studies are sensitive to minor changes in assumptions and model specification.

In general, however, the stock market evidence appears to be consistent with studies based on alternative measures of performance.

4.6. **Information technology and firm performance**

In addition to the literature reviewed above on R&D-based factors affecting firm performance, there is also a burgeoning empirical literature on the relationship between investment IT—computers and related equipment which embody the R&D of producers—and firm performance. In the United States in 2004, US firms invested nearly three times as much in IT (equipment and software) than in any other form of capital equipment. In 2004, such investments totaled about $560 billion, compared to total R&D performed in the United States of just over $300 billion.[2]

The results from selected empirical studies are presented in Table 4.7. Many of these studies begin with a Cobb–Douglas production function that includes

Table 4.6. Event studies of technology investment activities

Author(s)/Year	Technology event	Key results from the study
Anand and Khanna (2000)	Joint ventures, some of which were RJVs, and licensing contracts	Effect of learning though cooperative activity on value creation highest for RJVs
Chan, Martin, and Kensinger (1990)	Announcements of increases in R&D expenditures	Announcements of increase in R&D expenditures enhance share prices; firms whose R&D intensity exceeds the industry average have superior share price performance
Sundaram, John, and John (1996)	Announcements of increases in R&D expenditures	Announcements of increase in R&D expenditures enhance share price
Chan et al. (1997)	Strategic technology alliances	Announcements of joint R&D agreements enhance share price
Merchant and Schendel (2000)	Joint ventures, some of which were RJVs	Joint ventures that involve R&D activity enhance shareholder value
Madhavan and Prescott (1995)	Joint ventures, some of which were RJVs	Joint ventures that involve R&D activity enhance shareholder value
Reuer (2000)	Joint ventures, some of which are RJVs	Increases in shareholder value resulting from formation of joint ventures are positively correlated with R&D intensity
Dos Santos, Peffers, and Mauer (1993)	Major investments in IT	In general, investments in IT do not generate gains to shareholders; innovative investments in IT enhance shareholder wealth
Im, Dow, and Grover (2001)	Major investments in IT	Investments in IT enhance shareholder wealth for small firms, but not for large firms; market reacted more positively to more recent investment announcements; industry effects also important
Chen and Siems (2001)	Establishment of B2B e-marketplaces	B2B e-commerce initiatives result in an increase in shareholder wealth for both horizontal and vertical e-marketplace announcements
Subramani and Walden (2001)	E-commerce initiatives	E-commerce initiatives result in increase in shareholder wealth; higher returns associated with B2C initiatives than with B2B initiatives
Janney and Folta (2003)	Private equity placements of biotechnology firms	Private equity placements of biotechnology firms enhance shareholder wealth

Table 4.7. Studies of the relationship between information technology and firm performance

Author(s)/Year	Methodology	Key results from the study
Dunne et al. (2000)	Production function	Positive association between computers and labor productivity
Lehr and Lichtenberg (1999)	Production function with computer capital and computer labor	Excess returns to computer capital, especially personal computers; returns to computers peaked in 1986 or 1987
Licht and Moch (1999)	Production function including three types of computers (terminals, UNIX workstations, and PCs)	Terminals have positive impact on productivity in goods industries, but not in services; strong positive relationship between PCs and productivity in manufacturing and services
Gera, Wu, and Lee (1999)	Production function	Positive correlation between investment in computers and labor productivity growth
Stolarick (1999)	Production function	Positive relationship between spending on computers and plant productivity
Bharadwaj, Bharadwaj, and Konsynski (1999)	Profit analysis, Tobin's q	Positive relationship between investments in IT and Tobin's q
McGuckin, Streitwieser, and Doms (1998)	Production function	Plants using advanced computer-based technologies have higher levels of productivity; weaker evidence on the relationship between technology usage and productivity growth
Lehr and Lichtenberg (1998)	Production function	Excess returns to computer capital
Greenan and Mairesse (1996)	Production function	Positive impact of computers, equal to impact for other types of capital; returns appear to be higher in services than in manufacturing
Brynjolfsson and Hitt (1996)	Production function	Excess returns to computer capital and labor
Hitt and Brynjolfsson (1996)	Production function	Computers enhance productivity and consumer surplus, but not profitability
Lichtenberg (1995)	Production function	Excess private returns to computer capital and labor
Parsons, Gottlieb, and Denny (1993)	Cost function	Low returns on investments in computers for banks

an IT input variable serving a proxy for investment in computers, both computer capital and computer labor (Brynjolfsson and Hitt 1996; Lichtenberg 1995).

Much of the recent firm-level evidence suggests that there are excess returns to IT (i.e. the marginal product of IT capital is substantially higher than the marginal product of non-IT capital). There is also some evidence that these private or firm-level returns have become higher in recent years. This latter finding is important because there was a lack of a consensus regarding empirical results, at least in some of the early studies. Using country-level data, Oliner and Sichel (1994) concluded that IT did not make a significant contribution to output growth. Morrison (1997) reached a similar conclusion using industry-level data. On the basis of estimation of a more elaborate set of cost-function equations, including the price and quantity of IT equipment as separate arguments in the cost function, she reported that IT capital had only a very small impact on technical progress. Berndt, Morrison, and Rosenblum (1992) estimated production functions at the industry level and found that IT was uncorrelated with productivity growth in most industries. Parsons, Gotlieb, and Denny (1993) also found very low returns to IT investment by Canadian banks. Siegel and Griliches (1992), in contrast, reported a positive and significant correlation between a manufacturing industry's rate of investment in IT and its productivity growth across various time periods. At the firm level, Lichtenberg (1995) estimated production functions and similarly found strong evidence of excess returns to information systems equipment and labor.

Most of the recent papers find a strong relationship between IT and improvements in economic performance. Stiroh (2001) and Jorgenson and Stiroh (2000) reported some good news regarding the aggregate impact of investment in IT in the United States. In early studies, Jorgenson and Stiroh (1995) reported that computers did not make a large contribution to economic growth, reporting low estimates of the returns to IT that were quite similar to those presented in Oliner and Sichel (1994). However, in recent papers (e.g. Jorgenson, Ho, and Stiroh 2002), they concluded that the impact of IT on the aggregate economic performance has increased over time and especially in the last half of the 1990s.

On the basis of a comprehensive analysis of IT capital, Jorgenson, Ho, and Stiroh (2002) reported that computer hardware, software, and communications equipment accounted for a much larger fraction of economic growth in the last six years than in earlier periods. This may signify that there are substantial adjustment costs in implementing IT and that policymakers should not expect dramatic improvements in productivity growth in the short run. The economic payoff comes only after a substantial increase in IT investment or activity.

In a similar vein, Morrison and Siegel (1997) considered the possibility that conventional empirical studies of the connection between IT and productivity have underestimated the returns to IT, because they fail to take account of externalities that arise from investment in IT. The authors extended the simple Cobb–Douglas production framework by estimating a dynamic, flexible cost function—a Generalized Leontief functional form—for US manufacturing industries. This specification takes account of adjustment costs that might arise from IT and other capital investments. Their paper is a general critique and extension of various new growth studies that had used a simple production function approach to assess the impact of what the authors call external factors, such as investment in R&D, computers, and human capital, on growth. More importantly, they estimated the effects of external investments in computers on the productivity of a given industry, that is IT investments undertaken by other industries within the same broad sectoral category. The authors reported that an increase in investment in IT, and R&D, in a given industry has a positive effect on the productivity performance of other industries, both a positive impact on their suppliers and on their customers. These results are broadly consistent with the notion that IT, and the Internet in particular as discussed in Chapter 7, constitute what leading economists refer to as general purpose technology (GPT) (Helpman 1998), meaning a technology that has wide applications and productivity-enhancing effects in numerous downstream sectors.

Most of the firm-level evidence also suggests that IT has a positive impact on productivity. Lichtenberg (1995) found strong evidence of excess returns to information systems equipment and labor. Other production function studies reach the same conclusion, as reported in Table 4.7.

Siegel (1997) estimated a reduced form of the R&D capital stock model to assess the relationship between computers and productivity. He conjectured that investments in computers exacerbate errors in measuring output and input prices because computers improve both output quality and labor quality. Because these improvements are not properly accounted for in conventional productivity growth calculations, estimates of computer investments are biased downward. When statistical adjustments are made for measurement errors, computers do, in fact, enhance overall productivity growth.

McGuckin, Streitwieser, and Doms (1998) conducted the first plant-level study of the impact of IT investment on performance. The authors reported that plants using advanced computer-based technologies have higher levels of labor productivity. In a similar vein, Stolarick (1999) found a positive relationship between spending on computers and TFP growth at the plant-level. Using firm-level data from France, Greenan and Mairesse (1996), reported for US firms that the impact of computers on productivity growth is positive and at least as large as for other types of capital. Interestingly, the authors also found that the returns appear to be higher in services than in manufacturing.

Scholars who analyzed the impact of IT on worker or firm performance realize that the use of IT is often accompanied by dramatic changes in the work environment. Siegel (1999) found that the implementation of new advanced manufacturing technologies, including IT, induce companies to invest additional resources in training and to enhance employee empowerment. On the basis of supplemental case studies, it appears that organizational changes accompanying the technological changes are quite dramatic, in part because many of the technologies are integrative having an effect on numerous functional areas of the firm such as R&D, marketing, purchasing, logistics, manufacturing, and materials management. More importantly, in the aftermath of the technological change, the work environment changed with information and duties were more likely to be shared among workers performing different functional tasks.

Bresnahan, Brynjolfsson, and Hitt (2001) provided evidence on the relationship between technological change, organizational change, and performance. They hypothesized that decentralized decision-making and greater communication within an organization are required to successfully implement new technologies. The authors estimated a three factor Cobb–Douglas production function including labor, noncomputer capital, and computer capital. As they predicted, the interaction of applications of computer capital and organizational decentralization is positive and significant.

There have also been several useful case studies of the impact of IT, and the Internet, on firm performance. Carayannis, Alexander, and Geraghty (2001) presented interesting examples of how the Internet through business-to-business (B2B) commerce is used in two traditional US industries; petroleum and chemicals. They demonstrated how Internet and e-commerce technologies are used as a GPT resulting in improvements in quality and productivity in services.

Numerous examples of the economic benefits from the Internet are summarized in Litan and Rivlin (2001). Internet-related productivity improvements are varied; they include savings on transactions costs (with suppliers and customers), more efficient management, and other economic benefits including product variety and consumer choice, improvements in health care outcomes, and convenience. Litan and Rivlin (2001) concluded that the Internet will likely add only one-quarter to one-half of 1 percent per year to US productivity growth. Estimates for other countries have not been made.

McAfee's case study (2001) of Cisco Systems, which is not only the world's leading producer of routers and other Internet networking equipment but is also a leading user of the Internet in organizing its manufacturing through outsourcing, concluded that Cisco estimates that it saved about $650 million between 1995 and 1999—5 percent of its revenue in 1999—from intensive use of the Internet as a management tool. According to McAfee, many manufacturing firms have tried to emulate Cisco's success by forming virtual supply chains and B2B exchanges to generate cost savings.

Fine and Raff (2001) concluded that the largest productivity gains from the Internet in the automotive sector came from improvements in supply-chain management. They concluded that the clear winner in using information and communication technology (ICT) and the Internet is Daimler–Benz, which developed an approach called the extended enterprise. Daimler–Benz committed to long-term relationships with suppliers to develop complete subsystems and to share any cost savings benefit of ICT with them. Thus, the Internet facilitated for Daimler–Benz quasi vertical integration strategy, also commonly used among Japanese firms.

Clemons and Hitt (2001) asserted that productivity gains in the US financial services industry arose over time from transparency, pricing, and disintermediation. They defined transparency as the ability of consumers and corporate customers to assess the full range of prices and qualities of the various financial instruments and services. The authors estimated productivity gains, in terms of cost savings, of about $18 billion per year.

Nagarajan et al. (2001) presented case studies illustrating how firms in the trucking industry have used the Internet to enhance productivity. They identified new companies that have emerged to exploit Internet-related opportunities such as the use of direct links so that customers can access relevant data, and to exploit the implementation of programs to streamline efficiency in routing and shipments.

Danzon and Furukawa (2001) examined Internet initiatives in the US health care and pharmaceuticals industry. They disaggregated these efforts into those relating to connectivity, content, commerce, and care. The authors asserted that optimal connectivity could enable providers, payers, and patients to have seamless access to information, which could greatly reduce the demand for clerical labor, improve customer service, and most importantly, enable physicians to spend additional time with patients. They also found that significant cost savings can arise in supply chain management, through B2B e-commerce.

Fountain and Osorio-Urzua (2001) provided some facts about the use of Internet technology in the US governmental sector, and they found substantial cost savings arising from e-government initiatives, which appear to be strongly dependent on the extent to which Internet use is pervasive in the relevant community.

Goolsbee (2001) examined online higher education, and other Internet-related initiatives in the educational sector. He concluded that there is substantial potential cost savings to be derived from an industry that he characterizes as massive, regulated, and bureaucratic. He also included in this category uses of the Internet in corporate training. Several examples of the creative applications of the technology to graduate business education, such as the numerous on-line executive MBA programs at leading universities throughout the world are presented. The author identified

DigitalThink as the leading firm in this segment. This company provides computer training courses that are complete and delivered through the Web to clients such as Cisco Systems, Motorola, Intel, and other high-technology firms.

In summary, there are several key stylized facts that emerge from the IT and firm performance studies. These are:

- The use of IT typically results in an improvement in firm performance.
- The use of IT has transformed numerous industries in the service sector.
- The use of IT is often accompanied by dramatic changes in the work environment.

4.7. R&D, information technology, and worker performance

4.7.1. FRAMEWORK FOR ANALYSIS

Two additional dimensions of firm performance that are influenced by technology are the relative compensation of different types of workers and workforce composition. Economists refer to the technological change that favors highly skilled and highly educated workers as skill-biased technological change (SBTC). The SBTC hypothesis, originally proposed by Nelson and Phelps (1966), and later extended by Griliches (1969, 1970) and Welch (1970), asserts that the economic value of skilled workers is augmented by new technology. More specifically, workers embodied with a higher level of knowledge, or skill set, are able to implement new technology more efficiently and thus are more highly valued by the firm. Bartel and Lichtenberg (1987) proposed that the comparative advantage of highly skilled or highly educated workers in implementing new technology arises from their ability to solve problems and adapt to change in the work environment. The SBTC models predict that new technology is biased or nonneutral with respect to labor, having a disproportionate effect on different classes of workers.

A large number of empirical studies of SBTC have been based on estimation of a wage equation, with the inclusion of dummy variables serving as proxies for technological change:

$$w_i = f(X, D) \tag{4.6}$$

where, w_i is the wage of the ith worker, X is a vector of the workers human capital characteristics (e.g. level of education), and D is a dummy variable measuring if the ith worker works with technology (e.g. computers).

A more precise way to test for SBTC involves incorporating the technology variables in a cost function. Such a specification facilitates a formal test for the nonneutrality of technological change. More importantly, the cost function framework permits an examination of a more relevant dependent variable, changes over time in the relative share of highly skilled or highly educated workers (Berman, Bound, and Griliches 1994).

Several potential econometric problems plague these and related studies. One concern is the possibility that relative wages are endogenous. Another problem is simultaneity; the age of in place technology could be determined by changes in relative wages as well as by the rate of investment in technology. And, there may be multicollinearity among the technology indicator because they are measuring complementary phenomenon.

4.7.2. EMPIRICAL EVIDENCE

Despite these econometric issues, a vast literature has emerged on the impact of R&D and IT on worker performance, as summarized in Table 4.8. Despite the use of different methodologies and an analysis of data from many countries at different levels of aggregation (individual, plant, firm, and industry levels), all authors report that technological change—proxied by either R&D, computers, or adoption of advanced manufacturing technologies, etc.—is positively correlated with wages and changes in labor composition in favor of highly skilled or highly educated workers.

Many studies have reported findings based on industry-level regressions of changes in employment shares or wages on proxies for technological change, such as R&D investment. For example, Berman, Bound, and Griliches (1994) reported a positive association between investments in R&D and computers and changes in nonproduction workers' share of the industry wage bill. They interpreted this finding as indicative of skill upgrading. Using similar techniques, Mishel and Bernstein (1994) included the employment share of scientists and engineers in the industry as an additional indicator of technological change. They also found a positive correlation between proxies for technological change and shifts in demand in favor of highly educated workers. They also reported that the strength of this association has not become stronger in the 1980s.

Other industry-level studies are consistent with these results. Berndt, Morrison, and Rosenblum (1992) reported a positive correlation between high technology office equipment and the demand for white-collar workers. In a recent study, based on estimation of a latent variables model, Siegel (1997) found a positive association between proxies for labor quality and computer investments. Finally, Bartel and Lichtenberg (1987, 1990) reported that the demand for highly educated workers is inversely related to the age of an

Table 4.8. Empirical studies of the impact of R&D and information technology on wages and labor composition

Author(s)/Year	Methodology/Country	Technology	Labor input	Key results from the study
Bartel and Sicherman (1999)	Estimation of wage equations/US	Investments in computers, R&D	Production and nonproduction workers	Positive correlation between wages and technology, stronger for nonproduction workers; wage premium attributed to greater demand for ability in industries experiencing technological change
Haskel (1999)	Regressions of changes in relative wages of workers on computers/UK	Dummy variable denoting whether a plant introduced new equipment using microchip technology	Skilled and unskilled workers	Positive correlation between relative wages and computers; wage premium for skill rose by 13% in the 1980s; computers account for about half of the increase
Paul and Siegel (2001)	Dynamic cost function estimation with high tech capital/US	Computer capital and R&D	Four types of workers, classified by level of education	Workers with at least some college; trade has a strong indirect impact on the demand for less educated computer workers; R&D reduce demand for workers without college degrees but increase overall demand for workers because it stimulates additional investment in computers
Berman, Bound, and Machin (1998)	Cross country correlations of within-industry changes in the proportion of nonproduction workers/OECD countries	Expenditures on computers and R&D	Employment and wage shares for production and nonproduction workers	Positive correlation across OECD countries between investments and industry changes in shares of nonproduction workers
DiNardo and Pischke (1997)	Estimation of wage equations/Germany	Dummies for whether a worker sits down, or uses telephone, calculator, pen, or pencil	Detailed data on workers: age, sex, race, union status, region	Workers who use a computer earn a wage premium, but so do those who sit down while they work or use a calculator, telephone, pen, or pencil
Park (1996)	Regressions of changes in relative wages of skilled and unskilled workers on computers/Korea	Growth in labor productivity	All workers, excluding unskilled	Positive correlation between labor productivity growth and the proportion of multi-skilled workers in Korean manufacturing
Entorf and Kramarz (1995)	Estimation of wage equations/France	Firm-level data on usage of computer-based technologies	Occupational mix: unskilled and skilled blue-collar, clerks, managers, engineers, professionals	Positive correlation between technology usage and wages; highest wage premiums earned by those with the lowest level of skill
Regev (1995)	Estimation of production function/Israel	Technology index based on quality of labor and capital and R&D investment	No decomposition of labor	Technology intensive firms pay higher average wages, generated new jobs during a period of downsizing
Reilly (1995)	Estimation of wage equations/Canada	Dummy variable denoting access to computers	Detailed data on workers	Workers with access to computers earn a 13% wage premium

industry's technology. This is consistent with the authors' theoretical model that the demand for learning is highest when the firm implements a new technology. They argued that a higher wage is also needed to elicit higher levels of effort in the aftermath of technological change.

Results from studies in other countries are strongly consistent with the above evidence for the United States. Berman, Bound, and Machin (1998) found that changes in the employment structure in favor of highly educated workers are evident across many developed countries. The authors conclude that these wage and employment shifts can be linked to technological change. Also, the magnitudes of these linkages are quite similar across countries. Additional international evidence is presented in Park (1996), who reported a positive correlation between labor productivity growth and the proportion of multi-skilled workers in Korean manufacturing industries. Betts (1997) reported evidence of nonneutral technical change away from blue-collar labor in a number of Canadian manufacturing industries.

Many studies, especially those conducted by labor economists, have focused on the wage implications of innovation (Autor, Katz, and Krueger 1998; Davis and Haltiwanger 1991; Juhn, Murphy, and Pierce 1993; Katz and Murphy 1992; Levy and Murnane 1997; Mincer 1989; Murphy and Welch 1992). These researchers determined the extent of the rise in wage inequality and the concomitant increase in the demand for highly skilled and highly educated workers attributable to the use of new technologies. Davis and Haltiwanger (1991) documented a large increase in the 1980s in the earnings differential between nonproduction and production worker wages, attributing these changes to nonneutral technological change that has the effect of increasing the relative share of highly skilled workers.

Krueger (1993) authored the first major study to link changes in the wage structure at the individual level to technology usage. Krueger (1993) reported that workers during the mid-1980s in the United States who use computers on the job earn a wage premium of 10–15 percent relative to observationally equivalent workers. Reilly (1995) found that Canadian workers with access to computers earn a 13 percent wage premium during an earlier period. Autor, Katz, and Krueger's update (1998) of the earlier Krueger (1993) study showed an increase in the wage premium over the last decade to approximately 17 percent. More generally, the authors concluded that investments in computers could account for as much as 35–50 percent of the increase in the growth in demand for highly skilled workers.

There have also been several firm-level and plant-level studies of the effects of R&D and IT on the performance of workers in the United States, France, and the United Kingdom. The first firm-level study was by Lynch and Osterman (1989), who estimated labor demand curves for workers employed by a single firm in the telecommunications industry. The authors reported that technological innovations stimulated an increase in the demand for technical and professional workers.

Siegel (1999) collected comprehensive, firm-level panel data on the actual usage of advanced manufacturing technologies and concomitant, detailed changes in labor composition for selected US manufacturing firms. He found that implementation of a new technology leads to downsizing and a shift in labor composition and compensation in favor of white-collar workers, and that there is considerable heterogeneity in downsizing and skill upgrading across different types of technologies.

A cross-sectional, plant-level study was also conducted by Dunne and Schmitz (1995). The authors reported that US technology intensive plants pay higher wages than less technology intensive plants within the same industry. Evidence from labor markets in the United Kingdom and Israel is consistent with this finding. Van Reenen (1996) examined panel data on wages and innovation for sample of British firms with publicly traded shares for at least five years between 1976 and 1982, and he concluded that innovative firms pay above average wages. Regev (1995) estimated a simple production function model for a panel data-set of Israeli firms, and he reported that technology intensive firms pay above average wages and are consistently more productive than other firms in the same industry. He also found that these firms demonstrated net job creation during a period when many companies were downsizing.

One of the most important developments in empirical analysis of the impact of R&D and IT on worker performance is the creation of data-sets that match workers to their place of employment. Traditional studies of the labor supply behavior of individuals have suffered from limited information regarding the demand for a worker's labor. To understand the nature of this demand, and to help sort out the determinants of intra- and inter-industry wage differentials, it is helpful to simultaneously explore data on the characteristics of workers and firms. Note that conventional data-sets, which are relevant to the United States, that researchers use in labor market studies—the Current Population Survey (CPS), the National Longitudinal Survey (NLS), the Panel Study of Income Dynamics (PSID)—do not have detailed information on the employer.

Researchers at the US Census Bureau (e.g. Troske 1994) have constructed the Worker-Establishment Characteristic Database (WECD), a file that links detailed demographic data from the 1990 Decennial Census to comprehensive information on plants contained in the Longitudinal Research Database (LRD). The LRD is a compilation of data on establishments from the Census of Manufacturers (CM) and the Annual Survey of Manufacturers (ASM). This file has also been linked to the 1988 and 1993 US Survey of Manufacturing Technology (SMT), which provides detailed information on advanced manufacturing technology usage.

The linked version of the WECD and SMT has been analyzed by Dunne, Haltiwanger, and Troske (1996) and Doms, Dunne, and Troske (1997). Both studies reported a positive correlation between technology usage and levels, but not changes, in wages and education. The authors concluded that high-wage high-skill plants were more likely to adopt new technologies. They reported no evidence of workforce adjustment or skill-upgrading in the aftermath of technology adoption. While the cross-sectional analysis of wage and compositional effects is much richer than the previous Dunne and Schmitz (1995) Census study, the longitudinal analysis suffers from two important limitations: first, they can only measure changes in employment and wages for two types of employees: production and nonproduction workers, and second, they cannot identify the year of technology adoption, which precludes a precise analysis of timing effects.

Matched employee–employer data-sets have also been constructed in England and France. Chennells and van Reenen (1995) examined the 1984 Workplace Industrial Relations Survey (WIRS), a plant-level survey conducted in the United Kingdom. The WIRS survey contains a question which asks managers whether the plant has implemented a new computer technology. The authors reported that, for workers in all four skill categories (skilled, semi-skilled, unskilled, and clerical), there is a positive association between wages and technology usage. They find technological wage premiums of about 5 percent for skilled workers and about 10 percent for semi-skilled and unskilled workers.

Machin (1996) linked the WIRS survey to the Science Policy Research Unit (SPRU) data-set on innovations and found that R&D and innovations are positively associated with shifts in labor composition in favor of highly educated workers. However, computers are associated with skill upgrading only for workers with the highest level of education or skill.

Entorf and Kramarz (1995) examined a French matched employee–employer panel data-set with detailed measures of labor composition and technology usage. The authors also find a positive correlation between technology usage and wages. Interestingly, they found the highest wage premiums accrue to workers with the lowest level of skill. Their conclusion was that for many highly educated and skilled workers, proficiency with a new technology is expected, and thus, already factored into the current wage.

Note that both Chennells and van Reenen (1995) and Entorf and Kramarz (1995) concluded that it is unlikely that new technologies 'cause' higher wages, casting doubt on the conventional interpretation of the wage premium on computers or new technology as reflecting true economic returns (DiNardo and Pischke 1997). Of course, it is difficult to sort out these issues without more precise information on the timing of innovations.

Finally, Paul and Siegel (2001) simultaneously examined the impacts of trade, R&D, computers, and outsourcing on labor composition.

The authors found that technology has a stronger impact on shifts in labor composition in favor of highly educated workers than trade or outsourcing. The effects of computers and R&D do not appear to differ substantially. Trade also had a negative impact on the demand for less educated workers, but it is not associated with an increase in demand for more educated workers. Outsourcing appears to have a relatively small negative impact on demand across all education levels, with the strongest effects for workers with less than a college degree. And, they find that trade induces computerization, which exacerbates the negative impact that each factor has on the demand for workers without a college degree, and augments the positive effects that each factor has on the demand for workers with a college degree. Models that ignore these indirect effects may underestimate the overall impact of trade on labor composition.

Some recent studies have examined the relationship between technical and organizational change. These scholars have found that IT investment is often accompanied by substantial changes in the work environment. For example, Siegel, Waldman, and Youngdahl (1997) analyzed the effects of the adoption of advanced manufacturing technologies on human resource management practices, including proxies for employee empowerment, such as training, changes in job responsibilities, new career opportunities, and enhanced employee control. They report that there is strong positive correlation between the implementation of certain types of technologies and greater employee empowerment.

In a similar vein, Bresnahan, Brynjolfsson, and Hitt (2002) presented evidence on the connection among technological change, organizational change, and organizational performance. The authors studied the effects of declining IT prices, increased use of IT and a rise in the relative demand for highly educated workers. They conjectured that companies need to decentralize decision-making and adopt other 'high performance' workplace practices, in order to implement new technologies successfully. Such practices include an increased reliance on worker teams and quality circles, where employees can decide the pace and method of work to achieve the best results.

To test these theories, Bresnahan, Brynjolfsson, and Hitt (2002) estimated three variants of a regression model with IT demand, human capital investment, and value-added as dependent variables. They reported that proxies for workplace organization and human capital are strong determinants of the demand for IT capital, but not other types of capital. This finding is consistent with the argument that there are complementarities among IT, organizational change and human capital. Similarly, firms with higher levels of investment in human capital, as measured by a greater emphasis on selection, appraisal, and training of workers employees, tend to have higher levels of IT investment and more decentralized work organization. They reported that IT use is positively correlated with enhanced worker autonomy, management's need and ability to monitor workers, and the firm's desire to increase investment in human capital.

Several key stylized facts have emerged from the new interdisciplinary literature on the relationship between technological change and organizational change in developed countries. Bresnahan, Brynjolfsson, and Hitt (2002) reported that IT use in developed countries is associated with a cluster of complementary organizational practices. These include a transition from mass production to flexible manufacturing technologies, changing interaction with suppliers and customers (mostly resulting in closer relationships with customers and suppliers), decentralized decision-making and other organizational transformations, greater ease of coordination, and enhanced communication. Brynjolfsson, Hitt, and Yang (2000) found that these complementary technological and organizational changes enhance the market value of firms.

Thus, it appears that the manner in which IT is being used is changing organizational structure, design, and control systems. For instance, researchers have reported that back-office jobs are being replaced, while the importance of front-office skills and managerial leadership has increased. Networks of PCs are changing the way people work and the way they are compensated, in the sense that the rewards to multi-tasking are increasing and employers seem to prefer employees with broad-based education and conceptual and problem-solving skills, which are valued more and more by companies in developed countries.

The end result is that the returns to schooling are high and rising, which appears to be largely due to technological change and concomitant organizational changes that raise the value of knowledge workers to firms and other organizations. Despite this fairly substantial increase in the returns to education, the demand for computer literate workers continues to outstrip supply, which explains part of the wage premium economists have observed for these workers. This also explains why numerous multinational companies have begun outsourcing high-skilled labor to developing countries, as in the case of software programming in India (Lal 2002), much as they have always done with low-skilled labor. Paul and Siegel (2001) reported evidence that is consistent with this assertion, as they found that there is a positive correlation between IT investment and the propensity of US manufacturing firms to engage in foreign and domestic outsourcing of mostly business services.

There were other important IT-induced changes in the labor market: improved labor market outcomes for women through higher wages (reducing the gender gap in wages) and greater flexibility in the workplace and the work environment. That is, the diffusion of IT has facilitated the adoption of flexible work practices by firms, which has made it easier for employees, and especially women, to work from home. Thus, it appears as though technological and social developments are complementary because the so-called liberation of women has been accompanied by greater freedom to perform work-related tasks at home. This trend is likely to continue, provided, of course, that the infrastructure technology is available in many countries to effectively use IT equipment to perform one's job. In a similar vein, IT and the Internet have led to creation of new industries, especially in business and retail services. This has resulted in an increase in demand for workers who perform tasks that can be accomplished at home and a concomitant rise in women-owned small enterprises.

4.8. **Conclusions**

Firms invest in R&D and IT strategically, with an eye toward using such investments to build or sustain a competitive advantage. This is achieved through enhanced resources and capabilities. According to strategic management theory, these resources and capabilities can be generated internally through R&D and strategic investments in technology, as well as externally through RJVs, technology alliances, and networks.

In theory, such activities should enhance the absorptive capacity of the firm. The empirical evidence seems to be consistent with this view, although it is important to note that we have limited data on the output/outcomes/performance of RJVs, technology alliances, and networks. We believe that greater attention should be paid to gathering information on R&D and research partnership outputs, as opposed to the current data collection strategy that appears to be focused on R&D inputs. This approach could potentially yield more precise estimates of private returns and R&D spillovers. In a similar vein, it would also be useful to systematically collect information from as many firms as possible, including those who are not involved in research partnerships and those who apply for subsidies, yet fail to receive them. This would allow for a much more accurate assessment of the effects of private and public support of R&D and potentially enable us to identify those research partnerships that generate the highest private and social returns. Longitudinal analysis would also allow us to determine whether certain research partnerships are indeed effectively targeting market failures, since economic theory predicts that government intervention is warranted when there is a substantial divergence between private and social returns.

A vast, interdisciplinary body of research on the impact of internal and external investments in technology on firm and worker performance was reviewed in this chapter. The key methodologies used to assess performance impacts are the production and cost function framework, event studies, and other forms of regression analysis. All forms of technology investments—R&D, IT, RJVs, and other research partnerships—have been studied by scholars from various disciplines. Authors have examined many indicators of performance, such as TFP growth, patenting, short-run movements in stock prices, R&D expenditure, and R&D employment, technology licensing, citations of patents and scholarly articles, coauthoring between academic and industry scientists, and job creation.

Although the primary focus of this chapter has been the firm, it is also useful to consider the broader national technology framework policy. In the United States, and in selected other industrialized nations, there has been an important change in the national innovation system (Nelson 1993). Namely, the rise of the new economy has brought about a substantial increase in technology partnerships involving firms, universities, nonprofit organizations, federal research laboratories, and public agencies. Given the rise in the incidence and variety of such collaborative relationships, which are mostly public–private partnerships, government agencies should broaden their coverage of this activity. It would be particularly desirable to target the data collection effort to public–private partnerships, since there is typically interest from a public policy perspective in assessing the social, as opposed to the private, returns to R&D.

▢ NOTES

1. This section draws from Link and Siegel (2003).
2. Academics have been spurred to investigate the so-called productivity paradox based on the famous quip by Nobel Laureate Robert M. Solow that computers show up everywhere except in the productivity statistics.

5 The economics of R&D and economic growth

5.1. Introduction

In Chapter 4, we examined aspects of the economics and management literature on the relationship between both investments in R&D and in IT and firm performance. The objective of most empirical studies at this level of aggregation is to evaluate the private returns to investments in innovative capital. R&D is an investment into the stock of technical capital and IT is, generally, an investment into the stock of physical capital.

It is critical to assess these returns because they determine the extent to which firms have an incentive to invest in R&D. As noted in Siegel (1999) and Link and Scott (1998a, 1998b, 1998c), most companies have explicit hurdle rates which must be surmounted before the firm will consider investing in an R&D project. It is heartening to discover from the academic literature that the empirical evidence strongly suggests that such returns are positive.

In contrast, in this chapter the theoretical and empirical literature on the relationship between innovation and economic growth at the industry, regional, and national levels is reviewed.[1] Empirical analyses at these levels of aggregation allowed researchers to assess the social returns to innovation, or the benefits that accrue to society from innovation. Given the public good nature of knowledge, which was discussed in Chapter 1 with reference to the diffusion of bioscience, and difficulties in protecting intellectual property, firms typically cannot appropriate all of the benefits associated with innovation because externalities or spillovers that arise from investment in technology. Such social gains are reflected in the aggregate in terms of higher output, lower prices, and a greater variety of goods and services (or a weighted average of the three) resulting from higher productivity.

This is an important literature to examine because a primary objective of public policy is to enhance economic performance. The rapid diffusion of IT, and access and use of the Internet beginning in the 1990s, has also stimulated renewed policy interest in measuring and explaining economic growth, as has the technology-based emergence of more and more countries. It is critical to understand the evolution of this literature because there have been many theoretical developments in recent years and a large volume of empirical evidence.

The neoclassical and the so-called new growth theories of economic growth are reviewed in this chapter. Selected empirical evidence on the relationship between investments in technology and economic performance from various eras is also presented. Measurement issues are also considered throughout the chapter because such questions are critical in assessing the social returns to innovation.

5.2. **Early studies of economic growth**

The devastation caused by World War II sparked renewed interest in economic growth and its determinants as public policymakers in many countries sought to identify ways to rebuild their economies. In the 1950s, several economists articulated, Abramovitz (1956) being one of the first, the general importance of technological change as an underlying force for productivity growth, although his writings and the writings of others tended to be less formal than those of their disciples. Nelson (1981: 1030) perceptively observed that these early studies of economic growth were

. . . remarkable in foreshadowing the central conclusion of studies done somewhat later within the neoclassical framework.

The findings from selective studies are presented in Table 5.1. Note that each researcher used a variant of an output-over-input index to construct a productivity index, and then estimated so-measured increases in productivity, productivity growth, and overall resource efficiency. Presumably, measured efficiency gains were, in part, the result of economywide technological advances, a point that most researchers speculated about at that time but did not quantify formally, or even informally.

Abramovitz (1956) examined US economic activity in the post-Civil War economy, 1869–78 to 1944–53. He cautiously concluded from his quantitative

Table 5.1. Estimates of the rate of technological change, post-World War II studies of the US economy

Author	Time period	Measure of economic performance	Estimated average annual rate of technological change (%)
Schmookler (1952)	1869–78 to 1929–38	GNP per unit of input	1.36
Mills (1952)	1891–1900 to 1941–50	GNP per man-hour	3.6
Schultz (1953)	1910 to 1950	Agriculture output per unit input	0.8 to 1.35
Kendrick (1956)	1899 to 1953	Private domestic output per unit of input	1.7
Solow (1957)	1909 to 1949	GNP per unit of labor	1.5

investigation that the source of growth in output per unit of labor over that time period was not increased resources per head. Rather, the source of growth in output per unit of labor rested within the realm of such a little understood cause as the growth in the stock of knowledge. It is no wonder, then, that Abramovitz (1956) coined the descriptive phrase 'measure of ignorance' when referring to the determinants of productivity growth. He conjectured that the inputs into this stock of knowledge included such factors as research and education—both of which are bases for the generation of new knowledge.

Solow (1957) was the first to formalize the study of productivity growth within the context of an aggregate production function model. More importantly, he developed an explicit method for assessing the rate of technological change. Solow hypothesized the following production function in terms of capital (K) and labor (L):

$$Q = A(t) F(K, L), \tag{5.1}$$

where $A(t)$ is a disembodied shift factor. He also assumed, as previously discussed, that this production function has diminishing returns with respect to capital and labor and overall constant returns to scale.

Solow (1957) concluded from his empirical estimation of a version of equation (5.1) that in the United States over the period 1909–49 technological change was a critically important source of US economic growth. Specifically, Solow (1957: 320) concluded that:

... gross output per man-hour doubled over the [time] interval, with $87^1/_2$ percent of the increase attributable to technical change and the remaining $12^1/_2$ percent to increased use of capital.

Stated differently, $87^1/_2$ percent of the growth in aggregate output between 1909 and 1949 could not be explained by the growth of capital and labor.

Solow (1957) realized that his empirical results and interpretative conclusions were quite similar to findings presented in Fabricant (1954). Fabricant had also estimated that about 90 percent of the increase in output per capita between 1871 and 1951 was attributable to technical progress, but he did not do so within a production function model.

The quantitative research that followed from these early empirical studies had two objectives. One objective was to understand and refine the aggregate production function model posited by Solow (1957), which was expected at that time to be able to result in more accurate estimates of the impact of technological change on economic activity. A second objective was to improve the quality of input measures used to calculate productivity indices, as well as to expand the set of inputs considered. And a third objective was to disaggregate the yet unexplained residually measured portion of productivity growth. Each of these related areas of emphasis ultimately focused on understanding economic performance, of which economic growth was of primary emphasis.

Thus, before reviewing this literature, it is important to have a historical understanding of how economic growth, as conceptualized and measured in these investigations, fits within two larger bodies of theoretical literature, old growth theory and new growth theory.

5.3. Theories of economic growth

5.3.1. OLD GROWTH THEORY

It is critical to note that much of the theoretical work that falls under the heading of old growth theory was driven by the availability of data. That is, the development of National Income and Product Accounts and other macroeconomic data-sets on output and input usage in the early 1950s was a major breakthrough that influenced the development of this body of theory. These data-sets came about largely due to the influence of Kuznets and other scholars affiliated with the National Bureau of Economic Research, which was then located in New York City. The empirical studies cited in Table 5.1 were all attempts to measure and explain sources of economic growth over time. The authors referenced in that table used basically the same approach in their efforts to account for sources of economic growth. That is, the total contribution of input growth was computed by weighting each input—capital and labor—by their relative prices. As noted by Griliches (1996), this weighting of inputs seemed like such an obvious thing to do that no one felt compelled at that time to justify it theoretically.

The latter fact explains why Solow's (1957) aggregate production function research and estimation is regarded as seminal. He was the first to explicitly relate residually measured TFP growth, $\dot{A}/A$, to formal neoclassical growth theory (Solow 1956). A similar growth theoretic model was independently exposited in a contemporary study by Swan (1956). The Solow–Swan advancements can be construed as an example within the annals of economics, along with Adam Smith's pin factory, where empirical observations such as those in Table 5.1 lead to major theoretical contributions.

The papers by Solow (1956) and Swan (1956) formed the basis of what was then considered to be modern growth theory but which is now referred to as old growth theory. Solow and Swan drew heavily from the earlier works by Harrod (1946) and Domar (1947).

In any event, all of the early old growth theory models were based on a number of simplifying interrelated assumptions regarding producer behavior and factor markets. Specifically, these models assumed that perfect competition characterizes both input and output markets; production is characterized by constant returns to scale; and factors are paid their social marginal products.

The latter assumption implies that factor markets are perfectly competitive and all externalities are captured by a firm's behavior. That is, in these models, it is assumed that firms have no market power in output and factor (input) markets. For example, this means that the firm charges a price that is equal to marginal cost (i.e. no markups) and pays the prevailing market wage to its workers.

Looking ahead to the reasoning of many scholars who reflected on the well-known importance of knowledge as a source of innovation and innovation as a source for technological change, one obvious contradiction is present in these old growth theory models. Namely, it is well known that under perfect competition firms have little incentive to invest in R&D. Furthermore, investments in knowledge per se typically entail substantial up-front costs, and for such costs to be incurred it follows that there must be both increasing returns to scale and output prices are greater than the marginal cost of production otherwise the knowledge investment costs would not be recovered. These conditions of course violate the assumptions of perfect competition and constant returns to scale.

Two other results in Solow's growth model (1956) have also troubled many economists, even at the time when his paper was published. Following Nelson (1997), these concerns were and still are that technological change was modeled as an exogenous event and that changes in the saving rate were modeled to have no lasting effect on the rate of growth of output per worker. While certainly simplifying, the concept of technological change falling on firms like manna from heaven was problematic because it seemed fairly obvious, even at that time, that R&D was the result of purposive activity and that innovative behavior varied in response to such activities.[2]

Solow (1956) also hypothesized that diminishing returns to capital implied that the economy's steady-state growth rate would be independent of its savings rate. As also noted by Nelson (1997), this was a finding that many thought to be the most implausible.

Although some economists questioned the basic assumptions of the Solow model, a quiet consensus still emerged around this production function framework in the late 1960s and early 1970s, and as a result, there were few advances in growth theory for several decades. Furthermore, the oil price shocks and the resulting economic slowdown productivity growth in the early 1970s diverted the attention of economists to a debate on energy-capital substitution and the factors influencing business cycle fluctuations. While the productivity growth slowdown of the late 1960s and early 1970s did generate more interest in the determinants of long-run economic growth, it was the debate regarding convergence in rates of economic growth across countries, which followed directly from the Solow (1956) model that served as the catalyst for stimulating new theoretical research on growth.

Jorgenson (1996), among others, noted that much of the empirical evidence of the day on growth rates was not consistent with convergence. More specifically, Jorgenson pointed out that Solow's assumption (1956) of diminishing marginal returns to capital results in a growth process within a country in which it eventually reaches a steady state of per capital income growth. This steady state rate is hypothesized to be determined by several factors: the share of capital share in GDP, population growth, productivity growth, and the rate of depreciation of capital equipment. Using widely accepted values for each of these parameters, Jorgenson concluded that the actual rate of convergence is too low to be consistent with Solow's model.

5.3.2. NEW GROWTH THEORY

The anomalous finding regarding the lack of convergence in growth rates stimulated researchers, such as Romer (1986), to question the underlying assumptions of the neoclassical growth model. Romer's initial work has come to be generally regarded as the key initial contribution to new growth theory. He concluded that because the evidence on the slow rate of convergence was not consistent with the neoclassical growth theory, Solow's growth model (1956) needed to be revisited. Romer proposed allowing for increasing returns to scale in the aggregate production function and externalities arising from private capital investment to the rest of the economy. Romer's work is also more general in the sense that it refers to accumulation, which can mean accumulation of knowledge, physical capital, or human capital. Similar assumptions were also made in a highly influential new growth theory paper by Lucas (1988), although he focused specifically on the role of human capital.

Romer's subsequent work (1990) treated technological change as an endogenous factor of growth. This was an obvious departure from old growth theory, as well as an important extension of the literature on technology and productivity because he outlined a highly stylized equilibrium model in which agents engaging in R&D optimize. Romer's work can also be viewed as part of a general movement in economics, initiated by, for example, Lucas and Sargent and their disciples, to develop the micro-foundations of macroeconomics.

Aghion and Howitt (1990), Grossman and Helpman (1991a, 1991b), and Klette and Griliches (1997) also delineated models in which firms engage in R&D. Aghion and Howitt (1990) were the first to introduce the notion of Schumpeterian competition into new growth theory. They treat technological change as an endogenous process of creative destruction, where new technologies displace old technologies. Schumpeter's work (1934, 1950) had highlighted the role of the entrepreneur as an innovator and a key force in enhancing economic growth, as overviewed in Chapter 2. Grossman and Helpman (1991a, 1991b) advanced a quality ladder theory in which each product innovation is introduced by a new firm, while the firms selling the old products are driven out of business. The concept of a quality ladder refers to a model in which new, higher quality products affect the value of existing ones.

Caballero and Jaffe (1993) and Klette and Griliches (1997), among others, also delineated a fully specified endogenous growth model, which extended the Grossman and Helpman framework by drawing in elements from the patent race literature, as discussed in Gilbert and Newberry (1982, 1984) and in Reinganum (1985), and the discrete choice models of product differentiation, as discussed in Anderson, DePalma, and Thisse (1992) and Berry (1994).

New growth theory also more closely examines the role of infrastructure and government, as discussed by DeLong and Summers (1991) and Hall and Jones (1996). Barro and Sala-i-Martin (1998) also considered a wide range of institutional factors and organizations that influence growth. Other authors also attempted to examine sociological factors well. Like the earlier stream of growth theory, some of this theoretical work has been driven by the availability of a comprehensive data-set containing international comparisons of Real National Accounts across countries, constructed by Summers and Heston (1988).

Enthusiasm for new growth theory sparked an inevitable backlash for devotees of old growth theory and scholars who wanted to refine these theories. Several prominent economists demonstrated that if one extended the Solow model to include a human capital variable, then the empirical evidence is actually consistent with neoclassical theory. Mankiw, Romer, and Weil (1992) noted that the conventional production function can be expanded to include, along with capital (K) and labor (L), a stock of human capital (H):

$$Q = F(K, L, H) \tag{5.2}$$

Jones (1995) expanded this specification to allow for productivity gains to L from R&D.

There is a third school of thought, in addition to old and new growth theories, which has been referred to as embodiment hypothesis. This perspective can be traced to a seminal article by Solow (1960). Solow asserted that technical change is embodied in investment goods, not an all-encompassing force that influences the creation of all products and services. He also noted that these new investment goods are needed to reap the benefits of technical advances. Greenwood, Hercovitz, and Krusell (1997) and Hercowitz (1998) have recently resurrected this theory, in the context of a critique of the government's decision to hedonic or quality-adjusted measures of computers and other investment goods.

Table 5.2 summarizes the key differences between old and new growth theory. Old growth theories typically assumed constant returns to scale, price-taking behavior, an absence of spillovers associated with investment in private

Table 5.2. Comparison of old growth theory and new growth theory

Assumptions regarding	Old growth theory	New growth theory
Returns to scale	Constant returns to scale	Increasing returns to scale
Market structure of output and input markets	Perfect competition	Imperfect competition (some models allow for Schumpeterian competition)
Institutional factors influencing growth	Not considered	Considered in some models
Externalities (technological or otherwise)	No externalities	Allows for externalities
Technological change	Exogenous	Endogenous

capital, and exogenous technological change. These studies also ignore institutional factors and the role of government. New growth theory, in contrast, typically allows for increasing returns to scale, imperfect competition, externalities associated with private investment in physical or technical capital, and endogenous technological change. Some authors also consider institutional factors and the role of government.

5.4. **Technological or knowledge spillovers**

A critical aspect of new growth theory is the notion that technological or knowledge spillovers can arise when firms invest in innovation. Indeed, a fundamental feature of the seminal work of Romer (1986) was the possible existence of an externality that results when R&D investment undertaken by a firm augments the knowledge base that is accessible to all organizations. Spillovers or externalities can arise for several reasons. First, it is conceivable that technical know-how can leak from the innovator to other firms that have not invested in the technology due to imperfect protection of intellectual property (e.g. through patents) or the mobility of technical labor. Another possible source of spillovers is network effects, which could create an external benefit for consumers or firms that are already part of the network. Finally, it is important to note that even if technological spillovers are nonexistent, there is imperfect appropriability for the innovator, unless the company can engage in perfect price discrimination to rival firms (e.g. through licensing) and/or to downstream users.

Table 5.3 contains a summary of key studies of various channels of technological or knowledge spillovers. Arrow (1962) was the first to discuss one possible channel for the generation of such externalities: experience effects, resulting from learning by doing, which can result in higher productivity growth. Of course, as noted earlier, the seminal papers in new growth theory

Table 5.3. Potential sources of technological/knowledge spillovers

Author(s)	Potential source of spillovers
Arrow (1962)	Learning by doing
Romer (1990), Aghion and Howitt (1992), Caballero and Jaffe (1993)	R&D investment
Grossman and Helpman (1991a, 1991b), Coe and Helpman (1995)	International trade involving R&D intensive firms
Lucas (1988)	Human capital
DeLong and Summers (1991, 1992)	Equipment investment
Caballero and Lyons (1990, 1992), Bartelsman, Caballero, and Lyons (1994), Paul and Siegel (1999)	Supplier and customer-driven agglomeration effects
Helpman (1998)	General purpose technologies

(e.g. Romer 1986) all assumed that R&D investment generates externalities. Lucas (1986) highlighted the importance of human capital as a spillover mechanism. One could envision these externalities resulting from labor mobility in the aftermath of investments in education and training and the movement of knowledge from organization or industry to another. DeLong and Summers (1991, 1992) assert that inter-industry spillovers can arise from equipment investment.

Hall (1990) and Caballero and Lyons (1990, 1992) have outlined simple Cobb–Douglas production-function based models that allow for the existence of agglomeration externalities or thick market effects. These agglomeration effects are typically assumed to be transmitted via knowledge spillovers that arise from the activities of suppliers, customers, and even rivals. In endogenous growth models, these externalities appear as scale economies. Bartelsman, Caballero, and Lyons (1994) extended this analysis by distinguishing between short-run and long-run agglomeration externalities. They tested their model using detailed industry data and concluded that supplier-driven agglomeration externalities are more important than customer-driven agglomeration externalities in the long run.

Paul and Siegel (1999) found strong evidence of supply-side agglomeration in both the short run and long run. Their analysis is on a dynamic cost function framework, which imposes fewer restrictive assumptions on producer behavior than the Cobb–Douglas production function. This approach also provides a richer framework for assessing substitution patterns among internal and external capital inputs.

Morrison and Siegel (1997) and Paul and Siegel (1999) extended the literature on agglomeration externalities by simultaneously examining the impacts of several external capital factors, such as R&D, computers, and human capital, on long-run growth. Previous studies had typically examined the impact of a single external factor on growth. The authors found strong evidence of scale economies and that additional external investment in any of these factors (e.g. technology) would stimulate higher productivity growth. More importantly,

Table 5.4. Industry and aggregate-level empirical studies of the relationship between information technology and productivity growth

Author(s)	Methodology	Sector	Key results of the study
McGuckin and Stiroh (1999)	Cobb–Douglas production function with computer capital	Manufacturing and services	Evidence of excess returns on computer capital at each level of aggregation
Wolff (1999)	Regressions of nonparametric measures of TFP growth on IT	Manufacturing and services	No evidence of positive relationship between computers and productivity growth. Weak evidence of positive association in goods industries during 1977–87
Gera, Wu, and Lee (1999)	Cobb–Douglas production function with computer capital	Manufacturing	Positive correlation between investment in computers and labor productivity growth
Stiroh (1998)	Sectoral growth accounting methods and regression analysis based on Cobb–Douglas production function	Manufacturing and services	Computer-producing sector (SIC 35) has made a strong contribution to economic growth; computer-using sectors have not made a similar contribution. No evidence of positive relationship between computers and TFP growth at the sectoral level
Siegel (1997)	Latent variables model: regressions of parametric and nonparametric measures of TFP growth on rate of investment in computers	Manufacturing	When controls are included in the model for measurement errors, computers have statistically significant positive impact on productivity
Morrison and Siegel (1997)	Dynamic cost function estimation with 'high-tech' capital	Manufacturing	'External' investments in computers in related industries enhance productivity in a given industry
Oliner and Sichel (1994)	Growth accounting methods to estimate the contribution of computers to economic growth	United States/ economy wide	Under standard neoclassical assumptions, computers account for only a small percentage (0.15%) of average annual economic growth
Jorgenson and Stiroh (2000)	Sectoral growth accounting methods	United States/ economy wide	Growth contribution of computers increased substantially in mid- to late 1990s
Parsons, Gottlieb and Denny (1993)	Estimation of a translog cost function with computer capital	Banking	Very low returns on investments in computers for banks
Siegel and Griliches (1992)	Correlation between nonparametric measures of TFP and rate of investment in computers	Manufacturing	Positive correlation between the rate of investment in computers and TFP growth

they showed that ignoring fixities in capital and labor and the impact of external capital inputs, as one does with conventional estimation procedures, leads to biased estimates of scale economies and the magnitude of agglomeration externalities.

Finally, it is important to note that major technological advances, such as GPTs, can constitute an important spillover mechanism. According to Helpman (1998), GPTs have broad applications and productivity-enhancing effects in numerous downstream sectors. Thus, GPTs induce dramatic economic changes by creating new industries and rejuvenating existing sectors. Examples of GPTs include the steam engine, the electric dynamo, and lasers. More recently, several authors (e.g. Mowery and Simcoe 2002) have asserted that computers and the Internet are a GPT. Table 5.4 summarizes some of the related literature with an emphasis on computers' impact on productivity growth at the aggregate level. In Chapter 7, we consider two GPTs in detail: the Internet and nanotechnology.

5.5. Conclusions

In this chapter, we have reviewed some aspects of the extensive literature on economic growth. We distinguish between old and new growth theory and related empirics. Some key outcomes of the old growth theory literature were the first attempts to quantify the impact of investment in technology on economic growth, based on growth accounting methods. Although these models were useful and had important policy implications, many economists were skeptical about the empirical findings derived from these models because they were based on rather heroic, simplifying assumptions regarding producer behavior. Furthermore, they were not based on the type of highly stylized models featuring optimizing agents (based on neoclassical economic theory) that have become the norm at leading economics journals.

New growth theory and its associated burgeoning empirical literature on economic growth has been extremely useful in filling this void. The proponents of new growth theory also helped to shed further light on what was termed by Griliches (1992) as the 'search for spillovers'. The theoretical and empirical research on 'skilled-biased' technological change has also been illuminating.

These streams of research have greatly extended the earlier, simpler empirical analyses and generated some new stylized facts regarding the impact of technology on economic performance. Specifically highlighted is the relationship between investments in technology and human capital, which in turn lead to improvements in economic growth. The notion that external investments (i.e. external to the firm or industry) in computers, R&D, and human capital also have a positive effect on productivity growth has important policy implications. The end result is that the evidence suggests that the social returns to innovation are high, although we need better empirical evidence on spillover channels. We also need further exploration of the relationship among technological change, organizational change, and performance.

☐ NOTES

1. This chapter draws from Link and Siegel (2003).
2. As an aside, these are points that seem obvious to contemporary scholars in this field, although these ideas also follow logically from the writings of the Physiocrats nearly a century before, as discussed in Chapter 2.

6 Innovation in the service sector

6.1. Introduction

Most empirical research on the antecedents and consequences of innovative activity has been focused on the manufacturing sector. The emphasis on manufacturing is natural because most R&D is financed and performed within that sector. Furthermore, measures of economic performance, such as productivity, are considered more accurate in manufacturing.

As noted in Griliches (1994) and Nordhaus (2002), it is notoriously difficult to measure productivity in service industries, mainly due to problems with output deflators and in some cases, even defining the relevant output. To compute real output, data are required on turnover or receipts, as well as a price index to deflate nominal output. Unfortunately, until quite recently, producer or wholesale price indexes were not available for the outputs of many service industries because of the great difficulty in defining measurable units of output and adjusting for quality changes.

As predicted in the seminal paper by Baumol (1967), the service sector has continued to grow much more rapidly than the goods sector in advanced industrial economies. Unfortunately, this sector has not been studied intensely, from an empirical perspective.[1] Furthermore, the service sector is also an important innovation sector in all industrialized nations, especially in the United States. Given that service industries now constitute a large percentage of economic activity, the assessment of productivity in such sectors has become even more important on the public policy agenda.

Globally, much of the service sector's growth since the early 1980s has been based on new services with significant knowledge content. A large share of the knowledge content in services is being built on advances in hardware and software that were imported or purchased from the manufacturing sector. However, the service sector adds value in a different way than the manufacturing sector—by integrating purchased physical technology, which embodies others' R&D and innovative activity, into systems. To add this value, service sector firms have made considerable investments in capabilities such as systems-level integration.

For an industrialized nation to continue to experience historical rates of productivity growth, the future performance of the service sector will be critical.

6.2. The literature related to service sector innovation

To date, most researchers believe that an accurate model of service innovation is still absent from the literature (Howells 2000). With a few notable exceptions, such as, for example, Barras's reverse product cycle (Barras 1986), the extant literature related to service-sector innovation has focused on differentiating service activities from manufacturing innovation paradigms, as opposed to building on the specific nature of service-sector products and process.

This state of the literature suggests a need to integrate the unique traits of service-sector innovation into the existing taxonomies and innovation paradigms. The goal is to capture more diverse types of innovation in conceptual models of innovation, including what was once two distinct segments of the economy but has over time become increasingly less disparate (Gallouj and Weinstein 1997; Amable and Palombarini 1998). Although existing taxonomies have begun to address how innovation occurs in service sector firms, much more work remains to be done in terms of modeling an innovation system that incorporates services. The model we posit in this chapter is only one step toward that end, but it is an important step because it emphasizes the non-R&D role of innovation in the service sector.

Recent efforts to incorporate innovation into models of service-sector activity have included, for example, Pavitt's taxonomies (1984) for classifying sectoral patterns of technological change. By dividing a national economy into three sectors—supplier dominated, production intensive, and science based, Pavitt outlined a dynamic relationship between technology and service industries. Professional, financial, and commercial services are captured in the supplier-dominated category. However, the firms associated with this sector were primarily described as firms that expend few resources developing processes and products, usually having weak in-house R&D capabilities where most innovations come from the supplier of equipment and materials.[2]

Soete and Miozzo (1989) took the Pavitt model a step further by expanding on the supplier-dominated sector, offering two new classifications: a production-oriented category and an innovative-specialty category. The production category included those service firms performing large-scale processing and administrative activities and developing physical or information networks. The specialized technology suppliers' category included firms performing science-based activities to develop proprietary technology through innovation.

In addition to understanding the distinctions between manufacturing and service-sector innovative activities, a second line of research has focused on the differences between products (e.g. new services) and process (e.g. new organizational and delivery processes) within the service industry. Gallouj and

Weinstein (1997) made this distinction by dividing innovation for the service firm into two classifications: technical characteristics (front-office tangible technologies for the part of a firm in direct contact with clients) and process characteristics (both tangible and intangible back-office technologies such as methods, working tools, and organizational theory). Sirilli and Evangelista (1998) suggested that service-sector firms are able to distinguish between service and process innovations. These authors identified engineering, technical consultancy, and computing services as the most innovative service sectors.

Sundbo (1997) offered a strategic innovation paradigm where the firm's strategy is the core innovation determinant. He offered empirical evidence through a study of Danish service firms where he breaks services into three categories: top strategic organization, characterized by large- to medium-service-sector firms that are mass producing services; network organizations, described as a loosely tied association of small firms that innovate little on their own; and professional organizations, defined as collective action groups with shared interest in technology interoperability.

Evidence of the service sector's technological maturity has been established throughout the literature (Amable and Palombarini 1998; Pilat 2001). Service-sector firms are taking on more proactive roles in innovation activities and in some cases are leading the innovation process. Given the distributive and dynamic nature of the innovation process, both manufacturing and service-sector firms are beginning to collaborate through bilateral and multilateral networks. This collaboration of firms is referred to as a distributed innovation process (DIP) and suggests that service-sector firms are beginning to take more of a leading role in innovation.

The largest contribution to growth in the service sector is from a small subset of all services known as knowledge-intensive business services (KIBSs) (e.g. telecommunications, IT, networking, and organizational consultancy). In these areas, services are playing an increasingly important role in technological change and productivity growth by promoting standards and systems integration. Researchers predict that the developed economies of the world will soon enter a postindustrial period in which services drive economic growth (OECD 2001a).

Over the past two decades, the literature has attempted to develop a conceptual framework aimed at understanding how service firms innovate. In recent years, the discussion has turned from the sizable differences between the two sectors to their convergence. However, a growing number of authors point to such firms as IBM and/or Siemens (both large mass-production service firms) as examples of traditional manufacturers who now have a dominant share of their business activities associated with the sale of services (Howells 2000; OECD 2001b).

Over time the once sizable distinction between manufacturing industries and service-producing industries is narrowing (Amable and Palombarini

1998; OECD 2001*a*). The literature suggests that distinguishing between the primary (agriculture and raw material extraction), secondary (manufacturing), and tertiary (services) sectors of the economy is obsolete, as more firms in both manufacturing and services adopt the practice of encapsulating physical products with services (Howells 2000).

This broadening of scope is referred to as servicization, or the trend in manufacturing to encapsulate the physical product in a shell of services (i.e. finance, monitoring, maintenance, and repurchase). Servicization is also a growing trend in the automobile and aerospace industries, and, as it becomes more pervasive and better understood, researchers will begin to rethink how they characterize the service sector and its innovation activities.

6.3. **Measurement of service-sector innovation**

Recent empirical evidence has clearly demonstrated that service-producing industries innovate and have been doing so increasingly over time (Sirilli and Evangelista 1998). As national institutions began measuring innovation activities in the service sector, the original models and data collection instruments were based on an understanding of the technology innovation process as it applied to manufacturing firms. However, because of the intangible nature of the service sector's output, measuring the productivity of R&D performed using the historical measures of innovation, such as new products or patents (Gallouj and Weinstein 1997), is difficult. The manufacturing sector adds value to inputs—R&D is an explicit and direct input in the innovation process—by continuously improving the materials and design of their products, whereas the service sector applies accumulated knowledge to build organizational models or systems, a more abstract output than in manufacturing (Jankowski 2001). In the absence of such appropriate metrics, any resulting measure of innovative activity would by definition be limited.

Service innovations draw less directly on scientific breakthroughs and are often small or incremental in nature; this means that small changes can lead to new applications or reorganization of an existing technology or system (Pilat 2001). Some large service-sector firms actually have an innovation department that promotes and collects ideas. However, this organizational design may be the exception rather than the rule. Service-sector innovations are typically based on both market-wide and consumer-specific needs.

Innovation in service-sector firms is generally not a systematic process and often consists of spontaneous ideas developed internally to meet the real-time needs of a specific client. In contrast, innovation in manufacturing firms is typically highly structured, with a systematic approach to developing new products following the product life cycle. Although there is an attempt to systematically organize and account for innovation across all sectors, measuring innovation in the service sector is extremely subjective because of the intangible nature of its products (Pilat 2001). Measuring innovation is further complicated in the service sector because it occurs throughout the organizational process.

Patenting in the service sector is at times more difficult because of high visibility or the inexcludability of the product or process. If a manufacturing firm develops an innovative process or product, it can keep the process or product a secret by not allowing anyone outside the firm to see it. Service-sector firms offering intangible products have much higher visibility, which makes it hard to contain trade secrets and easier for other firms to imitate the product or process.

6.4. Models of innovation

For comparative purposes, a schematic model of innovation in the manufacturing sector is discussed below. It is followed by a similar schematic model and discussion of innovation in the service sector.

6.4.1. INNOVATION IN MANUFACTURING SECTOR FIRMS

One well-established schematic model of innovation activity relevant to technology-based firms in the manufacturing sector comes from Tassey (1997, 2005); it has been expanded on by Gallaher, Link, and Petrusa (2006) and Link (2006).[3] Figure 6.1 builds on the Tassey model; the figure illustrates different technology elements within the overall model of innovation. Each technology element has a slightly different degree of public good attributes. These distinctions in terms of public good attributes make the model especially relevant for policy analysis, but also useful as a benchmark for manufacturing and thus a point of departure for modeling service-sector innovation.

At the root of the model is the science base, referring to the accumulation of scientific and technological knowledge. The science base resides in the public domain. Investments in the science base come from basic research, primarily funded by the government and primarily performed globally in universities, federal laboratories, and a very few large companies.

Consider a representative manufacturing firm. Technology development, in the form of basic or applied research, generally begins within the firm's R&D laboratory. Technology development involves the application of scientific knowledge from the science base toward the proof of concept of a new technology. Such fundamental research, if successful, yields a generic

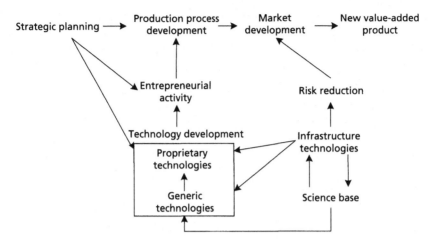

Figure 6.1. Model of innovation relevant to the manufacturing sector

Sources: NIST (2005) and Gallaher, Link, and Petrusa (2006).

technology. If the generic technology has potential commercial value, follow-on applied research takes place toward development, and if successful, a proprietary technology results.

Basic, applied, and development research occur within a firm as a result of the firm's overall strategic planning. Strategic planning defines the environment for entrepreneurial activities. And entrepreneurial activity influences production process development.

Figure 6.1 characterizes entrepreneurial activity in a Schumpeterian vein, as discussed in Chapter 2. Technology development corresponds to Schumpeter's concept of innovation being, among other things, the creation of a new good or new quality of good or the creation of a new method of production. In this sense, entrepreneurial activity involves 'the carrying out of new combinations' (Schumpeter 1934: 74).[4]

Technology infrastructure, the subject of Chapter 10, supports the processes that lead to both generic and proprietary technologies, and hence technology development. Infrastructure technologies are a diverse set of technical tools that are necessary to conduct efficiently all phases of R&D. Following Link, Tassey, and Zmud (1983b) and Tassey (1997, 2005), and as discussed in Chapter 10, examples of technology infrastructure include measurement and test methods, process and quality control techniques, evaluated scientific and engineering data, and the technical basis for product interfaces. Infrastructure technologies thus influence the science bases and are so influenced by it.

The managerial skills necessary for a firm to move its proprietary technologies to a value-added product or process are also shown along the top horizontal area of the schematic in Figure 6.1. After production, market development

Table 6.1. Public good characteristics of the elements of innovation in the manufacturing sector

Elements of the innovation model	Public good characteristics
Science base	Pure public good
Generic technologies	Quasi public good
Proprietary technologies	None
Entrepreneurial activity	None
Infrastructure technologies	Quasi public good
Risk reduction	Quasi public good
Strategic planning	None
Production process development	None
Market development	None
New value-added product	None

takes place. Markets do not always accept new technology for a number of reasons, including transaction costs associated with verifying the new technology's attributes and interoperability of the new technology with existing technologies. Infrastructure technologies can reduce such market risks and thus speed market development. And to conclude, if market development is successful, value added will result. Of course, all of the private-sector decision nodes in Figure 6.1 are influenced by the overall strategic planning of the manufacturing firm.

The ten elements in the model in Figure 6.1 can be categorized in terms of their public good characteristics, as listed in Table 6.1. This categorization is important because it highlights those aspects of manufacturing innovation that can be leveraged by public-sector innovation or technology policy. The knowledge that resides in the science base is a pure public good, as in knowledge per se. Generic technologies and infrastructure technologies are quasi public goods, and the results of risk reduction that stem from the use of infrastructure technologies also have a public good nature since the innovating manufacturing firm cannot appropriate fully these results.

6.4.2. INNOVATION IN SERVICE-SECTOR FIRMS

Many of the fundamental characteristics of the innovation process differ between the model relevant to manufacturing in Figure 6.1 and the model relevant to service-sector firms as shown in Figure 6.2.

Both manufacturing and service-sector innovation processes are driven by strategic planning. However, service-sector activities are more influenced by competitive planning because the technology-based service firm is more likely to innovate on the basis of customer input and on the basis of competitors that continually seek to challenge the firm for its customers. Whereas

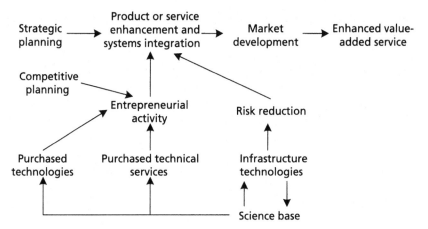

Figure 6.2. Model of innovation relevant to the service sector

Sources: NIST (2005) and Gallaher, Link, and Petrusa (2006).

manufacturing firms strategically formulate road maps for developing new emerging technologies; in the service sector, firms strategically formulate road maps for deploying modifications of existing products. Because manufacturing firms are more likely to target discrete technology jumps, creating new technologies that make their competition obsolete, their strategic plans are long-term and are linked less to current competitive planning. In contrast, service-sector firms' strategies are typically focused on retaining or gaining market shares and involve more continual or incremental transition strategies that are or will be integrated with competitive planning.

Strategic and competitive planning drive the firm's entrepreneurial activity. Whereas entrepreneurial activity in a manufacturing firm was related to innovation creating a state of disequilibrium, in a service-sector firm the entrepreneur is more of a manager or perhaps an arbitrageur. The service-sector entrepreneur collects and processes primarily existing knowledge and information. The identification and use of others' technologies are at the heart of entrepreneurial activity. R&D activity, subsumed under entrepreneurial activity in Figure 6.2, fulfills an adaptive role to ensure that purchased technologies and technical services are used efficiently. One could generalize about the service-sector entrepreneur as being an individual who allocates resources with an equilibrium state and to maintain an equilibrium state.

Whereas entrepreneurial activity, and its motivating perception of opportunity, drives the manufacturing firm toward producing new products and processes, the entrepreneurial activity of the service-sector firm drives redesigned or reconfigured enhancements of its existing products. At the root of entrepreneurial activity are others' intellectual capital and technologies that are licensed or purchased to meet the firm's road maps for deploying modifications of its existing products. Still, perception of opportunity is the defining entrepreneurial characteristic. These product and service enhancements often involve systems integration where systems integration facilitates the intersection of hardware, software, and the synthesis of application domains such as finance, manufacturing, transportation, and retail.

A key distinction between manufacturing and service-sector firms' R&D is that manufacturing firms conduct a larger share of their R&D in house, and the output of that internal activity is more likely to be a proprietary technology. In the service sector, little research (R) occurs in house, and the development (D) activity that occurs is primarily related to enhancing, redesigning, or reconfiguring others' proprietary technologies and is not often characterized internally as R&D.

Whereas manufacturing firms license or purchase others' technologies in the form of intellectual capital or equipment to be used to produce proprietary technology, service-sector firms purchase others' technology in the form of equipment to be modified and integrated into their operational system to deliver modifications to existing products. In addition, manufacturing firms strategically, through their research, introduce new technologically advanced products and processes to anticipate new consumer wants; service-sector firms strategically, through information gathering, modify existing products to meet existing consumer needs. These differences underscore the differences between entrepreneurial activities in the two sectors.

Both manufacturing and service innovation are built on the scientific base of knowledge. The manufacturing sector is more likely to build on the science base directly or in collaboration with universities. In contrast, the service sector purchases products and services as inputs which incorporate others' research, and which of course draws on the science base.

The role of technology infrastructure is also different between the two sectors. Whereas technology infrastructure reduces the market risk associated with the market introduction of a new product or process to the manufacturing firm, technology infrastructure ensures that purchased technologies interface or integrate with the service-sector firm's existing systems. Such infrastructure technologies emanate from the science base, and it is the science base that is at the root of the production of purchased technologies. Technology infrastructure, and the role of government to provide it, are the topics of Chapter 10.

An important component of the innovative process in both the manufacturing and service sectors is risk reduction. However, the focus of the activities differs. In the manufacturing sector, innovation is likely to be less integrated with marketing. Once a new product has been designed and tested, technical risk may be relatively low, but market risk may be significant because the product needs to be accepted and integrated into existing systems. In contrast, service sector innovation is more likely to involve enhancements to products in existing markets, lowering market risk. However, limitations and the cost of testing increase technical risk, making risk reduction a key objective of the product enhancement phase of service innovation.

As part of their risk reduction strategy, it is not uncommon for service-sector firms to outsource key components of product development or systems integration. However, many service-sector firms provide research as their primary service; thus, a component of their service is to assume the risk other firms are looking to outsource. These firms provide a key input into entrepreneurial activities similar to purchasing technology embedded in products or licensing technology.[5]

In summary, Figure 6.2 illustrates the process by which service-sector firms access and integrate technology toward the goal of developing and providing enhanced services to their customers. These firms lead the strategic planning and entrepreneurial activities, as well as market development. They are likely to be heavily involved in the final stages of developmental research but may outsource a large share of the applied research and early-stage developmental research. Their role is often an integrator of existing technologies; however, they may also outsource significant systems integration activities.[6]

6.5. Conclusions

The literature we have reviewed in this chapter has generated several stylized facts regarding innovation in the service-sector innovation processes. The first is that imitation tends to be much more prevalent in services, since process and systems-related patents are difficult to secure and protect. This suggests that intellectual property protection issues are somewhat less important in service firms than in manufacturing companies, since service firms are less likely to develop proprietary technologies. It also appears that formal R&D (e.g. patents, the employment of scientists and engineers) is less important in services than in manufacturing.

Another stylized fact is that innovation and entrepreneurial activity in services tends to be focused on incremental improvements rather than radical innovation. Gallaher, Link, and Petrusa (2006) suggested that this 'entrepreneurial' R&D is focused on systems design improvements and organizational/delivery modifications. This innovative activity also tends to be much more integrated across functional areas on the business and with broader IT systems.

A final stylized fact is that innovation in the service sector tends to be more customer-driven, or what von Hippel (1988) refers to as user innovation. In many instances, service-sector innovations must be tested on real consumers.

The openness and democratic nature of innovation in the service implies that the social returns to innovation may be high in this sector. A major challenge for scholars in this field is to estimate these returns.

☐ NOTES

1. This chapter draws from NIST (2005) and Gallaher, Link, and Petrusa (2006).
2. Howells (2000) suggests that this manufacturer-centrist view has permeated most attempts to reformulate how service sectors innovate.
3. The Tassey (1997, 2005) model has formed the conceptual basis for several US public–private partnership initiatives. See Link (1999, 2006) for an overview.
4. And the new combinations are the way through which the entrepreneur deals with the disequilibrium brought about by technology development.
5. These include biotechnology firms as well as systems integration firms in the information services sector.
6. Telecommunications and financial services sector firms are examples of technology integrators.

7 Technological spillovers and general purpose technologies

7.1. Introduction

We discussed in Chapter 5 two related concepts: technological spillovers or externalities and GPTs. Recall that GPTs have broad applications and productivity-enhancing effects in numerous downstream sectors. They induce dramatic economic changes by creating new industries and rejuvenating existing sectors. Examples of GPTs include the steam engine, the electric dynamo, and lasers. More recently, several authors (e.g. Mowery and Simcoe 2002) have asserted that computers and the Internet are GPTs.

In this chapter, we present a comprehensive historical analysis of two GPTs—the Internet and nanotechnology. A GPT is an enabling technology, one that when adopted and used is expected to change production and consumption activity and behavior. Bresnahan and Trajtenberg (1995) posit that a GPT has the following three characteristics: pervasiveness, an inherent potential for technological improvements, and innovational complexities that give rise to increasing returns to scale.[1] And, over time, nanotechnology is expected to possess these characteristics.[2]

Both of these technologies have benefited from public sector initiatives and public sector intervention. Such public sector influence is economically justifiable, in part, on the grounds that the technologies generate technological spillovers, thus the marginal social benefits of the technologies are greater than the marginal private benefits so firms will not invest in these technologies on their own to the level that is socially desirable.

7.2. The Internet

Mowery and Simcoe (2002) asserted that the Internet and the World Wide Web constitute a GPT. Note that the term Internet refers to a global network of computers, while the World Wide Web refers to the software that allows these computers to communicate with each other. According to Bresnahan and

Trajtenberg (1995), a GPT induces dramatic economic changes by stimulating new applications in downstream sectors or innovation complementarities, creating new industries, and rejuvenating existing sectors. Economic historians (e.g. Rosenberg and Trajtenberg 2001) have concluded that the steam engine, the electric dynamo, and lasers were GPTs.

The Internet has resulted in the creation of new industries, such as Internet service providers (e.g. America Online and Prodigy), producers of network communications equipment (e.g. Cisco Systems), firms that produce software and provide consulting services to help organizations use the Internet to enhance efficiency (e.g. Oracle and Anderson Consulting). Examples of innovation complementarities and the rejuvenation of existing industries associated with the use of the Internet abound in Litan and Rivlin (2001).

Mowery and Simcoe (2002) have presented an articulate in-depth historical analysis of the development of the Internet and the World Wide Web. They argued that the federal government and other elements of the US national innovation system played a key role in the creation of this GPT. For instance, the Department of Defense (DoD) and the NSF financed much of the research which resulted in the development of key infrastructure technologies, especially the creation of computer networks. Following the logic of Martin and Scott (2000), the main mode of innovation for this GPT was decentralized development of what they term a complex system. In addition to direct funding from federal agencies, policy instruments used included initiatives to foster R&D cooperation, targeted subsidies, and bridging institutions to stimulate the development of the infrastructure technology. Examples of bridging institutions include university research parks and federal research laboratories. Also, several university spin-offs, such as Bolt, Beranek, and Newman (BBN), and Sun Microsystems, out of MIT and Stanford, respectively, played a key role in the development of this technology.

Mowery and Simcoe (2002) argued that there were three distinct periods in the creation of the Internet and the World Wide Web. The first period, which began in 1960 and ended in 1985, was characterized by the early development of computer networks. Two innovations that facilitated the formation of these networks were digital packet-switching, the technology used to link computers, and the development of standards and protocols that facilitated the communication of information across networked computers. The first version of the Internet, called ARPANET, was funded by the Defense Advanced Research Projects Agency (DARPA) of the US DoD. In the mid-1970s, universities and other defense research organizations were added to the network.

The key standard developed during the initial period for communication via the Internet is transmission control protocol/Internet protocol or TCP/IP, which was also created by DARPA-funded engineers. TCP/IP is an open standard, which means that complete descriptions of it, as well as the rights to use this protocol, are both publicly available. Significant network externalities were generated when NSF adopted TCP/IP in forming its network of comput-ers with universities and other research institutions. Two other key events that occurred during this period were the development of e-mail, the first killer application for networks and the development of self-governance institutions. The latter refers to organizations, initially sponsored by NSF and DoD, which managed what became known as the Internet. The key institutions were the Internet Configuration Control Board (ICCB), which later became the Inter-net Activities Board (IAB). As the system grew, it became difficult for the IAB to manage the network while relying exclusively on government financing. Therefore, a public–private partnership, the Internet Society (ISOC), was established in 1992 to oversee the growth of the network and the continued development of open standards.

According to Mowery and Simcoe (2002), the second period in the devel-opment of the Internet and the World Wide Web was between 1985 and 1995. During these years, there was rapid growth in network infrastructure, in the public and private sectors. In the public sector, there was a transition from ARPANET to NSFNET in 1990. In the private sector, there was a large increase in the demand for corporate networks, as firms (and consumers) became heavy users of personal computers and organizations developed local-area networks (LANs) to allow these computers to communicate with each other.

Mowery and Simcoe (2002) asserted that the final period in the develop-ment of the Internet and the World Wide Web began in 1995 and continues to the present. During this period, there has been a rapid diffusion in use of the Internet for commercial purposes and by individuals and organizations. It is important to note that until 1991, the Internet was strictly a device for research and communication and not to be used for commercial purposes, as mandated by NSF, which controlled the network. After lobbying by com-mercial interests, NSF decided to abandon this policy. By 1995, management of the network had been completely transferred to four private companies, Ameritech, Sprint, MFS, and Pacific Bell.

A fundamental factor in the growth of the World Wide Web was the devel-opment of the HTML document format and the associated HTTP document retrieval protocol. HTML and HTTP facilitated the creation and dissemi-nation of multimedia documents. That is, these innovations made it quite simple for firms to create documents with text, pictures, and graphics and also enabled consumers to easily access these files. Furthermore, with HTML, it was easy for web-page authors to provide links to other documents, which greatly facilitated the value and use of the network. The combination of HTML and HTTP essentially transformed the Internet into the World Wide Web.

A key tool in using the World Wide Web is the Internet browser, which allows a user to access and read HTML files at the click of a mouse. One of the first browsers, called Mosaic, was created at the National Center for

Supercomputing Applications (an NSF-funded research center) at the University of Illinois by a graduate student named Marc Andreessen. Mosaic was ultimately replaced by Netscape's browser, which then battled with Microsoft's Internet Explorer browser for commercial dominance. Microsoft literally gave away its browser, including the browser in its standard 'Wintel' (Windows operating system combined with an Intel microprocessor) computer package.

The widespread, rapid diffusion of technologies that enabled consumers and firms to gain speedy access to the Internet and the World Wide Web was fueled by several factors. These include precipitous declines in inflation-adjusted computer prices and the cost of information transmission, along with a concomitant increase in speed of information delivery through high-speed communication networks. Consumers purchase computers to gain access to information and entertainment that is transmitted to them via the Internet. Now, consumers are reasonably confident about purchasing items online. The end result has been a substantial increase in e-commerce. IDC (2002) projected that global e-commerce would generate $4.6 trillion in revenue in 2005, and that forecast was surpassed. Note that this includes online shopping for consumers and B2B e-commerce. UNCTAD (2002) estimated that B2B e-commerce accounted for 58 percent of total global e-commerce activity, and that forecast was also surpassed.

The Internet and the World Wide Web provide an interesting example of government intervention to address innovation market failures. According to Martin and Scott (2000), causes of market imperfections include high risks associated with standards for new technology and the development of complex systems, limited appropriability of generic technologies (especially for infrastructure technology), and the high costs of creating new infrastructure technology and other basic research projects. These clearly applied in the case of the Internet and the World Wide Web.

It appears that there were several complementary bipartisan policy initiatives that, by either design or fortuitously, served to address these market failures. A key intervention was the enactment of antitrust and regulatory policies that made it difficult for incumbent telecommunications firms to exploit market opportunities, while at the same time, aiding new entrants and the emergence of Internet Service Providers (ISPs). With respect to intellectual property, we have noted that many of the key breakthroughs in this GPT were in the public domain, such as the open platforms and network architecture (e.g. TCP/IP and HTML/HTTP). Of course, there was also abundant direct public investment in basic research and technology infrastructure and the creation of high-technology bridging institutions and governance organizations such as the ICCB and IAB. Finally, we note that public–private partnerships, such as the ISOC, also facilitated the development of this technology.

7.3. **Nanotechnology**

The 21st century Nanotechnology Research and Development Act (PL 108-153; hereafter, the Act) was signed into law in December 2003 by US President George W. Bush.[3] It authorized $3.7 billion in federal nanotechnology-related R&D spending over four years, starting in FY 2005. Receiving broad bipartisan support in Congress, the Act put into law the programs and activities supported by the National Nanotechnology Initiative (NNI), one of the President's highest multiagency R&D priorities.[4] The Act formally made nanotechnology the highest priority funded science and technology effort since the efforts of the United States to win the space race (Choi 2003).

Although there is not a uniformly agreed on definition of nanotechnology, the widely accepted NNI definition states that:

[Nanotechnology refers to] the understanding and control of matter at dimensions of roughly 1 to 100 nanometers, where unique phenomena enable novel applications.[5]

The government fostered the NNI, and hence the Act, in part because of the expected economic impact associated with nanoscale science and technology. While estimates of nanotechnogy's economic impact vary widely across academic, government, and business experts—ranging from $1 trillion to $2 trillion in 2015[6]—all agree that its future potential is enormous.[7] According to the National Research Council (2002: 2):

With potential applications in virtually every existing industry and new applications yet to be discovered, nanoscale science and technology will no doubt emerge as one of the major drivers of economic growth in the first part of the new millennium.

Widespread commercial adoption of nanotechnology is already growing rapidly, and early commercial applications of nanotechnology have focused on improving existing products in such varied markets as cosmetics, coatings, textiles, and displays. Examples of areas in which nanotechnology is expected to have a high commercial impact in the future include improved chemical and biological sensors (within one to five years), new targeted drug therapies (within five to ten years), and new molecular electronics (in twenty plus years) (PCAST 2005). The extent to which commercial potential in these areas is achieved, however, and the speed with which the United States achieves it, will depend in large part on the extent to which barriers to companies' adoption and integration of nanotechnology can be identified and lessened.

Perhaps not surprisingly, given the recent origins of nanotechnology research, there has been heretofore no systematic research on barriers inhibiting the diffusion of nanotechnology from the laboratory to commercial application. The NNI serves as the US government's primary mechanism for supporting nanoscience research and nanotechnology development. Since its inception, the NNI's focus has been to develop an understanding of the novel properties that occur at the nanoscale and to harness the ability to control matter at the atomic and molecular level (PCAST 2005).

7.3.1. ACTIVITIES SETTING THE STAGE FOR THE NANOTECHNOLOGY ACT

Two motivations gave rise to the NNI. First, as mentioned above, nanoscale science and technology are predicted to have an enormous impact on the quality of life throughout the world. Second, at the time the NNI began there were no established major industrial markets for nanotechnology products. Government leadership and funds were deemed necessary to promote technology transfer activities to private industry by accelerating the time required for developing the infrastructure and technologies industry needs to exploit nanotechnology innovations and discoveries.

The NNI began long before the Act was passed. In early 1996, representatives from industry, government, and university laboratories convened to discuss the prospects for nanoscale science and technology. The attempt to coordinate at the federal-level scientific and technical work at the nanoscale began in November of that same year, when staff members from six agencies decided to meet regularly to discuss their respective plans for programs in nanoscale science and technology. This group met informally until September 1998, when the National Science and Technology Council (NSTC) designated the group the Interagency Working Group on Nanotechnology (IWGN) under the White House Office of Science and Technology Policy (OSTP).

The IWGN laid the groundwork for the NNI by sponsoring numerous workshops and studies to help define the state of the art in nanoscale science and technology and to forecast potential future developments in the field. Moreover, the group published several reports on the state of the science between July and September 1999, including:

- *Nanostructure Science and Technology: A Worldwide Study*, a report based on the findings of an expert panel that visited nanoscale science and technology laboratories around the world.

- *Nanotechnology Research Directions*, a workshop report with input from academic, private, and government participants.

These two documents supported the IWGN efforts to raise nanoscale science and technology to the level of a national initiative by pointing up the current and potential future impacts of nanotechnology innovations and discoveries, respectively. According to Mihail Roco, senior Adviser for nanotechnology at the NSF and primary author of the above reports, this was a crucial time for nanoscale science and technology (Bozeman and Boardman 2004: 17):

> At that moment many looked at nanotechnology as science fiction. So we developed [the NNI] like a science project, from the bottom up. We started first of all to look at the fundamentals that would justify investment and not just to the smallness. We emphasized the new properties, the new phenomena where you have only a few mechanisms that could potentially revolutionize fields from medicine to electronics, as well as benefit society. It was a process to convince people. The NNI was not a decision at the political level.

In August 1999, IWGN drafted its first plan for a national-scale initiative in nanoscale science and technology. Both the President's Council of Advisers on Science and Technology[8] (PCAST) and OSTP were involved in approving the plan. In January 2000, the White House officially announced its endorsement of the NNI and included the initiative in its 2001 budget submission to Congress.

To assist the Clinton administration convince Congress that the NNI should be a top priority, in February 2000 the IWGN prepared another report to supplement the President's budget request: *National Nanotechnology Initiative: Leading to the Next Industrial Revolution*. The report highlighted the nanotechnology funding mechanisms developed for the initiative as well as the funding allocations by each participating federal agency. Moreover, it outlined nanotechnology goals and benchmarks, infrastructure requirements, and contained examples of already-existing nanotechnology applications and partnerships that would become key components of the NNI.

After the February report, IWGN disbanded and the NSTC's Committee on Technology[9] established the Nanoscale Science, Engineering, and Technology subcommittee (NSET) to fill IWGN's shoes. This 'new' group, which was chaired by Roco and comprised of the same people who staffed IWGN, drafted the NNI implementation plan, *National Nanotechnology Initiative: The Initiative and Its Implementation Plan*. NSET submitted this plan to Congress in July 2000, which was identical to the February report save new sections on interagency management objectives and coordination.

In November 2000, Congress appropriated $422 million for the NNI for FY 2001, raising nanoscale science and technology to the level of a federal initiative. The subsequent activities paved the way to the formalized policies of the Nanotechnology Research and Development Act.

7.3.2. EVENTS SUBSEQUENT TO THE PASSAGE OF THE ACT

Consistent with that focus, approximately 95 percent of the funding authorized by the Act was targeted to scientific R&D—roughly 60 percent for academia and 35 percent for government laboratories. Thus, by design, and consistent with similar national programs of this type, the NNI's primary purpose is to provide a strong R&D foundation from which industry can select technologies to exploit for commercial purposes.

Even with this strong focus on R&D, advancing nanotechnology commercialization remains a critical component of the NNI. Two examples clearly illustrate this point. First, *The 2004 National Nanotechnology Initiative Strategic Plan* (hereafter, the *Strategic Plan*), mandated by the Act, outlined the following four national goals:

- maintain a world-class R&D program aimed at realizing the full potential of nanotechnology;
- facilitate transfer of new technologies into products for economic growth, jobs, and other public benefit;
- develop educational resources, as skilled workforce, and the supporting infrastructure and tools to advance nanotechnology; and
- support responsible development of nanotechnology.

Underlying the first three of the four goals, particularly the second one, is a fundamental appreciation of nanotechnology's importance to the economy and the need to harness nanotechnology for commercial purposes.

Second, the Act charged the NSTC with developing a plan to utilize federal programs, such as the SBIR program and the Small Business Technology Transfer (STTR) program, to support commercialization of nanotechnology.[10] Consistent with that charge, the *Strategic Plan*:[11]

Encourage[s] agencies participating in the NNI to have components of their SBIR and STTR programs focused on nanotechnology topics, and in particular on nanomanufacturing.... [and to]...Facilitate use of NNI-supported user facilities by small businesses that seek and receive SBIR and STTR grants and contracts.

In addition to these two examples, the *Strategic Plan* documented a number of current activities and plans to support the transfer of nanotechnology discoveries from the laboratory to commercial use. Among these are establishing industry liaison groups; supporting meetings involving industry, government, and industry; establishing and supporting user facilities available to researchers from all sectors; funding multidisciplinary research teams that include industry and university researchers; encouraging the exchange of researchers between universities and industry; establishing centers focused on nanomanufacturing research; and engaging with regional, state, and local nanotechnology initiatives.

Due to the brevity of the NNI's existence, efforts to assess how well it is meeting its goals have only recently begun (e.g. Bozeman and Boardman 2004). In 2005, the PCAST undertook the first formal US federal government assessment of the NNI: *The National Nanotechnology Initiative at Five Years:*

Assessment and Recommendations of the National Nanotechnology Advisory Panel (hereafter, the *Assessment*). The *Assessment's* executive summary stresses that (PCAST 2005: 1):

[The federal government's] substantial and sustained investment in nanotechnology has been largely based on the expectation that advances in understanding and harnessing novel nanoscale properties will generate broad-ranging economic benefits for our Nation.

With respect to the NNI's progress on issues related to nanotechnology's economic impact, the *Assessment* found that several industrial sectors have a high and growing level of interest and investment in nanotechnology and are likely to outpace levels of national investment in the near future.

In an effort to facilitate further nanotechnology transfer from the laboratory (company as well as federal) to the marketplace, the *Assessment* recommended two action steps beyond those outlined in the 2004 *Strategic Plan* (PCAST 2005: 3):

(1) the NNI's outreach to, and coordination with, the States should be increased, and
(2) the NNI should examine how to improve knowledge management of NNI assets.

These recommendations stem from PCAST's position that, while the federal government can take steps to help promote technology transfer, the primary responsibility for funding product manufacturing should be left to the private sector with appropriate assistance from state and local governments.

7.4. **Conclusions**

The growth of public investment in R&D, through national innovation systems and other programs, has led to greater interest in evaluating the social returns to publicly funded R&D. A missing element in the assessment of the social returns to publicly funded R&D conducted at universities, federal research labs, and other nonprofit/public institutions is the role that public R&D plays in the creation of new industries.

Currently, the government does a poor job of tracking economic activity in embryonic industries and the emergence of new industries within existing sectors. The statistical agencies (e.g. US Census Bureau) that collect such data do not have sufficient coverage of embryonic sectors and are not charged with the responsibility of measuring spillovers across industries.

This lack of coverage could result in a downward bias in estimates of the social returns to public R&D because it might lead to an underestimation of the impact of public R&D on economic efficiency. Thus, we have relied on retrospective information to illustrate the development and aspects of the economic impact of two GPTs. There is no doubt that both technologies have widespread applications and have transformed existing industries. These cases also illustrate the importance of standards and openness, which both serve to accelerate the rate of technological diffusion. Although there is always the counterfactual (e.g. perhaps the Internet and nanotechnology would have developed in the absence of public sector involvement and/or initiatives), it appears that both initiatives have successfully addressed innovation market failures that provide the theoretical justification for government intervention.

▢ NOTES

1. Jovanovic and Rousseau (2005) referred to the latter characteristic as innovation spawning.
2. David (1990) emphasized that general purpose technology does not deliver productivity gains on arrival, hence our emphasis on expectations over time.
3. This section draws from Bozeman, Hardin, and Link (2006).
4. The NNI was promulgated in FY (2001) as part of the Clinton administration's efforts to raise nanoscale science and technology to the level of a federal initiative.
5. 'Encompassing nanoscale science, engineering and technology, nanotechnology involves imaging, measuring, modeling, and manipulating matter at this length scale' (http://www.nano.gov/).
6. The $1 trillion estimate is from the National Science Foundation; the $2 trillion estimate is from Lux Research.
7. Zucker and Darby (2006) provide technology-based information (e.g. patent activity) to support indirectly this conjecture.
8. PCAST was originally established by President George Bush in 1990 to enable the President to receive advice from the private sector and academic community on technology, scientific research priorities, and math and science education. The organization follows a tradition of Presidential advisory panels on science and technology dating back to Presidents Eisenhower and Truman. Since its creation, PCAST has been expanded and currently consists of twenty-three members plus the Director of the Office of Science and Technology Policy who serves as the Council's Co-Chair. The council members, distinguished individuals appointed by the President, are drawn from industry, education, and research institutions, and other nongovernmental organizations (NGOs).
9. The purpose of the Committee on Technology was to advise and assist the NSTC in improving the overall effectiveness and productivity of Federal Research and Development (R&D) efforts. The Committee will address significant national policy matters that cut across agency boundaries and shall provide a formal mechanism for interagency policy coordination and the development of federal technology activities. The Committee will act to improve the coordination of all federal efforts in technology. This includes creating balanced and comprehensive R&D programs, establishing structures to improve the way the federal government plans and coordinates R&D, and advising the Director, Office of Science and Technology Policy, and the Director, Office of Management and Budget, on R&D budget crosscuts and priorities.

10. The National Science and Technology Council (NSTC) was established by an Executive Order on November 23, 1993. This Cabinet-level Council is the principal means for the President of the United States to coordinate science, space, and technology to coordinate the diverse parts of the federal research and development enterprise. See, http://www.ostp.gov/NSTC/html/NSTC_Home.html

11. Here, too, the NNI's recognition of nanotechnology's potential importance to the economy is clear.

8 University technology transfer

8.1. Introduction

Many university administrators in the United States and other industrial nations have asserted that university technology transfer can potentially provide substantial revenue for universities.[1] Public policymakers in these nations have also pointed to the possibility that technology transfer can enhance national and regional economic growth. The key university technology transfer commercialization mechanisms are licensing agreements between the university and private firms, RJVs, and university-based start-ups. These activities could potentially result in financial gains for the university, other benefits to these institutions (e.g. additional sponsored research and hiring of graduate students and post-doctoral fellows), and job creation in the local region. Given the importance of these commercialization mechanisms, many universities and public policymakers continually seek guidance on how to evaluate and enhance effectiveness in university technology transfer.

Organizations such as the Association of University Technology Managers (AUTM) in the United States, the University Companies Association (UNICO), and the Association for University Research Industry Links (AURIL) in the United Kingdom have helped to promote technology transfer activity by publishing benchmarking surveys. These surveys have been used by scholars to explore key research questions relating to the drivers of effective university technology transfer. While such studies have been useful, the academic literatures remains somewhat embryonic with many unresolved managerial and policy issues.

In many nations, national governments have provided support for these initiatives through legislation to facilitate technological diffusion from universities to firms (e.g. the Bayh–Dole Act 1980 in the United States) and collaborative research (e.g. the National Cooperation Research Act (NCRA) of 1984 in the United States as discussed in Chapter 10), subsidies for RJVs involving universities and firms (e.g. the EU's Framework Programs and the US Commerce Department's Advanced Technology Program (ATP)), and shared use of expertise and laboratory facilities (e.g. the NSF's Engineering Research Centers, Science and Technology Centers, and Industry–University Cooperative Research Centers). Along these lines, national, state, and regional government authorities have also provided support for science parks and incubators.

The growth in public and private investments in university-based technology initiatives has raised important policy questions regarding the impact of such activities on researchers, universities, firms, and local regions where such investments occur. Given that many of these initiatives are relatively new, university officials and policymakers seek guidance on best practices. More specifically, they seek evidence on specific organizational practices related to incentives, strategic objectives, and measurement and monitoring mechanisms, which might enhance technology transfer effectiveness. Inductive, qualitative research is also useful in this context, since notions of effectiveness are likely to vary across different types of initiatives (e.g. incubators vs. TTOs) and for different players involved in such activities (e.g. university scientists, university administrators, and corporations interacting with the university).

In this chapter we review and synthesize research on the antecedents and consequences of university-based technology transfer and we explore the implications for practice and future research in this domain. We also include an appendix, which presents material on methods used to assess the relative performance of universities in transferring technologies.

In the late 1970s, US research universities were often criticized for being more adept at developing new technologies than facilitating their commercialization into the private sector (General Accounting Office 1998). Furthermore, it was asserted that the long lag between the discovery and commercialization of new knowledge at the university level had weakened the global competitiveness of US firms (Marshall 1985). While such conclusions glossed over the principal mission of research universities as creators of new knowledge, they generated sufficient concern for public policymakers. In response, in 1980, the US Congress attempted to remove potential obstacles to university technology transfer by passing the Bayh–Dole Act.[2] Bayh–Dole instituted a uniform patent policy across federal agencies, removed many restrictions on licensing, and allowed universities to own patents arising from federal research grants. The framers of this legislation asserted that university ownership and management of intellectual property would accelerate the commercialization of new technologies and promote economic development and entrepreneurial activity.

In the aftermath of this landmark legislation, almost all research universities in the United States established TTOs to manage and protect their intellectual property. The number of TTOs increased eightfold, to more than 200 by 2004, this increase resulting in a sixfold increase in the volume of university patents registered (AUTM 2004). TTOs facilitate commercial knowledge transfers through the licensing to industry of patents or other forms of intellectual property resulting from university research. AUTM reported that from 1991 to 2004, university revenues from licensing IP have increased over 533 percent, from $220 million to $1.385 billion (AUTM 2004). The number of firms that utilize university-based technologies has also increased. Evidence also suggests that venture capitalists are increasingly interested in ventures founded on the basis of basic research (Small Business Administration 2002).

8.2. The institutional contexts of university technology transfer

Tables 8.1 and 8.2 summarize recent quantitative and qualitative studies on university technology transfer through licensing and new business formation, respectively. As demonstrated from the summaries in these tables, recent research related to university technology transfer includes, but is not limited to, faculty participation in technology commercialization (Bercovitz and Feldman 2004; Owen-Smith and Powell 2003); university licensing strategies (Feldman et al. 2002); university incentives and licensing revenues (Lach and Schankerman 2004; Siegel, Waldman, and Link 2003); US and Swedish policies on invention commercialization (Goldfarb and Henrekson 2003); firm linkages to universities (Cohen, Nelson, and Walsh 2002; Rothaermel and Thursby 2005; Thursby and Thursby 2002); issues of moral-hazard problems in technology licensing (Jensen and Thursby 2001); the performance of licensing firms (George, Zahra, and Wood 2002); antecedents to commercialization speed of university-based inventions (Markman et al. 2005*a*); and the performance of university-based start-up companies (Link and Scott 2005*a*; Lockett and Wright 2005; Shane and Stuart 2002).

The success of a university's licensing program depends on its institutional structure, organizational capability, and incentive systems to encourage participation by researchers. Pursuing this line of inquiry, Siegel, Waldman, and Link (2003) presented quantitative and qualitative evidence on the efficiency of university technology transfer, derived from the AUTM survey and from 55 structured, in-person interviews of 100 university technology transfer stakeholders (i.e. academic and industry scientists, university technology managers, and corporate managers and entrepreneurs) at 5 research universities in the US states of Arizona and North Carolina. Siegel, Waldman, and Link (2003) concluded that intellectual property policies and organizational practices can potentially enhance (or impede) technology transfer effectiveness. Specifically, they found that informational and cultural barriers existed between universities and firms, especially for small firms, and that if these were not explicitly considered in the transfer process, the perceived attractiveness of university technology to commercial innovators is attenuated.

This result was consistent with Clarke (1998), who found evidence on the importance of institutional norms, standards, and culture. On the basis of a qualitative analysis of five European universities that had outstanding performance in technology transfer, he concluded that the existence of an entrepreneurial culture at those institutions was a critical factor in their success (Clarke 1998). Additionally, Roberts (1991) found that social norms and MIT's tacit approval of entrepreneurs were critical determinants of successful academic entrepreneurship at MIT.

Interestingly, the availability of venture capital in the region where the university is located and the commercial orientation of the university, proxied by the percentage of the university's research budget that is derived from industry, were found to have an insignificant impact on the rate of start-up formation in the United States (DiGregorio and Shane 2003). Lockett and Wright (2005) and Wright et al. (2006) found, in contrast, that the presence of venture capital in university spin-offs made a statistically significant difference in the United Kingdom.

Degroof and Roberts (2004) examined the importance of university policies related to start-ups in regions where environmental factors (e.g. technology transfer and infrastructure for entrepreneurship) are not particularly conducive to entrepreneurial activity. They offered a taxonomy for four types of policies: an absence of start-up policies, minimal selectivity/support, intermediate selectivity/support, and comprehensive selectivity/support. Consistent with the Roberts and Malone (1996) study, Degroof and Roberts (2004) found that comprehensive selectivity/support is the optimal policy for generating start-ups that can exploit ventures with high growth potential. However, while such a policy is ideal, it may not be feasible given the resource constraints faced by universities. Degroof and Roberts (2004) concluded that while spinout policies matter in the sense that they affect the growth potential of ventures, it may be more desirable to formulate such policies at a higher level of aggregation than the university.

Franklin, Wright, and Lockett (2001) analyzed perceptions at UK universities regarding entrepreneurial start-ups that emerge from university technology transfer. They distinguished between academic and surrogate (external) entrepreneurs and old and new universities in the United Kingdom. Old universities have well-established research reputations, world-class scientists, and they are typically receptive to entrepreneurial start-ups. New universities tend to be somewhat weaker in academic research and less flexible with regard to entrepreneurial ventures. They found that the most significant barriers to the adoption of entrepreneurial-friendly policies are cultural and informational and that the old universities generating the most start-ups are those that have the most favorable policies regarding surrogate or external entrepreneurs.

Finally, Mustar et al. (2006) reviewed the literature on research-based spin-offs (RBSOs) and concluded that there were a number of common dimensions around which the processes of spin-off creation and spin-off development could be described. Specifically, they could be described in terms of the types of resources being employed in the processes (e.g. technical, human, social, and financial), the business model of the spin-off, and the institutional links to which the spin-offs were connected.

8.3. The organizational context of university technology transfer

Bercovitz et al. (2001) examined the organizational structure of the TTO and its relationship to the overall university research administration. On the basis of the writings of Chandler and Williamson, they analyzed the performance implications of four organizational forms: the functional or unitary form (U-Form), the multidivisional (M-form), the holding company (H-form), and the matrix form (MX-form). They noted that these structures have different implications for the ability of a university to coordinate activity, facilitate internal and external information flows, and align incentives in a manner that is consistent with its strategic goals with respect to technology transfer. To test these assertions, they examined TTOs at Duke University, Johns Hopkins University, and Penn State University and found evidence of alternative organizational forms at these three institutions. Finally, they creatively linked these differences in structure to variation in technology transfer performance along three dimensions: transaction output, the ability to coordinate licensing and sponsored research activities, and incentive alignment capability.

Related to this issue of organizational structure, a surprising conclusion of Markman et al. (2005b) was that the most attractive combinations of technology stage and licensing strategy for new venture creation—early-stage technology, combined with licensing for equity—are least likely to be favored by the university and thus not likely to be used because universities and TTOs are typically focused on short-term cash maximization, and extremely risk-averse with respect to financial and legal risks. Their findings are consistent with evidence presented in Siegel et al. (2004), who found that TTOs appear to do a better job of serving the needs of large firms than small, entrepreneurial companies. The results of these studies imply that universities should modify their technology transfer strategies if they are serious about promoting entrepreneurial development. Markman et al. (2005a) found that speed of process matters in the sense that the faster TTOs can commercialize technologies that are protected by patents. They also found that the faster commercializable technologies are protected, the greater the returns to the university and the higher the rate of start-up formation. These authors also reported that there are three key determinants of the speed of the process: the level of the TTO's resources, the competency of the TTO in identifying licensees, and the participation of faculty-inventors throughout the licensing process.

Along the same lines of inquiry, Lockett and Wright (2005) assessed the relationship between the resources and capabilities of UK TTOs and the rate of start-up formation at their respective universities. Here, these authors applied the RBV of the firm to the university. The RBV asserts that an organization's superior performance (in the parlance of strategic management, its competitive advantage) is related to its internal resources and capabilities. They are able to distinguish empirically between a university's resource inputs and its routines and capabilities. The results from their analysis suggest that universities seeking to spawn numerous start-ups should devote greater attention to recruitment, training, and development of technology transfer officers with broad-based commercial skills.

Markman, Gianiodis, and Phan (2006) showed that bypassing, or so-called gray market, activity is reduced when universities professionalize their technology licensing offices and when monitoring is delegated to dual agents who can better monitor agents, namely scientists/faculty departments. They also showed that increased bypassing activity is associated with more valuable discoveries and heightened entrepreneurial activities, highlighting the conundrum found in other studies; that universities focused on entrepreneurial start-ups may do well to reduce restrictions over intellectual property flows.

In a comprehensive review of the literature, Mustar et al. (2006) offered a typology of RBSOs from university technology transfer. In the review, they suggested that RBSOs can be described according to a resource-based perspective with a focus on internal capabilities, a business model perspective with a focus on the value creation process, and an institutional perceptive with a focus on the governing constraints exhibited by their parent institutions (i.e. the universities, research laboratories, and so on). The conclusion of their review is that RBSOs are not homogeneous with respect to the focuses that create them and therefore cannot be analyzed (from a dependent variable standpoint) without reference to the institutional contexts, internal capabilities, and strategic mission.

Siegel, Waldman, and Link (2003) found that the high rate of turnover among licensing officers was detrimental toward the establishment of long-term relationships with firms and entrepreneurs. Other concerns they found were insufficient business and marketing experience in the TTO and the possible need for incentive compensation, as indicated by other studies. In a subsequent paper, Link and Siegel (2005) found that the royalty distribution formula, which determines the fraction of revenue from a licensing transaction that is allocated to a faculty member who develops the new technology, can potentially enhance technology licensing (as distinct from start-up formation).

Siegel, Waldman, and Link (2003) also found, based on TTO-based data, that universities allocating a higher percentage of royalty payments to faculty members tend to be more efficient in technology transfer activities (closer to the production frontier). Organizational incentives for university technology transfer therefore appear to be an important determinant of success. This finding was independently confirmed in Friedman and Silberman (2003) and Lach and Schankerman (2004) using slightly different methods and data. Finally, Markman, Gianiodis, and Phan (2006) found that increasing royalty revenues to scientists' departments is associated with increased gray market activity and patent citations.

According to Thursby and Thursby (2004), TTOs can be modeled as dual agents seeking to obtain discoveries from faculty and seeking to manage the commercialization process to industry incumbents for the university. TTOs assess the potential rents derived from discoveries, seek IP protection for promising discoveries, solicit research sponsors and potential technology licensees, and manage and enforce contractual agreements with partners and licensees. Hence, the structure of the TTO, as Markman et al. (2004) found, was critical to the success of the transfer process.

Using an agency theoretic approach, Jensen, Thursby, and Thursby (2003) modeled the process of faculty disclosure and university licensing through a TTO as a game, in which the principal is the university administration and the faculty and TTO is a dual agent who maximizes expected utilities. The game is played when faculty members decide whether to disclose the invention to the TTO and at what stage. If an invention is disclosed, the TTO decides whether to search for a firm to license the technology and then negotiates the terms of the licensing agreement with the licensee. The university administration influences the incentives of the TTO and faculty members by establishing policies for the distribution of licensing income and/or sponsored research. According to Jensen, Thursby, and Thursby (2003), the TTO engages in a balancing act in the sense that it can influence the rate of invention disclosures, evaluate the inventions once they are disclosed, and negotiate licensing agreements with firms as the agent of the administration.

The Jensen, Thursby, and Thursby (2003) theoretical analysis generates a number of interesting empirical predictions. For example, in equilibrium, the probability that a university scientist discloses an invention and the stage at which he or she discloses the invention is related to the pecuniary reward from licensing, as well as faculty quality. The authors test the empirical implications of the dual agency model based on an extensive survey of the objectives, characteristics, and outcomes of licensing activity at sixty-two US universities.[3] Their survey results provide empirical support for the hypothesis that the TTO is a dual agent. They also demonstrated that faculty quality is positively associated with the rate of invention disclosure at the earliest stage and negatively associated with the share of licensing income allocated to inventors.

Related to the above issue, Siegel, Waldman, and Link (2003) identified a mismatch between incentive systems for faculty involvement and the commercialization goals for university technology transfer. This includes both pecuniary and nonpecuniary rewards, such as credit toward tenure and promotion. Some respondents in the study even suggested that involvement in technology transfer could be detrimental to their careers. Other authors have explored the role of incentives in university technology transfer. For example, Markman et al. (2004, 2005*b*) assessed the role of incentive systems in stimulating academic entrepreneurship and the determinants of innovation speed, or time to market. An interesting result of Markman et al. (2004) was that there is a positive association between compensation to TTO personnel and both equity licensing and start-up formation. Paradoxically, DiGregorio and Shane (2003) found that a royalty distribution formula that is more favorable to faculty members reduced start-up formation, a finding that is confirmed by Markman et al. (2005*b*). DiGregorio and Shane (2003) attributed this result to the higher opportunity cost associated with launching a new firm, relative to licensing the technology to an existing firm.

O'Shea, Allen, and Chevalier (2005) extend these findings in several ways. First, they employed a more sophisticated econometric technique, originally used by Blundell, Griffith, and van Reenen (1995) on innovation counts, to account for unobserved heterogeneity across universities due to history and tradition. This type of path dependency would seem to be quite important in the university context since university policies tend to evolve slowly. Indeed, O'Shea, Allen, and Chevalier (2005) found that a university's previous success in technology transfer is a key explanatory factor of start-up formation. Consistent with DiGregorio and Shane (2003), they also found that faculty quality, commercial capability, and the extent of federal science and engineering funding are significant determinants of higher rates of university start-up formation.

Moray and Clarysse (2005) adopted an institutional perspective on spinning-off ventures as a venue for commercializing research. The central question they considered was the following: Are the resource endowments of science-based entrepreneurial firms at time of founding influenced by the way in which technology transfer is organized by the parent? Using archival data sources, standardized questionnaires, and semi-structured interviews from science-based entrepreneurial ventures, they found that changes in the internal institutional set up—the technology transfer policy in particular—go together with a changing overall tendency in the resources endowed to the science-based entrepreneurial firms.

Moray and Clarysse's paper (2005) built on existing research that demonstrated that Public Research Institutes (PRIs) could undertake different generic approaches to spinning-out new ventures (Clarysse et al. 2005). IMEC—Europe's leading independent research center in nanoelectronics and nanotechnology—is an interesting case where the PRI became, in effect, an incubator over time; the third phase outlined by Moray and Clarysse. Their research showed that the strategy of the PRI to become an incubator has an effect on the type of new ventures being created.

Powers and McDougall (2005a, 2005b) tested a model of PRIs selectivity and support policy orientation for technology licensing and its interaction with the external environment for entrepreneurship. They found that both selectivity and entrepreneurial density are significant positive predictors of the number of licenses held with private companies that subsequently went public. However, a university's selectivity and support orientation was not found to be significantly influenced by the density or sparseness of the external entrepreneurial environment. Further, university technology transfer performance measured in terms of IPO firms did not appear to depend on the policy orientation, and policy orientation did not appear to be significantly influenced by the external environment for entrepreneurship. With respect to product royalties, they found that universities that are more selective about their choices for what to patent and license via the start-up and small company route appear to be especially disadvantaged in terms of royalty flows when they provide a high degree of support for their technology transfer program. Conversely, universities that are less selective appear to be advantaged by a stronger support orientation. For those universities in the middle third of the support range, an increase in selectivity results in a decreasing royalty benefit up to a point. The same benefits were not evident for those universities that pursue either a high selectivity and high support policy orientation or a low support and low selectivity policy orientation.

Lockett and Wright (2005) utilized data from a UK survey of all research universities that are active in spinning-out ventures and found that the presence of sufficient experience and expertise within what are historically noncommercial environments may be central to their ability to generate gains from spinout ventures. They asserted that it is important to distinguish between the roles of the stock of universities' resource inputs and their routines/capabilities in affecting the creation of spinout companies.

Lockett and Wright (2005) reported that both the number of spinout companies created and the number of spinout companies created with equity investment are significantly positively associated with expenditure on intellectual property protection, the business development capabilities of TTOs and the royalty regime of the university. In contrast, they did not find that the number of start-ups is associated significantly with the size of the TTO staff, the years the TTO has been in existence, or the available technology.

Markman, Gianiodis, and Phan (2006), using interview data from US university TTOs, concluded that the shorter the time to market, the greater the returns to the university and the higher the rate of start-up formation. They surmised that during the discovery and disclosure stage, the lack of TTO resources—time, capital, and poor central administration support for licensing activity—are less of a hindrance to speedy commercialization than the limitations posed by inventor-related impediments such as resistance, indifference, and poor-quality disclosures. However, during advanced commercialization stages, faculty-inventors seem to play a more positive role in accelerating the process. It could be that some faculty-inventors are the founders of these technology-based start-ups, which means that their interest in the new venture extends beyond the licensing process, involving the management of the commercialization process itself.

Rothaermel and Thursby (2005) considered the importance for incubator firms of linkages to universities. They focused on two types of university linkages, a license obtained from the university by the incubator firm and links to university faculty. They proposed that a university link to the sponsoring institution reduces the probability of new venture failure and, at the same time, retards timely graduation. Furthermore, they suggested that these effects are more pronounced the stronger the university-incubator link. Their empirical analysis was based on longitudinal data from start-up firms incubated in the Advanced Technology Development Center at the Georgia Institute of Technology over the six-year period between 1998 and 2003.

Ensley and Hmieleski (2005) analyzed differences among firms that are spun out from university-affiliated business incubators and technology parks and those who emerged without such assistance. The authors drew on institutional isomorphism theory to predict that university-affiliated new venture top management teams (TMTs) will be more homogeneous in composition, will display less developed team dynamics, and as a result, will perform below those without university affiliation. These authors adopted the view that university-affiliated firms will institutionalize themselves toward the norms of the university and the successful ventures that have been launched through their nurturing rather than toward the norms of their own industry. This is a phenomenon that they call localized isomorphic behavior. The costs associated with localized isomorphism are used to explain why the benefits of university affiliation might fail to translate into performance gains.

The issue of geographic location has been highlighted in two key papers. First, Link and Scott (2005a, 2005b, 2005c, 2005d) analyzed the determinants of the new venture formation within US university research parks. They focused on research parks because these institutions or property-based incubators are designed to enhance knowledge spillovers between universities and park tenants, as well as to enhance regional economic growth. Adopting an institutional environment perspective, they conjecture that there are two critical factors that explain the rate of spin-off formation: the research environment of the university and the characteristics of the research park to which the spin-off companies locate.

Link and Scott (2005a) conjectured that the more research-intensive a university is, the greater the probability that its faculty will innovate; and, the more innovative the faculty, the greater the probability that technologies will develop around which a spin-off company could be based. They also hypothesized that the formation of university spin-off companies into the university's park will occur more often in older parks than in newer ones as these have developed the expertise to facilitate opportunity recognition and development. There hypotheses were confirmed with survey data from the population of US university-based research parks.

Audretsch and Lehmann (2005) examined the importance of location. They hypothesized that proximity to the university is shaped by different spillover mechanisms—research and human capital—and by different types of knowledge spillovers—natural sciences and social sciences. Their primary source of data consisted of young high-technology start-ups in Germany between 1997 and 2002. The Audretsch and Lehmann's results suggest that spillover mechanisms as well as spillover types are heterogeneous. More importantly, they found that firm spin-offs, at least in the knowledge and high-technology sectors, are influenced not only by the traditional regional and economic characteristics but also by the opportunity to access knowledge generated by universities.

Contrary to some of the maintained assumption of conventional economic models, researchers have found that the variation in relative TTO performance cannot be completely explained by environmental and institutional factors. Instead, the extant literature on TTOs suggests that the key impediments to effective university technology transfer tend to be organizational in nature (Siegel, Waldman, and Link 2003; Siegel et al. 2003, 2004). These impediments include problems with differences in organizational cultures between universities and firms (especially small firms), incentive structures (including both pecuniary and nonpecuniary rewards, such as credit toward tenure and promotion), and staffing and compensation practices of the TTO itself.

Finally, this strand of the literature suggests that there are multiple exit markets for university technological discoveries (Wright, Birley, and Mosey 2004). Much of the early literature looked at licensing revenues and licensing productivity, since many were motivated by the policy implications of Bayh–Dole, while an increasing number of the later research focused on spinouts or new firm formation, and joint ventures between researchers and large corporations in the form of sponsored research. What seems to be evident is that the organizational context is both the antecedent to the type of outcomes favored, with licensing representing overwhelming share of exit strategy, and the constraint, with licensing policies often conflicting with the institutional context and organizational resources required for successful spinouts. It turns out, as we note later in this chapter, that such issues related to the productivity of technology transfer figured prominently in the earlier research and is now increasingly of interest to organizational researchers who want to marry economic models of scientific discovery with organization-level drivers of success.

8.4. **The individual contexts of university technology transfer**

Several studies have focused on individual scientists and entrepreneurs in the context of university technology transfer. Audretsch (2000) examined the extent to which entrepreneurs at universities are different than other entrepreneurs. He analyzed a data-set on university life scientists in order to estimate the determinants of the probability that they will establish a new biotechnology firm, and he found that university entrepreneurs tend to be older and more scientifically experienced.

Zucker and Darby, and their various collaborators, explored the role of star scientists in the life sciences on the creation and location of new biotechnology firms in the United States and Japan. Zucker, Darby, and Armstrong (2000) assessed the impact of these university scientists on the research productivity of US firms. A star scientist is defined as a researcher who has discovered over forty genetic sequences, and affiliations with firms are defined through coauthoring between the star scientist and industry scientists. Some of these scientists resigned from the university to establish a new firm or kept their faculty position, but worked very closely with industry scientists. Research productivity is measured using three proxies: number of patents granted, products in development, and products on the market. They found that ties between star scientists and firm scientists have a positive effect on these three dimensions of research productivity, as well as other aspects of firm performance and rates of entry in the US biotechnology industry (Zucker, Darby, and Armstrong 1998; Zucker, Darby, and Brewer 1998).

Zucker and Darby (2001) examined detailed data on the outcomes of collaborations between star university scientists and biotechnology firms in Japan. Similar patterns emerge in the sense that they find that such interactions substantially enhance the research productivity of Japanese firms, as measured by the rate of firm patenting, product innovation, and market introductions of new products. However, they also reported an absence of geographically localized knowledge spillovers resulting from university technology transfer in Japan, in contrast to the United States, where they found that such effects were strong. The authors attributed this result to the following interesting institutional difference between Japan and the United States in university technology transfer. In the United States, it is common for academic scientists to work with firm scientists at the firm's laboratories; in Japan, firm scientists typically work in the academic scientist's laboratory. Thus, according to the authors, it is not surprising that the local economic development impact of university technology transfer appears to be lower in Japan than in the United States.

The unit of analysis in Bercovitz and Feldman (2004) was also the individual faculty member. They analyzed the propensity of US medical school researchers at Duke University and Johns Hopkins University to file invention disclosures, a potential precursor to technology commercialization. The authors found that three factors influence the decision to disclose inventions: norms at the institutions where the researchers were trained and the disclosure behaviors of their department chairs and peers, respectively.

On the basis of an in-depth case study of Stanford University in the early 1990s, Roberts and Malone (1996) conjectured that much of the entrepreneurial activity that was stimulated through technology transfer was a direct result of university policies. They noted that during this period, Stanford refused to grant exclusive licenses to inventor-founders.

DiGregorio and Shane (2003) directly assessed the determinants of start-up formation using AUTM data. They concluded that the two key determinants of start-ups are faculty quality and the ability of the university and inventor(s) to assume equity in a start-up in lieu of licensing royalty fees.

Louis, Blumenthal, Gluck, and Stoto (1989) analyzed the propensity of life science faculty to engage in various aspects of technology transfer, including commercialization. Their statistical sample consisted of life scientists at the fifty US research universities that received the most funding from the US National Institutes of Health. The authors found that the most important determinant of involvement in technology commercialization was local group norms; they reported that university policies and various types of organizational structures had little effect on this activity.

In a similar vein, Nicolaou and Birley (2003) investigated the consequences of considering the social networks of academic entrepreneurs as a determinant of spinout types. Similar to Mustar et al. (2006), they adopted a structural contingency view of spinout types and sought to describe the various forms with reference to the social network structure of the academic entrepreneurs involved in the spinouts. Academics with strong ties to the external environment that are nonredundant were found to be more likely to engage in spinouts.

To the extent that the successful commercialization of university-based technology depends on the individual incentives, risk-taking propensities, and skill sets of academic entrepreneurs, the extant research seems to suggest that paying attention to the individual level of analysis matters in building more complete models of technology transfer effectiveness. Specifically, the ability for academics to identify commercial opportunities is determined by their technical expertise, experience in their previous attempts to commercialize university-based technologies, and their personal networks outside the university context. Their willingness to engage in such activities is primarily related to the incentives they are offered and/or the perceived risk/return outcomes.

8.5. **Measuring the effectiveness of university technology transfer**

One useful way to assess and explain the effectiveness of university technology transfer is to model this activity within a production function framework. Referring to the literature summarized in Table 8.1, we note that effectiveness usually refers to a measure of productivity, which have been constructed from indicators of outputs and inputs of university technology transfer (e.g. Chapple et al. 2005; Friedman and Silberman 2003; Siegel, Waldman, and Link 2003; Thursby and Thursby 2002).

Siegel, Waldman, and Link (2003) employed stochastic frontier analysis to assess and explain the relative productivity of 113 US university TTOs. In their model, licensing activity is treated as the output and invention disclosures, full-time equivalent employees in the TTO, and legal expenditures are considered to be inputs. They found that the production function model yields a good fit. Based on estimates of their marginal product, it appears that technology licensing officers add significant value to the commercialization process. The findings also imply that spending more on lawyers reduces the number of licensing agreements but increases licensing revenue. Licensing revenue is subject to increasing returns, while licensing agreements are characterized by constant returns to scale. An implication of increasing returns for licensing revenue is that a university wishing to maximize revenue should spend more on lawyers. Perhaps this would enable university licensing officers to devote more time to eliciting additional invention disclosures and less time to negotiating with firms.

While licensing has traditionally been the most popular mechanism for commercialization of university-based technologies, universities are increasingly emphasizing the entrepreneurial dimension of technology transfer; see Table 8.2. AUTM reported that the number of start-up firms at US universities rose by more than tenfold between 1980 and 2003—from 35 to 374. This rapid increase in start-up activity has attracted considerable attention in the academic literature. Some researchers have focused on the university as the unit of analysis, while others analyze entrepreneurial agents (either academic or nonacademic entrepreneurs).

Franklin, Wright, and Lockett (2001) concluded that the best approach for universities that wish to launch successful technology transfer start-ups is a combination of academic and surrogate entrepreneurship. This would enable universities to simultaneously exploit the technical benefits of inventor involvement and the commercial know-how of surrogate entrepreneurs. In a subsequent paper, Lockett, Wright and Franklin (2003) found that universities that generate the most start-ups have clear, well-defined strategies regarding the formation and management of spinouts. These schools tended to use

Table 8.1. Quantitative and qualitative research on the effectiveness of licensing of university-based inventions

Author(s)	Data-sets	Methodology	Key results from the study
Jensen and Thursby (2001)	N/A	Theoretical analysis	Faculty involvement in the licensing of a university-based technology increases the probability of its success
Thursby, Jensen, and Thursby (2001)	AUTM, authors' survey	Descriptive analysis of authors' survey/ regression analysis	Inventions tend to disclose at an early stage of development; elasticities of licenses and royalties with respect to invention disclosures are both less than unity; faculty members are increasingly likely to disclose inventions
Bercovitz et al. (2001)	AUTM and case studies, interviews	Qualitative and quantitative analysis	Analysis of different organization structures for technology transfer at Duke, Johns Hopkins, and Penn State; differences in structure may be related to effectiveness
Thursby and Kemp (2002)	AUTM	Data envelopment analysis and regression analysis on efficiency scores	Faculty quality and number of TTO staff has positive impact on licensing; private universities appear to be more efficient than public universities; universities with medical schools are less efficient
Friedman and Silberman (2003)	AUTM, NSF, NRC, and Milken Institute Tech-Pole Data	Regression analysis and systems equations estimation	Higher royalty shares for faculty members are associated with greater licensing income
Carlsson and Fridh (2002)	AUTM	Regression analysis	Research expenditure, invention disclosures, and age of TTO have a positive impact on university licensing
Siegel, Waldman, and Link (2003)	AUTM, NSF, and US Census data, interviews	Productivity of university licensing; stochastic frontier analysis and field interviews	TTOs exhibit constant returns to scale with respect to licensing; increasing returns to scale with respect to licensing revenue; organizational and environmental factors have considerable explanatory power
Lach and Schankerman (2004)	AUTM, NSF, and NRC	Regression analysis	Higher royalty shares for faculty members are associated with higher licensing income
Chapple et al. (2005)	UK-NUBS/UNICO Survey-ONS	Data envelopment analysis and stochastic frontier analysis	UK TTOs exhibit decreasing returns to scale and low levels of effectiveness; organizational and environmental factors have considerable explanatory power
Link and Siegel (2005)	AUTM, NSF, and US Census data, interviews	TFP of university licensing; stochastic frontier analysis	Land grant universities are more efficient in university technology licensing; higher royalty shares for faculty members are higher levels of effectiveness in university technology licensing
Debackere and Veugelers (2005)	Interviews and survey data of 11 European research universities	Case studies	Universities allocating a higher percentage of royalty payments to faculty members tend to be more effective in technology transfer; critical success factor is decentralized management style.
Chapple et al. (2005)	US-AUTM, UK-NUBS/UNICO survey-ONS	Stochastic distance function	US universities are more efficient than UK universities; TTOs exhibit decreasing or constant returns to scale; universities with medical schools and incubators are closer to frontier

Table 8.2. Quantitative and qualitative research on university-based entrepreneurial activity

Author(s)	Unit of analysis	Data/methodology	Key results from the study
Louis et al. (1989)	US faculty members in the life sciences	Faculty members from universities; regression analysis	Key determinant of faculty-based entrepreneurship: local group norms; university policies and structures have little effect
Zucker, Darby, and Brewer (1998)	Relationships involving star scientists and US biotechnology firms	Scientific papers reporting genetic-sequence discoveries, data on biotech firms from the North Carolina Biotechnology Center and Bioscan; regression analysis	Location of star scientists predicts firm entry in biotechnology
Zucker, Darby, and Armstrong (2000)	Relationships involving star scientists and US biotechnology firms	Scientific papers reporting genetic-sequence discoveries, data on Biotech firms from the North Carolina Biotechnology Center and Bioscan; regression analysis	Collaboration between star scientists and firm scientists enhances research performance of US biotech firms, as measured using three proxies: number of patents granted, number of products in development, and number of products on the market
Audretsch (2000)	Entrepreneurs in the life sciences	Founders of Biotech firms/regression analysis	University entrepreneurs tend to be older; more scientifically experienced
Zucker and Darby (2001)	Relationships involving star scientists and Japanese biotech firms	Data on biotechnology firms and the Nikkei Biotechnology Directory	Collaboration between star scientists and firm scientists enhances research performance of Japanese biotech firms; as measured using three proxies: number of patents granted, number of products in development, and number of products on the market
Franklin, Wright, and Lockett (2001)	TTOs and university-based start-ups	Authors' quantitative survey of UK TTOs	Universities that wish to launch successful technology transfer start-ups should employ a combination of academic and surrogate entrepreneurship
Lockett, Wright, and Franklin (2003)	TTOs and university-based start-ups	Authors' quantitative and qualitative surveys of UK TTOs	Universities that generate the most start-ups have clear, well-defined spinout strategies, strong expertise in entrepreneurship, and vast social networks
DiGregorio and Shane (2003)	US university-based start-ups	AUTM survey; count regressions of the determinants of number of start-ups	Two determinants of start-up formation: faculty quality and ability of the university and inventor(s) to take equity in a start-up, in lieu of licensing royalty fees; royalty distribution formula that is more favorable to faculty members reduces start-up formation
Lockett and Wright (2005)	TTOs and university-based start-ups	Quantitative survey of UK TTOs; count regressions of determinants of number of start-ups	University's rate of start-up formation positively associated with its expenditure on intellectual property protection, business development capabilities of TTOs, and the extent to which royalty distribution formula favors faculty members

(Cont.)

Table 8.2. (Continued)

Author(s)	Unit of Analysis	Data/Methodology	Key Results from the Study
Nerkar and Shane (2003)	University-based start-ups	Longitudinal data from MIT start-ups; hazard function analysis	Radicalness of new technology and patent scope increase probability of survival more in fragmented industries than in concentrated sectors; effectiveness of technology strategies of new firms appears to depend on industry conditions
O'Shea, Allen, and Arnaud (2005)	US university-based start-ups	AUTM survey; count regressions of determinants of number of start-ups	University's previous success in technology transfer key determinant of rate of start-up formation
Markman et al. (2004)	US TTOs and university-based start-ups	AUTM survey; authors' survey; linear regression analysis	Equity licensing and start-up formation positively correlated with TTO wages; uncorrelated or even negatively correlated with royalty payments to faculty members
Markman et al. (2005b)	US TTOs and university-based start-ups	AUTM survey; authors' survey; linear regression analysis	Three determinants of time-to-market (speed): TTO resources, competency in identifying licensees, and participation of faculty-inventors in licensing process
Markman et al. (2005a)	US TTOs and university-based start-ups	AUTM survey; authors' survey; linear regression analysis	Most attractive combinations of technology stage and licensing strategy for new venture creation—early-stage technology and licensing for equity; least likely to be favored by university
Lockett and Wright (2005)	TTOs and university-based start-ups	Authors' quantitative survey of UK TTOs; regression analysis	University's rate of start-up formation is positively associated with expenditures on intellectual property protection, business development capabilities of TTOs, and extent to which its royalty distribution formula favors faculty members
O'Shea, Allen, and Arnaud (2005)	US university-based start-ups	AUTM survey; regression analysis	University's previous success in technology transfer determinant of rate of start-up formation
Leitch and Harrison (2005)	UK university-based start-ups	Case studies of UK university spinouts	In nontechnology intensive regions, TTOs focus on regional economic development and commercialization of university-based research

Study	Context	Method	Findings
Thursby and Thursby (2005)	Faculty members at US universities	Authors' database of faculty members; regression analysis	Female faculty members less likely to disclose inventions than male faculty members, even though they appear to publish at roughly the same rate; evidence that rate of disclosure activity of women and men converging over time
Powers and McDougall (2005a)	US university-based start-ups	AUTM survey; regression analysis	University financial, human capital, and organizational resources significant predictors of rate of start-up formation and number of initial public offering (IPO) based on university technology license
Powers and McDougall (2005b)	US university-based start-ups	AUTM survey; regression analysis	Universities with more supportive licensing and entrepreneurial policies have better technology transfer performance
Brouwer (2005)	N/A	Theoretical analysis	Outside inventors have stronger incentives to invent than incumbents; embryonic inventions best commercialized by new enterprises due to uncertainty of outcomes; cooperative invention and commercialization might boost consumer welfare but provides little incentive to invent
Campbell (2005)	UK universities	Case studies	Asserts that UK universities developed new ways to create value through technology commercialization because new initiatives promote flexibility and cutting-edge approaches
Markman, Gianiodis, and Phan (2006)	TTOs and university-based start-ups	AUTM survey, interview surveys, TTO Documents; regression analysis and content analysis	Gray market activity reduced when TTOs professionalized, but such activity is associated with more valuable discoveries and heightened entrepreneurial activities
Renault (2006)	Faculty members	Interviews	Significant determinant of entrepreneurial behavior is professor's belief about proper role of universities in dissemination of knowledge; institutional policies as royalty distribution formulas are also important

surrogate or external entrepreneurs, rather than academic entrepreneurs, to manage this process. It also was the case that the more successful universities have greater expertise and vast social networks that help them generate more start-ups. However, the role of the academic inventor was not found to differ between the more and less successful universities. Finally, equity ownership was found to be more widely distributed among the members of the spinout company in the case of the more successful universities.

Markman et al. (2005*b*) developed a model linking university patents to new-firm creation in university-based incubators, with university TTOs acting as the intermediaries. While there have been some qualitative studies of university originated new business formation (e.g. Bercovitz et al. 2001; Mowery et al. 2001; Siegel, Waldman, and Link 2003), these studies have been based on data from only the elite US research universities (e.g. Stanford University, University of California, Berkeley and Massachusetts Institute of Technology) or from a small sample of more representative US institutions. To build a theoretically saturated model of TTOs' entrepreneurial development strategies, the authors collected qualitative and quantitative data from virtually the entire population of university TTOs. In a subsequent paper, Markman, Gianiodis, and Phan (2006) found that entrepreneurial activity was positively correlated to gray market activities, which raises a conundrum for university administrators interested in pursuing greater level of entrepreneurial intensity.

Nerkar and Shane (2003) analyzed the entrepreneurial dimension of university technology transfer, based on an empirical analysis of 128 firms that were founded between 1980 and 1996 to commercialize inventions owned by MIT. They began by noting that there is an extensive literature in management that suggests that new technology firms are more likely to survive if they exploit radical technologies (e.g. Tushman and Anderson 1986) and if they possess patents with a broad scope (e.g. Merges and Nelson 1990). The authors conjectured that the relationships between radicalness and survival and scope and survival are moderated both by the market structure or level of concentration in the firm's industry. Specifically, they asserted that radicalness and patent scope increase the probability of survival more in fragmented industries than in concentrated sectors. They estimated a hazard function model using the MIT database and find empirical support for these hypotheses. Thus, the effectiveness of the technology strategies of new firms may be dependent on industry conditions.

In an elaboration of studies in university spinouts, Nicolaou and Birley (2003) as well as Mustar et al. (2006) offered typologies of spinouts, suggesting that for further theory development to take place, particularly with respect to the antecedents of spinout rates and success, a contingency approach utilizing social network theory, the RBV, and institutional theory would allow researchers to avoid assumptions of homogeneity with respect to these entities. Clearly, the reasons for and consequences of spinouts can vary by institutional mission, technology class, and available expertise and resources to administer them. Similarly, Vohora, Wright, and Lockett (2004) employed a case-based research methodology and found that spinouts must pass through a series of well ordered phases in order to enjoy success. They also found that these phases are iterative and nonlinear, with critical junctures in terms of the resources and capabilities the spinouts need to move to the next phase. The four critical junctures are: opportunity recognition, entrepreneurial commitment, credibility, and sustainability. Thus, the problems faced by university spinouts, in the main, are similar to new start-ups in other contexts. While there are distinctions between types of spinouts, there is also a general model of spinout process that can be applied to the data.

Technology incubators are university-based technology initiatives that are designed to facilitate knowledge transfer from the university to firms located on such facilities. Rothaermel and Thursby (2005) investigated the research question of how knowledge actually flows from universities to incubator firms. The authors assessed the effect of these knowledge flows on incubator firm-level differential performance. Based on the RBV of the firm and the absorptive capacity construct, they hypothesized that knowledge flows should enhance incubator firm performance and found some support for knowledge flows from universities to incubator firms based on a sample of specific technology ventures sponsored by Georgia Institute of Technology. Their evidence suggested that incubator firms' absorptive capacity is an important factor when transforming university knowledge into firm-level competitive advantage.

The transfer of scientific and technological know-how into valuable economic activity has become a high priority for many nations and regions. The emphasis on the role and the nature of industry science links during this transfer process is an important dimension of this emerging policy orientation. Debackere and Veugelers (2005) explored the diverse and evolutionary nature of industry science links, as well as the major motivations driving them. The establishment of TTOs can be seen as providing both a strategic and a structural response toward embedding industry science links within academic institutions.

Consistent with evidence from the United States (e.g. Link and Siegel 2005), they found that incentives and organization practices are important in terms of explaining variation in relative performance. Specifically, they reported that universities allocating a higher percentage of royalty payments to faculty members tend to be more effective in technology transfer. On the organizational side, the authors found that another critical success factor is what they call a decentralized management style, which apparently allows the TTO to be much more sensitive to the needs of its stakeholders.

Audretsch and Lehmann (2005) examined the success of technical universities in facilitating the spillover and commercialization of knowledge by firms. The authors compared the impact of technical and general universities on the performance of knowledge-based firms. Technical universities are expected to have a stronger impact than general universities in stimulating such spillovers. These institutions, which were established in Germany in the mid-nineteenth century, focused on science engineering. They have received more research grants and state funding, compared to general universities. They tested the hypothesis of differential impact based on a unique data-set, consisting of publicly held high-technology firms in Germany. The authors reported that firm performance is not influenced by the type of university it interacts with. That is, technical universities do not have a differential impact on firm performance, relative to more general universities.

Chapple et al. (2005) extended previous research on the relative performance of university TTOs (Siegel, Waldman, and Link 2003; Thursby and Kemp 2002) in two important ways. First, the authors reported the first evidence based on data from university TTOs in the United Kingdom. A second contribution is that they simultaneously employed parametric and nonparametric methods, which provides for more accurate and robust measurement and explanation of relative productivity. Specifically, they compared and contrasted stochastic frontier estimation (SFE) and data envelopment analysis (DEA).

Several stylized facts emerge from this empirical analysis. Relative to the United States, there appears to be greater variation in relative performance in technology transfer across UK universities using both nonparametric and parametric approaches. More importantly, in contrast to the United States, there appears to be decreasing returns to scale to licensing activity and relatively low levels of absolute efficiency at UK universities. This indicated that substantial improvements can be made with respect to the efficiency of UK TTOs. Consistent with US evidence, the authors found that organizational and environmental factors explain substantial variation in relative performance. Specifically, authors reported that older TTOs are less productive than comparable institutions, suggesting an absence of learning effects. Universities located in regions with higher levels of R&D and GDP appeared to be more efficient, implying that there may be regional spillovers in technology transfer.

Link and Scott (2005a) investigated the conditions when a RJV will involve a university as a research partner. They hypothesized that larger RJVs are more likely to invite a university to join the venture as a research partner than smaller RJVs because larger ventures are less likely to expect substantial additional appropriability problems to result because of the addition of a university partner and because the larger ventures have both a lower marginal cost and a higher marginal value from university R&D contributions to the ventures' innovative output. The authors tested this hypothesis using data from the NSF-sponsored CORE database, and those data confirmed the hypothesis.

8.6. **Theoretical implications from the literature**

Our literature review clearly suggests some theoretical frameworks that can be applied to advancing academic research related to university technology transfer. Because the research is still relatively nascent, much of it has not only been descriptive, but also it has been approached from the perspective of inventorying the phenomenon. However, we also reviewed examples of theoretically based approaches. The concept of path dependency goes a long way to explain the persistent difference in commercialization success rate between experienced universities and those that are new to the game. In contrast to phenomena that can be described by productivity frontiers, there does not appear to be evidence of diminishing returns (i.e. a regression to the mean) in technology transfer activities. One reason could be that we have not been able to measure technology transfer activities over a sufficiently long time period to observe diminishing returns, but a more compelling rationale could be that TTOs eventually learn how to do this well. They also learn the extent to which such tacit knowledge becomes embedded in an institutional context. In addition, because of the geographically localized nature of successful technology transfer, it appears that the situations into which such expertise can be successfully transplanted may be limited. Hence, scholars have used institutional theory and evolutionary economics perspectives to explain the persistence of differences in effectiveness of technology transfer across regions.

At the level of the organization, our review clearly concludes that the consistency and congruency of organization design, incentive systems, information process capacity, and organization-wide values matter a great deal in technology transfer success and new venture creation. Theoretical underpinnings from the organization sciences—such as the RBV of the firm, structural contingency theory, and social network theory—could provide a basis for deriving even more sophisticated insights in future research, particularly because the phenomenon is going international and therefore, attempts to generalize theory must take a more systematic tact than has heretofore been employed in the literature. In particular, if the dependent variable is carefully defined as an economic outcome (e.g. technological commercialization) of a largely sociopsychological phenomenon (e.g. university scientists discovering knowledge), one should be able to apply standard organization theories in the nonprofit setting of a university.

At the individual level of analysis, there is an emerging literature that has attempted to model the TTO-scientist and TTO-university relationship from an agency theory perspective. This is a highly useful direction to pursue, which we believe can be taken a step further. Assumptions relating to principal–agent decisions are based largely on Bayesian rationality. Based on recent research on prospect theory, we can incorporate the notion of prior losses or gains into the choice models (e.g. to a faculty member's decision to disclose or not to disclose an invention, to license or not license a technology, or to launch a new venture or not) to the problem of opportunity costs faced by the scientists and transactions costs faced by the university and/or commercial enterprise. The specificity with which we can specify theoretically the TTO relationships will allow us to seek latent constructs that determine the institutional, organizational, and individual relationships to technology transfer effectiveness and thus build more predictive normative models.

8.7. **Conclusions**

For technology transfer to succeed, it is critical for university administrators to think strategically about that process. Most of the academic studies strongly suggest that university administrators are often more concerned about protecting intellectual property and appropriating the fruits of the transfer than they are about creating the appropriate context or environment in which such activities are to take place. This implies that they must address numerous formulation and implementation issues, which we now consider in turn.

A key formulation issue is the establishment of institutional goals and priorities, which must be transparent, forthright, and reflected in resource allocation patterns. Establishing priorities also relates to strategic choices regarding technological emphasis (e.g. life sciences vs. engineering and the physical sciences) for the generation of licensing and start-up opportunities (Bercovitz and Feldman 2004; Mustar et al. 2006; Nerkar and Shane 2003). Opportunities for technology commercialization and the propensity of faculty members to engage in technology transfer vary substantially across fields both between and within the life sciences and physical sciences. Universities must also be mindful of competition from other institutions when confronting these choices. For example, many universities have recently launched initiatives in the life sciences and biotechnology—many through the establishment of a university-based research park—with high expectations regarding enhanced revenue and job creation through technology transfer. It is conceivable that any potential financial gains from these fields may be limited.

Resource allocation decisions must also be driven by strategic choices the university makes regarding various modes of technology transfer (Chapple et al. 2005; Markman et al. 2005*b*). As previously mentioned, these modes are licensing, start-ups, sponsored research, and other mechanisms of technology transfer that are focused more directly on stimulating economic and regional development, such as incubators and research parks. Licensing and sponsored research generate a stream of revenue, while equity from start-ups could yield a payoff in the long term. Universities that stress economic development outcomes are advised to focus on start-ups because these companies could potentially create jobs in the local region or state. Note that a start-up strategy entails higher risk because the failure rate of new firms is quite high. However, a start-up can also potentially generate high returns if the start-up is taken public. It is also important to note that a start-up strategy entails additional resources, if the university chooses to assist the academic entrepreneur in launching and developing their start-up.

Organizational incentives are also important. The evidence implies that shifting the royalty distribution formula in favor of faculty members (e.g. allowing faculty members to retain 75% of the revenue, instead of 33% of the revenue) would elicit more invention disclosures (Lach and Schankerman 2004) and greater efficiency in technology transfer (Link and Siegel 2005; Markman et al. 2004). A more controversial recommendation is to modify promotion and tenure guidelines to place a more positive weight on technology transfer activities in such decisions. Clearly, this is a matter that relates to the very core of what it means to be an academic researcher and therefore, impinges on issues of norms and shared values. However, while we do not underestimate the difficulty, and indeed the appropriateness, with which norms, standards, and values among tenured faculty can be changed, such changes are necessary at institutions that wish to place a high priority on technology commercialization. A more straightforward and simple recommendation to consummate more licensing agreements is to switch from standard compensation to incentive compensation for technology licensing officers. This has been attempted at several US universities (e.g. University of North Carolina at Chapel Hill and New York University).

The extant research also clearly demonstrates the importance of the effective implementation of technology transfer strategies. Examples of implementation issues include choices regarding information flows, organizational design/structure, human resources management practices in the TTO, and reward systems for faculty involvement in technology transfer. There are also a set of implementation issues relating to different modes of technology transfer, licensing, start-ups, sponsored research, and other modes that are focused more directly on stimulating economic development, such as incubators and research parks.

For university administrators to effectively deal with implementation issues, they should adopt a value chain perspective of technology transfer. In a corporate setting, the production function is conceptualized as a chain of value adding activities linked by cross functional processes, information flows, material flows, and risk flows. Seen this way, the production function can be reengineered, reordered, re-sequenced, and even cut short. Similarly, value-adding activities can also be sliced into smaller pieces and assigned to partners, suppliers, and customers. In a similar manner, a university's technology licensing process need not remain exclusively in-house. It is seldom that there is sufficient technical, legal, and managerial expertise in a TTO to manage the scope and depth of technologies and potential technology customers that emanate from a university's laboratories. Hence, by dicing up the set of activities related to technology transfer, from technology identification and selection to technology customer matching, a university can concentrate on those activities it is best equipped to manage and partner with resource providers and outside experts for those areas that it cannot or should not expend resources to build.

Human resource management practices, for example, appear to be quite important. Several qualitative studies (e.g. Siegel et al. 2004) indicate that there are deficiencies in the TTO, with respect to marketing skills and entrepreneurial experience. Unfortunately, field research (e.g. Markman et al. 2005*b*) has also revealed TTOs are not actively recruiting individuals with such skills and experience. Instead, representative institutions appear to be focusing on expertise in patent law and licensing or technical expertise.

One method of dealing with this problem is to enhance training and development programs for TTO personnel, along with additional administrative support for this activity, since many TTOs lack sufficient resources and competencies to identify the most commercially viable inventions. Training in portfolio management techniques would be extremely useful in this context. Selection, training, and development of TTO personnel with such portfolio management skills are necessary if the screening mechanism is to be improved. Furthermore, incentives should be directed toward creating immediate feedback and rewards (i.e. cash) to motivate TTO personnel to improve their expertise through training.

Another solution, taking a value chain approach, is to partner with technology experts in corporations or consulting firms. Research has shown that career opportunities for university technology licensing officers are limited and often of short duration (Markman et al. 2004; Siegel et al. 2004), which implies recruiting appropriate talent is, at best, a stochastic outcome.

Finally, the extant research suggests that improving information flows between academics and the university administration matters to technology transfer effectiveness. In the first instance, technology licensing officers and university administrators share an interest in promoting technology commercialization and therefore should devote more effort to eliciting invention disclosures. The lack of full invention disclosure is partly due to insufficient faculty incentives (publications are usually regarded as mutually exclusive to patents). However, a more important reason for the lack of full disclosure is the lack of formal and rich communication channels between university laboratories and the TTO.

Maintaining effective communication is resource intensive (with respect to time) for the technology licensing officer and especially, for the academic researcher. Filing reports and giving seminars to potential technology licensees is a strong deterrent to faculty, even if they are interested in profiting from their discoveries. The opportunity costs are such (by some estimates, eight peer reviewed papers for each patent filed) that the 'hurdle rate' for an embryonic discovery would be so high as to minimize potential block-busters that would only be apparent with additional, usually incremental, research (Markman et al. 2004). Hence, the institution must be prepared to bear the costs of maintaining communication, such as providing admin-istrative support within the individual laboratories to manage information flows and paperwork for licensing projects. Related to this, it is also impor-tant to provide information and support for faculty members who express an interest in forming a start-up. Given that business formation requires skills that academic scientists typically do not possess and they involve activities that are somewhat alien to their culture (e.g. assessing market demand for their invention), universities could partner with and reward business school faculty to train and mentor potential academic entrepre-neurs.

Universities will also have to confront a set of issues related to ethics and social responsibility as they more aggressively pursue technology commercial-ization and assume additional equity/ownership in start-up firms. For exam-ple, the recent $25 million agreement between Novartis and the plant biology department at the University of California at Berkeley raised eyebrows among those concerned that technology commercialization might be exacerbating inequalities across departments and colleges and destroying the traditional openness of university culture.

Nelson (2001) pointed out that tensions that may arise between depart-ments and colleges within a university that are successful and unsuccessful in technology transfer, as well as potential conflicts of interest. His greatest concern, however, is that aggressive exercise of intellectual property rights by universities is inconsistent with the long-standing tradition of open science and training. Consistent with this view, Blumenthal et al. (1997) have found that university scientists engaged in technology transfer-related activities are less likely to share their data with fellow scientists and are, in general, more 'secretive' than comparable university scientists who are involved in technol-ogy transfer.

It is also important to note that technology commercialization can make universities more vulnerable to pressure from NGOs and stakeholders to be socially responsible. Yale University, for example, recently created a patent pool for an AIDS drug known as Zerit, which it parlayed into a $150 million up-front payment from Bristol–Myers Squibb. The university then came under intense pressure from activists to ensure that Bristol–Myers Squibb would make generic versions of the drug available in African countries, espe-cially in South Africa.

☐ APPENDIX: METHODS USED TO MEASURE PRODUCTIVITY IN UNIVERSITY TECHNOLOGY TRANSFER

One potentially useful way to assess and explain the effectiveness of university technology transfer is to model this within a production function/frontier framework. Such a production function is typically estimated econometrically. Production frontiers are also estimated using nonparametric models, which offer some advantages, relative to the parametric approach. For instance, these methods obviate the need to specify a functional form for the production frontier and also enable us to identify best practice universities. Nonparametric techniques can also handle multiple outputs.

Perhaps the most popular nonparametric estimation technique is DEA. The DEA method is essentially a linear program, which can be expressed as follows:

$$\max h_k = \frac{\sum_{r=1}^{s} u_{rk} Y_{rk}}{\sum_{i=1}^{m} v_{ik} X_{ik}} \tag{A8.1}$$

subject to

$$\frac{\sum_{r=1}^{s} u_{rk} Y_{rj}}{\sum_{i=1}^{m} v_{ik} X_{ij}} < 1; \quad j = 1, \ldots, n \tag{A8.2}$$

for all $u_{rk} > 0$; $v_{ik} > 0$, and where Y = a vector of outputs, X = a vector of inputs, i = inputs (m inputs), r = outputs (s outputs), and n = number of decision-making units (DMUs), or the unit of observation in a DEA study.

The unit of observation in a DEA study is referred to as the decision-making unit (DMU). A maintained assumption of this class of models is that DMUs attempt to maximize efficiency. Input-oriented DEA yields an efficiency score, bounded between 0 and 1, for each DMU by choosing weights (u_r and v_i) that maximize the ratio of a linear combination of the unit's outputs to a linear combination of its inputs (see equation A8.2). These scores are often expressed as percentages. A DMU having a score of 1 is efficient, while those with scores of <1 are (relatively) inefficient. Multiple DMUs have scores of 1.

DEA fits a piecewise linear surface to rest on top of the observations. This is referred to as the efficient frontier. The efficiency of each DMU is measured relative to all other DMUs, with the constraint that all DMUs lie on or below the efficient frontier. The linear programming technique identifies best practice DMUs, or those that are on the frontier. All other DMUs are viewed as being inefficient relative to the frontier DMUs.

The SFE is a parametric method developed by Aigner, Lovell, and Schmidt (1977) and Meeusen and van den Broeck (1977). SFE generates a production or a cost frontier with a stochastic error term that consists of two components: a conventional random error (i.e. white noise) and a term that represents deviations from the frontier, or relative inefficiency. Following Battese and Coelli (1995), the stochastic frontier model in cross sectional form is

$$Y_i = \exp(x_i \beta + V_i - U_i) \tag{A8.3}$$

where, Y_i represents the output or production of the ith observation ($i = 1, 2, \ldots, N$); x_i is a $(1 \times k)$ vector of values of inputs or resources used in production; and i denotes the ith firm. β is a $(k \times 1)$ vector of unknown parameters to be estimated. The V_is are assumed to be independent and normally distributed $N(0, \sigma_V^2)$ random errors, distributed independently of the U_is. The U_is are the nonnegative random variables associated with technical inefficiency of production, which are assumed to be independently distributed, such that U_i is obtained by truncation (at zero) of the normal distribution with a mean $z_i \delta$ and a variance, σ^2. Z_i is a $(1 \times m)$ vector of explanatory variables associated with technical inefficiency of the production of observations and finally δ is a $(1 \times m)$ vector of unknown coefficients.

Equation (A8.3) specifies the stochastic frontier production function in terms of the original production values. In order to explain technical efficiency, this model needs to be extended to make technical efficiency conditional on exogenous variables. Following Battese and Coelli (1995), we can model explanatory variables in a one stage SFE model. That is, the technical inefficiency effects, the U_is, are assumed to be a function of a set of explanatory variables, the z_is and the unknown vector of coefficients δ. If all the elements of the δ vector are equal to 0, then the technical inefficiency effects are not related to the z variables, and so the half normal distribution specified in Aigner, Lovell, and Schmidt (1977) is obtained.

The technical inefficiency effect, U_{it}, in the stochastic frontier model (3) can be specified as:

$$U_i = z_i \delta + W_i \qquad (A8.4)$$

where, the random variable, W_i is defined by the truncation of the normal distribution with zero mean and variance, σ^2.

The method of maximum likelihood is used for the simultaneous estimation of the parameters of the stochastic frontier model and the model for the technical inefficiency effects. The likelihood function is expressed in terms of the variance parameters, $\sigma_S^2 \equiv \sigma_V^2 + \sigma_U^2$ and $\gamma \equiv \sigma_U^2 / \sigma_S^2$. Therefore γ is the ratio of the standard error of technical inefficiency to the standard error of statistical noise, and is bounded between 0 and 1. Note that $\gamma = 0$ under the null hypothesis of an absence of inefficiency, indicating that all of the variance can be attributed to statistical noise. The technical efficiency of production for the ith observation is defined by:

$$TE_i = \exp(-U_i) = \exp(-z_i \delta - W_i) \qquad (A8.5)$$

Choosing between the parametric SFE and the nonparametric DEA is not without controversy (Gong and Sickles 1993). A main attraction of stochastic frontier analysis is that it allows hypothesis testing and construction of confidence intervals. A drawback of the approach, however, is the need to assume a functional form for the production function and for the distribution of the technical efficiency term. The use of DEA obviates the need to make these assumptions and, as noted earlier, also allows for multiple outputs in the production function. However, a major weakness of DEA is that it is deterministic. Hence, DEA does not distinguish between technical inefficiency and noise.

Chapple et al. (2005) assert that the technology transfer is characterized by multiple outputs: licensing and start-up activity. With multiple outputs, it is appropriate to employ a 'distance' function approach, which can be considered as a generalization of the single output production (or cost) frontier. Distance functions can be estimated using nonparametric or parametric methods. A simple parametric distance function can be expressed as:

$$\ln D_o = a_0 + \sum_{m=1}^{M-1} a_m \ln y_m + \sum_{k=1}^{K} \ln x_k + \ln \varepsilon \tag{A8.6}$$

Noting that homogeneity implies that:

$$D_o(x, \omega y) = \omega D_o(x, y) \tag{A8.7}$$

Thus, if we arbitrarily choose one of the outputs, such as the Mth output, and set $\omega = 1/Y_M$, we obtain:

$$D_o\left(\frac{x, y}{y_M}\right) = \frac{D_o(x, y)}{y_M} \tag{A8.8}$$

For the Cobb–Douglas case, this yields:

$$\ln(D_{o/ym}) = a_0 + \sum_{m=1}^{M-1} a_m \ln y^* + \sum_{K=1}^{k} \beta_K \ln x_k + \ln \varepsilon \tag{A8.9}$$

where, $y^* = y_m/y_M$.

The distance function can be expressed more concisely as:

$$-\ln(D_o) - \ln(y_M) = CD\left(\frac{x, y}{y_M, a, \beta}\right) \tag{A8.10}$$

and thus:

$$-\ln(y_M) = CD\left(\frac{x, y}{y_M, a, \beta}\right) + \ln(D_o) \tag{A8.11}$$

Thus, if we append a symmetric error term, v to account for statistical noise and rewrite $\ln(D_o)$ as μ, we can obtain the stochastic output distance function, with the usual composite error term $\varepsilon = v + \mu$. We make the standard assumptions that the vs are normally distributed random variables while the μs are assumed to have at truncated normal distribution:

$$-\ln(y_M) = CD\left(\frac{x, y}{y_M, a, \beta}\right) + v - \mu \tag{A8.12}$$

As in the stochastic frontier approach, the predicted value of the output distance function for the ith firm, $D_{oi} = \exp(-\mu)$ is not directly observable but must be derived from the composed error term, ε_i. Therefore, predictions for D_o are obtained from the conditional expectation $D_{oi} = E\left[(-\mu)\varepsilon_i\right]$.

☐ NOTES

1. This chapter draws from Phan and Siegel (2006).
2. Known as the Bayh–Dole Act, the University and Small Business Patent Protection Act of 1980 reformed federal patent policy by providing increased incentives for diffusion of federally-funded innovation results. Universities, nonprofit organizations, and small businesses were permitted to obtain titles to innovations developed with government funds; federal agencies were also permitted to grant exclusive licenses to their technology to industry.
3. See Thursby, Jensen, and Thursby (2001) for a detailed description of the survey.

9 University research parks

9.1. Introduction

In recent years there has been a substantial increase in investment in university research parks (URPs, and the term research park is more prevalent in the United States and the term science park is more prevalent in Europe and Asia) and other property-based institutions that facilitate technology transfer (e.g. incubators). Many universities have established research parks and incubators in order to foster the creation of start-up firms based on university-owned (or licensed) technologies. Public universities (and some private universities) also view these institutions as a means of fostering regional economic development.

URPs are important as a mechanism for the transfer of academic research findings, as a source of knowledge spillovers, and as a catalyst for national and regional economic growth. This generalization follows from a vast literature in economics on the impact of basic research, which is largely performed in universities. These studies link investment in basic research to improvements in productivity growth at the firm and societal levels (e.g. Adams 1990; Griliches 1986; Lichtenberg and Siegel 1991; Link 1981*a*, 1981*b*; Link and Siegel 2003; Mansfield 1980). There is also a related literature in economic development, which focuses on the impact of research clusters on regional economic growth (Porter 2001*a*, 2001*b*; Swann, Prevezer, and Stout 1998).

The growth in URPs has stimulated an important academic debate concerning whether such property-based initiatives enhance the performance of corporations, universities, and economic regions. More practically, it has also led to an interest among policymakers and industry leaders in identifying best practices. Unfortunately, few academic studies address such issues. This can be attributed to the somewhat embryonic nature of URPs and the fact that most URPs are public–private partnerships, indicating that multiple stakeholders (e.g. community groups, regional, and state governments) have enormous influence over their missions and operational procedures. Thus, developing theories to characterize the precise nature of their business models and managerial practices can be somewhat complex.

That is, there are few managerial benchmarks to follow to ensure the growth and possible success of URPs; and, more generally, the place of URPs in a national innovation system is not well understood. In large part, URPs are not well understood and attendant research on them is just beginning to burgeon. We speculate that this gap in understanding stems from the lack of well-defined constructs about what constitutes a university research park, the variety of goals of a URP, and the general lack of clear metrics for measuring their success.

In this chapter, we discuss the formation of URPs as a strategic response by universities to transfer their intellectual property, employ their graduates, and contribute to regional economic growth and development.[1] We also review the burgeoning literature on this topic.

9.2. Definitions of a university research park and park formations

9.2.1. ALTERNATIVE DEFINITIONS

A number of definitions of a research park have been proffered in recent years. Beginning with the international definitions, the International Association of Science Parks (IASP) offers the following:[2]

A Science Park (or Technology Park, or Technopole or Research Park) is an organisation managed by specialised professionals, whose main aim is to increase the *wealth of its community* [emphasis added] by promoting the culture of innovation and the competitiveness of its associated businesses and knowledge-based institutions.

To enable these goals to be met, a Science Park stimulates and manages the flow of knowledge and technology amongst universities, R&D institutions, companies and markets; it facilitates the creation and growth of innovation-based companies through incubation and spin-off processes; and provides other value-added services together with high quality space and facilities.

The United Kingdom Science Park Association's (UKSPA) definition is more focused:[3]

A science park is essentially a cluster of knowledge-based businesses, where support and advice are supplied to assist in the growth of the companies. In most instances, science parks are associated with a center of technology such as a university or research institute. In more detail, they are business support and technology transfer initiatives that:

- encourage and support the start up, incubation and further *growth of innovative businesses with good growth potential* [emphasis added].

- provide an environment where larger, frequently international businesses can develop scientific and close interactions with a particular center of technology for their mutual benefit, and

- usually have a formal and operational link with such a reservoir of technology.

The United Nations Educational, Scientific and Cultural Organization (UNESCO) defines a science park as:[4]

...an economic and technological development complex that aims to foster the development and application of high technology to industry. Research facilities, laboratories, business incubator, as well as training, business exchange and service facilities are located in the complex. It is formally linked (and usually physically close) to a center of technological excellence, usually a university and/or research center. Most science parks focus on information technology (including electronics and computers), telecommunication, biotechnology and new materials.

The general characteristic of a science park is as follows:

- promote research and development by the *university in partnership with industry* [emphasis added], assisting in the growth of new ventures, and promoting economic development;
- facilitate the creation and growth of innovation-based companies through incubation and venturing;
- stimulate and manage the flow of knowledge and technology amongst universities, R&D institutions, companies and markets; and
- provide an environment where knowledge-based enterprises can develop close interactions with a particular centre of knowledge creation for their mutual benefit.

More specific to the United States, the Association of University Related Research Parks (AURRP) defined a research park in the following terms:[5]

The definition of a research or science park differs almost as widely as the individual parks themselves. However, the research and science park concept generally includes three components:

- A real estate development
- An organizational program of activities for technology transfer
- A partnership between academic institutions, government and the private sector

The AURRP recently changed its name to the Association of University Research Parks (AURP), and it set forth the following definition for a university research park:[6]

A university research *park or technology incubator* [emphasis added] is defined by AURP as a property-based venture which has:

- Existing or planned land and buildings designed primarily for private and public research and development facilities, high technology and science based companies, and support services.
- A contractual and/or formal ownership or operational relationship with one or more universities or other institutions of higher education, and science research.

- A role in promoting research and development by the university in partnership with industry, assisting in the growth of new ventures, and promoting economic development.
- A role in aiding the transfer of technology and business skills between the university and industry tenants.

The park or incubator may be a not-for-profit or for-profit entity owned wholly or partially by a university or a university related entity. Alternatively, the park or incubator may be owned by a non-university entity but have a contractual or other formal relationship with a university, including joint or cooperative ventures between a privately developed research park and a university.

Each of the above definitions had limitations, and based on previous research none of these definitions is an accurate characterization of either the US or the UK growth phenomenon.[7] In particular, the IASP definition only emphasizes the regional economic growth aspects associated with park activity, but in some European countries that is the founding objective of many of the parks. The UKSPA definition appropriately emphasizes technology transfer from the university, but it is narrow in that it focuses on park company growth. Although the recognition of 'mutual benefit' suggests a two-way flow of knowledge, the UNESCO definition like that of the UKSPA emphasizes a one-way knowledge flow from the university to the private sector. The AURP definition appropriately acknowledges that knowledge does flow in two directions between park tenants and the university. The AURP definition is appealing and formed the foundation for our working definition of a university research park.

Here, following Link and Scott (2006*a*, 2006*b*), we proffer the following succinct definition of a URP:[8]

A university research park is a cluster of technology-based organizations that locate on or near a university campus in order to benefit from the university's knowledge base and ongoing research. The university not only transfers knowledge but expects to develop knowledge more effectively given the association with the tenants in the research park.

Generally, if the park is on or adjacent to a university campus the university owns the park land and either oversees or at least advises on aspects of the activities that take place in the park as well as on the strategic direction of the park's growth. Such oversight may include tenant criteria for leasing space in the park (Link and Link 2003). Such criteria may specify particular technologies or state that the tenant must maintain an active research relationship with university departments and their students.

In the United States, when the park is located off campus, it is often the case that the park land is owned by a private venture—and sold or leased to tenants—but the university had contributed financial capital to its formation and/or intellectual capital to its operation; therefore, there are elements of an administrative relationship between the university and these research parks. In the United Kingdom, all science parks are located on a university campus.

The form of the relationship between the university and the research park can be very explicit, as in the case when the university owns the park land and buildings and leases space to criteria-specific tenants; or very implicit, as in the case when the privately owned park is juxtaposed to the university and the university owns and operates buildings on park land. Certainly, a physical relationship between the university and the park does not necessarily imply an administrative or strategic relationship.

Universities are motivated to develop a research park on their own or in partnership by the possibility of financial gain associated with technology transfer, the opportunity to have faculty and students interact at the applied level with technology-based organizations, and the responsibility of contributing to a regional-based economic development effort. Research organizations are motivated to locate in a research park to gain access to faculty, students, and research equipment, and to foster research synergies.

The most complete time series of data on research park formations applies to the United States (Link and Scott 2003a, 2006a, 2006b). According to Link and Scott (2003a, 2006a, 2006b), there were, as of 2002, eighty-one active URPs in the United States. The UKSPA reports that there are 100 science parks in the United Kingdom, most of which are based on or near UK universities. According to Lindelof and Lofsten (2003), there are twenty-three science parks in Sweden. Phan, Siegel, and Wright (2005) identified, as of 2003, over 200 science parks in Asia, with 111 based in Japan. China has over 100; Hong Kong and South Korea each report two parks; and Macau, Malaysia, Singapore, Taiwan, and Thailand have one each. India established thirteen parks in the late 1980s, but with the exception of Bangalore, India's Silicon Valley, all have failed.

With regard to park formation in the United States, between 1951 and 1980 a number of parks were founded but only twelve are still active. Stanford Research Park (established in California in 1951), Cornell Business & Technology Park (established in New York in 1952), and the Research Triangle Park of North Carolina (established in North Carolina in 1959). Unfortunately, there has not been any systematic accounting of failed parks, but Danilov (1971) suggested that those parks that did fail did so due to restraints on corporate R&D and uncertainty about economic conditions. The formation of new URPs increased rapidly throughout the 1980s and early 1990s, it was sporadic in the late 1990s, and park formations are continuing to grow.

Concomitant with this trend, during the early and mid-1970s, real industrial R&D spending decreased in the United States. Based on NSF data reported in the National Science Board's *Science and Engineering Indicators, 2002* (2002), the real R&D performed in industry decreased in 1970 and 1971,

and then again in 1974 and 1975. It was not until 1977 that real R&D performed in industry was able to return to its 1969-predecline level, and relatedly, in 1978 park formations began to increase. It is reasonable to hypoth-
esize that private sector demand for research park space increased during
this R&D growth period because firms were looking for cooperative research
partnerships to expand their research portfolios, as opposed to development
portfolios.

The period of the relatively rapid increase in park formation corresponds to
a period of significant public policy initiatives to encourage university-with-
industry relationships, increases in industrial R&D spending, and the formation of cooperative research partnerships. In the United States, the Bayh–Dole
Act was passed in 1980, the R&E tax credit was enacted in 1981, and the NCRA
was legislated in 1984. All of these public initiatives fostered additional private
sector R&D activity, which could have stimulated states and universities to
establish potentially beneficial locations for that R&D to take place.

9.3. Empirical studies of university research parks

There have been numerous empirical studies of URPs, although the overwhelming majority of these studies have been based on non-US data. The
paucity of US-based studies has been primarily due to the lack of data availability. The key empirical studies are summarized in Table 9.1.

A number of case studies have also been conducted but are not discussed
in detail in the table. These include, for completeness of this chapter, the
following: Castells and Hall (1994) and Saxenian (1994) described the Silicon Valley (California) and Route 128 (around Boston, MA) phenomenon;
Luger and Goldstein (1991), Link (1995a, 1995b, 2002), and Link and Scott
(2003b) detailed the history of Research Triangle Park (North Carolina); Gibb
(1985), Grayson (1993), Guy (1996a, 1996b), and Vedovello (1997) summarized aspects of the research park phenomenon in the United Kingdom; Gibb
(1985) also chronicles the research park phenomenon in Germany, Italy, the
Netherlands, and selected Asian countries; and Chordà (1996) reports on
French research parks, Phillimore (1999) on Australian research parks, and
Bakouros, Mardas, and Varsakelis (2002) and Sofouli and Vonortas (2007) on
the development of research parks in Greece.

The key empirical studies on US URPs were conducted by Link (1995a,
1995b, 2002) and Link and Scott (2003a, 2003b, 2006a, 2006b). Link and Scott
(2003a, 2003b) examine the evolution and growth of US science parks and
their influence on academic missions of universities, employing econometric
methods and qualitative analysis. They use two data sources: a data-set constructed by the AURRP containing a directory of science parks and limited

Table 9.1. Selected empirical studies of university research parks

Author(s)	Data-set/country	Methodology	Key results from the study
Westhead and Storey (1994)	Authors' longitudinal data-set; UK	Analysis of the probability of survival	URP environments did not significantly increase the probability of firm survival
Westhead and Cowling (1995)	Authors' longitudinal data-set; UK	Descriptive statistics	No difference in employment growth rates of firms located on URPs and similar firms not located on URPs
Westhead, Storey, and Cowling (1995)	Authors' longitudinal data-set; UK	Regression analysis	URP environments did not significantly increase the probability of firm survival
Siegel, Westhead, and Wright (2003a, 2003b)	Authors' longitudinal data-set; UK	Productivity of research efforts; estimation of R&D production function; includes controls for endogeneity bias	URP firms more efficient than non-URP firms in generating new products and services and patents
Lofsten and Lindelof (2003)	Authors' longitudinal data-set; Sweden	Regression analysis	Insignificant differences between URP and non-URP firms, along two dimensions of R&D output: counts of patents and new products; however, URPs place a stronger emphasis on innovative ability, sales and employment growth, market orientation, and profitability than non-URP firms
Link and Link (2003)	AURRP survey of parks; survey of park directors; United States	Regression analysis	Real estate parks are the fastest growing type of URP, but their growth is not related to being close to a university; directors view employment growth as primary objective
Link and Scott (2003b)	Research Triangle Park data/United States	Gompertz curve fitting case study	Organizations entering Research Triangle Park follow S-shaped (Gompertz) pattern of growth

Link and Scott (2003a)	AURRP survey; authors' survey of university provosts; United States	Hazard function analysis employment growth; impact analysis of park on university mission	Proximity to a university and the availability of venture capital have a positive impact on growth; URPs enable universities to generate more publications and patents, more easily place graduates, and hire pre-eminent scholars
Lofsten and Lindelof (2004)	Authors' longitudinal data-set; Sweden	Regression analysis	Insignificant differences in R&D output among URP and non-URP firms; however URP firms with stronger links and networks to universities have higher levels of R&D output and growth than comparable non-URP firms
Ferguson and Olofsson (2004)	Authors' longitudinal data-set; Sweden	Regression analysis	URP firms have a higher survival rate than non-URP firms; however, there is no difference in sales and employment growth
Fukagawa (2006)	Authors' data-set; Japan	Regression analysis	Firms located on science parks are more likely to develop links with universities; the range of these linkages is not necessarily localized; on-park firms are not encouraged to develop linkages with universities more than off-park firms
Link and Scott (2006a, 2006b)	Authors' survey of research parks; United States	Regression analysis	Factors associated with URP growth are proximity to the university, if park is managed by a private organization, if park has biotechnology or IT focus
Leyden, Link, and Siegel (2007)	Compustat data and authors' survey of research parks; United States	Probability analysis	Firms locating on URPs are more R&D active and more diversified than observationally equivalent firms

information on their characteristics, and their own qualitative survey of provosts at eighty-eight major research universities. The provosts were asked several questions about the impact of the university's involvement with science parks on various aspects of the academic mission of the university.

The authors concluded that research parks can be viewed as an innovation, and the formation of a URP is an entrepreneurial response by the university. In fact, park formations in the United States have followed, over time, an S-shaped or Gompertz pattern of growth. Their results suggest that the existence of a formal relationship with a research park enables a university to generate more scholarly publications and patents and also allows them to more easily place Ph.D. students and hire pre-eminent scholars. They also found that there appears to be a direct relationship between the proximity of the research park to the university and the probability that the academic curriculum will shift from basic toward applied research.

In a subsequent study, Link and Scott (2005*a*) analyzed the determinants of the formation of university spin-off companies within the university's research park and reported that university spin-off companies constitute a greater proportion of the companies in older parks and in those parks with richer university research environments. The authors also found that university spin-off companies comprise a larger proportion of firms in parks that are located closer to their university and in parks that have a biotechnology focus.

Finally, Leyden, Link, and Siegel (2007) outlined a highly stylized theoretical model of the selection process onto a US URP. They tested this model empirically using the population of US publicly traded firms that report positive R&D expenditures. The authors conclude that firms locating on URPs are more research active and more diversified than observationally equivalent firms.

The best available evidence on the economic effects of being located on a URP on tenant performance is from the United Kingdom. Several studies were based on longitudinal data consisting of performance indicators for firms located on URPs and a control group of firms not located on URPs (Monck et al. 1988; Westhead and Storey 1994; Westhead, Storey, and Cowling 1995). This method is referred to in the academic literature as a matched pairs approach. The authors found no difference between the closure rates of firms located on URPs and similar firms not located on URPs (32% vs. 33%), implying that sponsored park environments did not significantly increase the probability of business survival or enhance job creation.

With respect to the importance of the university, Westhead and Storey (1994) found a higher survival rate among science park firms with a university link (72%) than firms without such a link (53%). Westhead (1997), examining differences in R&D outputs (i.e. counts of patents, copyrights, and new products or services) and inputs (i.e. percentage of scientists and engineers in total employment, the level and intensity of R&D expenditure, and information on the thrust and nature of the research undertaken by the firm) of firms located on URPs and similar firms located off URPs, found no significant differences between the park and off-park firms.

However, Siegel, Westhead, and Wright (2003*a*, 2003*b*) found that science park firms have higher research productivity than comparable nonscience park firms, in terms of generating new products and services and patents, but not copyrights. These findings are relatively insensitive to the specification of the econometric model and controls for the possibility of an endogeneity bias. This preliminary evidence suggests that university science parks could constitute an important spillover mechanism since they appear to enhance the research productivity of firms.

There have also been several evaluation studies of Swedish science parks. Lindelof and Lofsten (2003, 2004) conducted a 'matched pairs' analysis of 134 on-park and 139 off-park Swedish firms using techniques similar to those employed by Westhead and Storey (1994). The authors reported that there are insignificant differences between science park and nonscience park firms in terms of patenting and new products. However, they found that companies located on science parks appear to have different strategic motivations than comparable off-park companies. More specifically, they seem to place a stronger emphasis on innovative ability, sales and employment growth, market orientation, and profitability. Lindelof and Lofsten (2004) also found that the absolute level of interaction between the university and companies located on science parks is low, but that science park firms were more likely to have a relationship with the university than nonscience park firms. Considered together with other evidence presented in Ferguson and Olofsson (2004), their results imply that science park firms interacting with nearby universities will achieve higher levels of R&D output than comparable nonscience park firms.

Another interesting study was undertaken by Fukugawa (2006), who analyzed the value added to firms by science parks in Japan, and in Japan not all science parks are associated with a university. He found that firms located on these parks are more likely than observationally equivalent nonpark firms to develop links with universities. It appears that the range of these is not necessarily localized. The author also reported that on-park firms are not encouraged to develop linkages with such institutions more than off-park firms are. Taken together, these findings suggest that localized spillovers from parks are not as great as they could be.

9.4. **Conclusions**

In sum, empirical research on these institutions suggests the importance of a university link in enhancing the performance of firms located on research parks. In part, this may be because many research parks were created to incubate the spinouts created from university-based technology. What has been less clear is the exact nature of this link that contributes to the differences between park and off-park firms. Speculation has ranged from explanations of knowledge spillovers to the proximity of the requisite competencies to staff these firms. Nonetheless, given the technological nature of such firms, we conjecture that there may be an important role for the technology transfer process in the success of the university-related research parks and their business tenants.

The academic literature reveals that URPs have numerous objectives in terms of their impact on organizations and their local regions. Those goals relating to firms include facilitating university technology transfer, promoting the formation and growth of start-ups and existing high-technology firms, attracting firms involved in leading-edge technologies, and fostering strategic alliances/networks. Goals relating to regional impacts include economic development, job creation, and enhancement of the image of the location. The jury is still out on the question of whether these institutions are actually accomplishing all of these objectives.

☐ NOTES

1. This section draws from Link and Scott (2003*b*, 2006*b*).
2. http://www.iaspworld.org/information/definitions.php
3. http://www.ukspa.org.uk/htmlfiles/index1.htm
4. http://www.unesco.org/pao/s-parks/what.htm
5. AURRP (1997).
6. http://www.aurp.net/whatis/
7. See Link (1995*a*, 2002), Link and Link (2003), Link and Scott (2003*a*, 2003*b*, 2006*b*), and Siegel, Westhead, and Wright (2003*a*, 2003*b*). According to Link and Scott (2006b): 'If you've seen one research park ... you've seen one research park.'
8. This is used by the National Science Board in *Science and Engineering Indicators, 2006* (National Science Board 2006).

10 Government as entrepreneur and innovator

10.1. Introduction

The government, primarily at the national level, provides technology infrastructure and thus acts as an entrepreneur in the innovation process. Technology infrastructure supports the design, deployment, and use of both individual technology-based components and the systems of such components that form the knowledge-based economy. As such it plays a central role in the innovation process and in the regulation of the diffusion of technologies and is thus an important element contributing to the operation of innovation systems and innovation performance in any modern economy.

Government, by providing technology infrastructure, acts in a Schumpeterian manner as entrepreneur. In a dynamic fashion, government exhibits leadership by perceiving opportunity and acting on that perception. According to Schumpeter (1928: 380), leadership aptitudes mean that:

... some are able to undertake uncertainties incident to what has not been done before; [indeed] ... to overcome these difficulties incident to change of practice is the function of the entrepreneur.

The opportunity at hand is the provision of a public good—the technology itself—that leverages the ability of firms and other actors to participate efficiently in the innovation process and thereby contribute to technology-based economic growth.

10.2. Technology infrastructure

Technology infrastructure has many dimensions. It can be classified first, legitimately, by the set of physical and virtual tools, methods, and data that enable all three stages of technology-based economic activity: the conduct of R&D, the control of production processes to achieve target quality and yield, and the consummation of market place transactions at minimum time and cost. The underlying infratechnologies—including measurement and test methods, process and quality control techniques, evaluated scientific and engineering data, and the technical dimensions of product interfaces—are ubiquitous in the typical technology-based industry. The collective economic benefits of such infrastructure are therefore considerable, as are the consequences of not having it in place at critical points in a technology's life cycle.

Technology infrastructure can also, although done less frequently, be interpreted broadly as an organizational or institutional form, often tied to national measurement systems, that leverages knowledge creation and knowledge flows in technology developers and users, including research parks, incubators, university research centers, and focused public–private partnerships. The efficiency of these institutions in providing technology and related infrastructure services are essential to an efficiently functioning national innovation ecology and to the capacity of that ecology to form and reform innovation systems around innovation problems.

Technology infrastructure, either in the narrow or in the broad sense, is not well understood as an element of a sector's technology platform or national innovation system. Similarly misunderstood are the processes by which such infrastructure is embodied in standards or diffused through various institutional frameworks. In fact, because of the public good nature of technology infrastructure, firms as well as public sector agencies and organizations underinvest in it, thus inhibiting long-term technological advancement and economic growth. Thus, government has an economically justifiable role to play in its support of infrastructure technology.

Recall from Chapter 3 (in equation (3.1) rewritten here as equation (10.1)) that much of the literature on technological change stems from production function models in which the output (Q) of an economic unit (a plant, a firm, or an industry) is represented simply as a function of capital (K) and labor (L):

$$Q = A(t)\,F(K, L) \tag{10.1}$$

where $A(t)$ is a disembodied time-related shift factor. Introducing the firm's stock of technical capital, T, as a third input, the model becomes:

$$Q = A(t)\,F(K, L, T) \tag{10.2}$$

If equation (10.2) is Cobb–Douglas in nature, then it can be written as:

$$Q = A(t)\,K^{\alpha}L^{\beta}T^{\gamma} \tag{10.3}$$

where α is the relative share of K, β the relative share of L, and γ the relative share of T. Technology infrastructure can be thought to leverage the efficiency of technical capital (T) or R&D, which is the relevant investment into the stock of T. Thus, a framework for conceptualizing the economic impact of infrastructure technology would include a specification for γ being a function of publicly provided technology infrastructure, *TechInfra*:

$$\gamma = F(\textit{TechInfra}) \qquad (10.4)$$

10.3. **Government's role in innovation**

The theoretical basis for government's role in market activity is based on the concept of market failure.[1] Market failure is typically attributed to market power, imperfect information, externalities, and public goods. The explicit application of market failure to justify government's role in innovation—in R&D activity in particular—is a relatively recent phenomenon within public policy.

Martin and Scott (2000: 438) observed:

Limited appropriability, financial market failure, external benefits to the production of knowledge, and other factors suggest that strict reliance on a market system will result in underinvestment in innovation, relative to the socially desirable level. This creates a *prima facie* case in favor of public intervention to promote innovative activity.

There are several technological and market factors that will cause private firms to appropriate less return from investments in infrastructure technology, as well as from R&D, and to face greater risk than society does. Link and Scott (1998a, 2004, 2005b) noted a number of factors that are barriers to innovation and new technology. These include: high technical risk associated with the underlying R&D; high capital costs to undertake the underlying R&D; long time to complete the R&D and commercialize the resulting technology; underlying R&D spills over to multiple markets and is not appropriable; market success of the technology depends on technologies in different industries; property rights cannot be assigned to the underlying R&D; resulting technology must be compatible and interoperable with other technologies; and high risk of opportunistic behavior when sharing information about the technology.

These factors underlie what Arrow (1962) identified as the nonexclusivity and public good characteristics of investments in the creation of knowledge. The private firms' incomplete appropriation of social returns in the context of technical and market risk can make risk in its operational sense unacceptably large for the private firm considering an investment.

The design of appropriate public policy should match the policy with the specific source of underinvestment. In that light, Martin and Scott (2000) identified several roles for government research related to infrastructure technology. Appropriate institutions such as the National Institute of Standards and Technology (NIST) in the United States match their intramural research programs with specific sources of underinvestment.

The NIST provides direct infrastructural and research resources to leverage both public and private R&D. The Act of March 3, 1901, also known as the Organic Act, established the National Bureau of Standards within the Department of the Treasury, where the Office of Standard Weights and Measures was administratively located. In 1913, the Bureau was formally housed in the Department of Commerce. National Bureau of Standards was renamed under the guidelines of the Omnibus Trade and Competitiveness Act of 1988:

The National Institute of Standards and Technology [shall] enhance the competitiveness of American industry while maintaining its traditional function as lead national laboratory for providing the measurement, calibrations, and quality assurance techniques which underpin United States commerce, technological progress, improved product reliability and manufacturing processes, and public safety...[and it shall] advance, through cooperative efforts among industries, universities, and government laboratories, promising research and development projects, which can be optimized by the private sector for commercial and industrial applications...[More specifically, NIST is to] prepare, certify, and sell standard reference materials for use in ensuring the accuracy of chemical analyses and measurements of physical and other properties of materials...

NIST's mission is to promote US economic growth by working with industry to develop and apply technology, measurements, and standards. As a group, these represent infrastructure technologies. All industrial countries have agencies similar to NIST.

More generally, government, working through such an institution, which is part of a national innovation system, facilitates the promulgation and adoption of standards for new technology as inputs in industries such as in the sectors developing software, equipment, and instruments. The term standards is used in this context in a general sense to refer to voluntary performance protocols and interoperability standards, test methods, and standard reference materials. More specifically, a standard is a prescribed set of rules, conditions, or requirements concerning: definitions of terms; classification of components; specification of materials, their performance, and their operations; delineation of procedures; and measurement of quantity and quality in describing materials, products, systems, services, or practices.

Although one can find examples where observers have thought that product standards were used in anticompetitive ways, the role for public research institutions is quite general and important, encompassing several types of standards. Government provision of such technology infrastructure is a response to industry's needs for standards that cannot be met by firms on their own because of appropriability issues. Government thus serves as an honest broker providing impartial mediation of disputes that could not be provided by a private firm with a proprietary interest in the outcomes. Industry's scientists and engineers frequently interact with scientists in government through conferences and workshops and together they enable the public research laboratories to develop the standards needed as the technological requirements for industry to remain competitive evolve. In the absence of the government's provision of infrastructure technology, industry would have incurred higher costs to replace the public standards activities than the actual costs to the public institution for those activities. Further, the quality of the more costly private standards activities would have been less than the quality of the public standards activities.

Another role in a national innovation system for the government that is related to the provision of technology infrastructure is to facilitate the diffusion of advances from research in application areas that have high science content such as in biotechnology, chemistry, materials science, and pharmaceuticals. This role is one of facilitating communication and dissemination of ideas from science that can then be used by many sectors to advance applied R&D. In many cases, government funds will have been used by universities to develop the basic science, because the ideas have a strong public good component and there would not have been sufficient incentive to develop them without government funding. Once the basic science is available, the government's infrastructure technology program, with expertise in both research and connections to industry, can help to disseminate the information widely.

Following the analytical framework proffered by Tassey (1997) and Jaffe (1998) and applied to various theoretical situations and case study applications by Link and Scott (1998a, 2001, 2005b), one can think of public sector intervention into the market by providing technology infrastructure using the model in Figure 10.1.

To explain this figure, consider a marketable technology to be produced through an R&D process where conditions prevent full appropriation of the

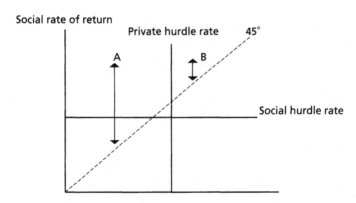

Figure 10.1. Spillover gap between social and private rates of return to R&D

benefits from technological advancement by the R&D-investing firm. Other firms in the market or in related markets will realize some of the profits from the innovation, and of course consumers will typically place a higher value on a product than the price paid for it. The R&D-investing firm will then calculate, because of such conditions, that the marginal benefits it can receive from a unit investment in such R&D will be less than that could be earned in the absence of the conditions reducing the appropriated benefits of R&D below their potential, namely the full social benefits. Thus, the R&D-investing firm may underinvest in R&D, relative to what it would have chosen as its investment in the absence of the conditions. Stated alternatively, the R&D-investing firm may determine that its private rate of return is less than its private hurdle rate and therefore it will not undertake socially valuable R&D.

In Figure 10.1, the social rate of return is measured on the vertical axis along with society's hurdle rate on investments in R&D. The private rate of return is measured on the horizontal axis along with the private hurdle rate on R&D. A 45° line (dashed) is imposed on the figure under the assumption that the social rate of return from an R&D investment will at least equal the private rate of return from the same investment. Two separate R&D projects are labeled as project A and project B. Each is shown, for illustrative purposes only, with the same social rate of return.

For project A, the private rate of return is less than the private hurdle rate because of barriers to innovation and technology. As such, the private firm will not choose to invest in project A, although the social benefits from undertaking project A would be substantial.

The principle of market failure illustrated in the figure relates to appropriability of returns to investment. The vertical distance shown with the double arrow for project A is called the spillover gap; it results from the additional value society would receive above what the private firm would receive if project A were undertaken. What the firm would receive (along the 45° line) is less than its hurdle rate because the firm is unable to appropriate all of the returns that spill over to society. Project A is the type of project in which public resources should be invested to ensure that the project is undertaken.

In comparison, project B yields the same social rate of return as project A, but most of that return can be appropriated by the innovator, and the private rate of return is greater than the private hurdle rate. Hence, project B is one for which the private sector has an incentive to invest on its own or, alternatively stated, there is no economic justification for public resources being allocated to support project B.

For projects of type A where significant spillovers occur, government's role has typically been to provide funding or technology infrastructure through public research institutions that lowers the marginal cost of investment so that the marginal private rate of return exceeds the private hurdle rate.

Note that the private hurdle rate is greater than the social hurdle rate in the figure. This is primarily because of management's (and employees') risk aversion and issues related to the availability and cost of capital. These factors represent an additional source of market failure that is related to uncertainty. For example, because most private firms are risk averse (i.e. the penalty from lower than expected returns is weighted more heavily than the benefits from greater than expected returns), they require a higher hurdle rate of return compared to society as a whole that is closer to being risk neutral.

To reduce market failures associated with inappropriability and uncertainty, government typically engages in activities to reduce technical and market risk (actual and perceived). These activities include, but are not limited to, the activities of public research institutions, as discussed below. The following section discusses several circumstances—termed barriers to technology—that cause market failure and an underinvestment in R&D.

There are a number of factors that can explain why a firm will perceive that its expected private rate of return will fall below its hurdle rate. Individuals will differ not only about a listing of such factors because they are not generally mutually exclusive, but also they will differ about the relative importance of one factor compared to another in whatever taxonomy is chosen.

First, high technical risk (i.e. outcomes may not be technically sufficient to meet needs) may cause market failure given that when the firm is successful, the private returns fall short of the social returns. The risk of the activity being undertaken is greater than the firm can accept, although if successful there would be very large benefits to society as a whole. Society would like the investment to be made; but from the perspective of the firm, the present value of expected returns is less than the investment cost and is thus less than the amount yielding its acceptable return on investment.

Second, high technical risk can relate to high commercial or market risk (although technically sufficient, the market may not accept the innovation—reasons can include factors listed subsequently such as imitation, or competing substitutes, or interoperability issues) as well as to technical risk when the requisite R&D is highly capital intensive. The project may require too much capital for any one firm to feel comfortable with the outlay. The minimum cost of conducting research is thus viewed as excessive relative to the firm's overall R&D budget, which considers the costs of outside financing and the risks of bankruptcy. In this case, the firm will not make the investment, although society would be better off if it had, because the project does not appear to be profitable from the firm's private perspective.

Third, many R&D projects are characterized by a lengthy time interval until a commercial product reaches the market. The time expected to complete the R&D and the time until commercialization of the R&D results are long, and the realization of a cash flow from the R&D investment is in the distant future. If a private firm faces greater risk than society does, and as a result requires a greater rate of return and hence applies a higher discount rate than society does, it will value future returns less than does society. Because the private discount rate exceeds the social discount rate, there may be underinvestment, and the underinvestment increases as the time to market increases because the difference in the rate is compounded and has a bigger effect on returns further into the future.

Fourth, it is not uncommon for the scope of potential markets to be broader than the scope of the individual firm's market strategies so the firm will not perceive or project economic benefits from all potential market applications of the technology. As such, the firm will consider in its investment decisions only those returns that it can appropriate within the boundaries of its market strategies. While the firm may recognize that there are spillover benefits to other markets and while it could possibly appropriate them, such benefits are ignored or discounted heavily relative to the discount weight that would apply to society. A similar situation arises when the requirements for conducting R&D demand multidisciplinary research teams; unique research facilities not generally available with individual companies; or 'fusing' technologies from heretofore separate, noninteracting parties. The possibility for opportunistic behavior in such thin markets may make it impossible, at a reasonable cost, for a single firm to share capital assets even if there were not R&D information sharing difficulties to compound the problem. If society, perhaps through a technology-based public institution, could act as an honest broker to coordinate a cooperative multifirm effort, then the social costs of the multidisciplinary research might be less than the market costs.[2]

Fifth, the evolving nature of markets requires investments in combinations of technologies that, if they existed, would reside in different industries that are not integrated. Because such conditions often transcend the R&D strategy of firms, such investments are not likely to be pursued. That is not only because of the lack of recognition of possible benefit areas or the perceived inability to appropriate whatever results, but also because coordinating multiple players in a timely and efficient manner is cumbersome and costly. Again, as with the multidisciplinary research teams, society may be able to use a technology-based public institution to act as an honest broker and reduce costs below those that the market would face.

Sixth, a situation can exist when the nature of the technology is such that it is difficult to assign intellectual property rights. Knowledge and ideas developed by a firm that invests in technology may spill over to other firms during the R&D phase or after the new technology is introduced into the market. If the information creates value for the firms that benefit from the spillovers, then other things being equal, the innovating firms may underinvest in the technology. Relatedly, when competition in the development of new technology is very intense, each firm, knowing that the probability of being the successful innovator is low, may not anticipate sufficient returns to cover costs.

Further, even if the firm innovates, intense competition at the application stage can result because of competing substitute goods, whether patented or not. Especially, when the cost of imitation is low, an individual firm will anticipate such competition and may therefore not anticipate returns sufficient to cover its R&D investment costs. Of course, difficulties appropriating returns need not always inhibit R&D investment (Baldwin and Scott 1987). First-mover advantages associated with customer acceptance and demand, as well as increasing returns as markets are penetrated and production is expanded, can imply that an innovator wins most (or at least a sufficient portion to support the investment) of the rewards even if it does not take all.

Seventh, industry structure may raise the cost of market entry for applications of the technology. The broader market environment in which a new technology will be sold can significantly reduce incentives to invest in its development and commercialization because of what some scholars have called technological lock-in and path dependency.[3] Many technology-based products are part of larger systems of products. Under such industry structures, if a firm is contemplating investing in the development of a new product but perceives a risk that the product, even if technically successful, will not interface with other products in the system, the additional cost of attaining compatibility or interoperability may reduce the expected rate of return to the point that the project is not undertaken. Similarly, multiple submarkets may evolve, each with its own interface requirements, thereby preventing economies of scale or network externalities from being realized. Again, society, perhaps through a technology-based public institution, may be able to help the market's participants coordinate successful compatibility and interoperability.

Eighth, situations exist where the complexity of a technology makes agreement with respect to product performance between buyer and seller costly. Sharing of the information needed for the exchange and development of technology can render the needed transactions between independent firms in the market prohibitively costly if the incentives for opportunistic behavior are to be reduced to a reasonable level with what Teece (1986) calls obligational contracts. Teece emphasizes that the successful transfer of technology from one firm to another often requires careful teamwork with purposeful interactions between the seller and the buyer of the technology. In such circumstances, both the seller and the buyer of the technology are exposed to hazards of opportunism. Sellers, for example, may fear that buyers will capture the know-how too cheaply or use it in unexpected ways. Buyers may worry that the sellers will fail to provide the necessary support to make the technology work in the new environment; or they may worry that after learning about the buyer's operations in sufficient detail to transfer the technology successfully, the seller would back away from the transfer and instead enter the buyer's industry as a technologically sophisticated competitor. Once again, if society can use a technology-based public institution to act as an honest broker, the social costs of sharing technology may be less than market costs.

These eight factors create, individually or in combination, barriers to innovation and technology and thus lead to a private underinvestment in R&D. While these factors were discussed individually above and listed in the table as if they are discrete phenomena, they are interrelated and overlapping, although in principle any one factor could be sufficient to cause a private firm to underinvest in R&D.

10.4. **Technology infrastructure: Public sector infratechnologies**

Much of the empirical analysis of technology infrastructure has been funded by government agencies, NIST being the agency in the United States that has dominated the literature through primarily contracted studies. For the most part, the empirical literature has focused on assessing the economic impacts associated with public investments in infrastructure technology. These studies, which generally take the form of an evaluation case study, conclude across the board that the social returns to public investments in infrastructure technology are significant, so public investments in such technology are socially valuable.

Support of technology infrastructure generally takes one of two forms: the underlying research is either publicly funded, publicly performed or it is publicly funded, privately performed.

Based on economic theory, publicly funded, publicly performed research programs should be evaluated using what Link and Scott (1998a) call the counterfactual evaluation method. The relevant evaluation question is: What would the private sector have had to invest to achieve the same benefits as the publicly funded, publicly performed research program but in the absence of the public sector's investments? The answer to this question gives the benefits of the public's investments in such research—namely, the costs avoided by the private sector.

Based on economic theory, publicly funded, privately performed research programs should be evaluated using what Link and Scott (1998a, 1998b, 1998c) call the spillover evaluation method. Public funding is needed when a socially valuable project would not be undertaken by the private sector because the expected private rate of return from the research project falls short of the private hurdle rate (or rate required for the private sector to view the research program as valuable). The relevant evaluation question is: What is the net social rate of return from the research program compared to the net private rate of return? The answer to this question determines whether the public's investment in such research is warranted.

As summarized in Table 10.1, the vast majority of the empirical literature related to the role of technology infrastructure has been case studies that utilize a counterfactual evaluation method for assessing the social impact of related public investments. The impact of a particular technology infrastructure—such as a test method, standard reference material, a standard—is identified, interviews are conducted with affected parties in the private sector (and sometimes in the public sector) to determine what amount of investment they would have had to invest to achieve the same benefits as the publicly funded, publicly performed research has provided, but in the absence of the public sector's investments.

Representative retrospective studies from this literature are summarized in Link (1996a). One example applicable to the United States related to the watt-hour revenue meter. The basic instrument used by power companies to measure the flow of electric energy is the watt-hour revenue meter. Manufacturers of standard meters must calibrate each one against a standard meter that has been calibrated at NIST. In turn, all domestic manufacturers of watt-hour meters must maintain traceability to NIST. Their watt-hour meters are tested against their standard meter, which has been calibrated at NIST. Finally, the American National Standard Code for Electricity Metering has recommended that each electric utility company and each state utility commission establish and maintain traceability to NIST. On the basis of extensive interviews with parties involved in this traceability chain, Link (1996a: 90) concluded that:

...the manufacturers of standard meters estimated that the collective [industry wide] annual (ongoing) economic benefit associated with NIST's maintenance of the national standard for the watt-hour is $600,000 (quantified in terms of the estimated cost to duplicate NIST's measurement environment). The annual economic benefit associated with NIST's research to lower the level of [measurement] uncertainty is estimated at $70,000 (quantified in terms of estimated production savings).

Similarly, manufacturers of revenue meters estimated economic benefits from NIST's maintenance of the national standard for the watt-hour at $1.21 million, and utilities and state commissions estimated it between $1.21 and $0.19 million. When compared to the annual NIST cost of $80,000, it is clear that benefits far exceed costs and thus the value to society from this NIST-provided technology infrastructure is positive.

As another example (Link and Scott 1998a; TASC 1998a), NIST is often called on to contribute specialized assistance to industry in areas of national importance. Historically, chlorofluorocarbons (CFCs) have been used extensively as refrigerants, aerosol propellants, solvents, and industrial agents. Globally, refrigerants manufactured with CFCs were used because of their physical and economic properties. However, research has shown over time

Table 10.1. Empirical studies of the economic impact of public investments in technology infrastructure

Author(s) (Year)	Technology infrastructure	Type of infrastructure technology	Economic impacts
Link (1996a)	Intelligent control systems	Generic architecture	Increase productivity
Link (1996a)	Structured Query Language	Test method	Reduce transaction costs
Link (1996a)	ISDN technology	Interoperability standards	Reduce transaction costs
Link (1996a)	Maintain values of primary electric units	Calibration test method	Reduce transaction costs
Link (1996a)	Electromigration characterization	Test method	Increase R&D efficiency
Link (1996a)	Fiber-optic test procedures	Acceptance test method	Reduce transaction costs
Link (1997); Coursey and Link (1998)	Radiopharmaceuticals	Standard reference materials	Increase product quality
TASC (1997); Link and Scott (1998a)	Thermocouple calibration	Standard reference materials	Reduce transaction costs; increase product quality
Link and Scott (1998a)	Optical detector calibrations	Test method	Increase product quality; reduce transaction costs
Link and Scott (1998a)	Spectral irradiance standard	Calibration test method	Reduce transaction costs
Link and Scott (1998a)	Quality control algorithm	Test method	Increase product quality; reduce transaction costs
TASC (1998a); Link and Scott (1998a)	Alternative refrigerants	Standard reference data	Increase R&D efficiency; increase productivity
TASC (1998b); Link and Scott (1998a)	Ceramic phase diagrams	Standard reference data	Increase R&D efficiency; increase productivity
RTI (1999a, 1999b)	Power device simulation modeling	Software model	Increase R&D efficiency; increase productivity
RTI (2000a)	Role-based access controls	Generic technology; reference model	Enable new markets; increase R&D efficiency
RTI (2000b)	Standard reference materials for sulfur	Standard reference materials	Increase productivity; reduce transaction costs
TASC (2000a)	Cholesterol standards	Standard reference materials	Increase productivity; reduce transaction costs
TASC (2000b)	Power and energy calibration	Standard calibrations	Increase productivity; reduce transaction costs
Link and Scott (2001, 2006a)	Quality performance measures	Performance standards	Increase performance; increase product quality
TASC (2001a)	Data encryption	Standard conformance test method	Increase R&D efficiency; enable new markets
TASC (2001b)	Volt standards	Standard reference materials	Increase R&D efficiency; increase productivity
RTI (2002a)	Traceable reference materials	Standard reference data; calibration services	Increase efficiency of regulatory compliance
RTI (2002b)	Data exchange models	Standards development; conformance test methods and services	Increase product quality; accelerate standards development

that release of CFCs into the atmosphere causes damage to the ozone layer of the earth. In response to such evidence, international legislation for a phase out of the production and use of CFCs resulted in the signing of the Montreal Protocol in 1987.

The Montreal Protocol was adopted under the 1985 Vienna Convention for the protection of the ozone layer, and became effective in 1989. By 1994, 136 nations had signed the agreement. For CFCs, the protocol called for a production and consumption cap at 100 percent of 1986 levels by 1990, a decrease to 80 percent by 1994, and to 50 percent by 1999. In the United States, affected industries could not do the requisite research to final alternative refrigerants with the time frames set forth in the Montreal Protocol. In response to this industrial need, NIST developed a refrigerant properties (REFPROP) program for manufacturers and users of CFCs to help them model the behavior of various refrigerant mixtures that could replace existing CFC mixtures.

Based on extensive interviews with manufacturers of alternative refrigerants, refrigerant manufacturers estimated the benefits of NIST's technology infrastructure embodied in REFPROP in terms of the (Link and Scott 1998a: 99):

...additional person-years of research effort, absent the NIST-conducted research program, that would have been needed since the Montreal Protocol to achieve the same level of technical knowledge about alternative refrigerants that they have now.

From 1989 through 1996, this amount totaled, in nominal terms, over $6.5 million.

Refrigerant users who were interviewed as part of the study to obtain these values were asked (Link and Scott 1998a: 100) to estimate:

...the additional number of person-years of effort that would have been needed to achieve the same level of product reliability as they currently have.

From 1990 through 1996, this amount totaled, in nominal terms, over $5.0 million. When these benefits are compared to NIST's alternative refrigerant research costs of $3 million, in nominal terms between 1987 and 1993, the technology infrastructure provided by NIST has been socially worthwhile.

In more detail, specific evaluation tools were used in these studies and those surveyed in Table 10.1, as well as in most studies in other nations that have sought to quantify the net social benefits of government investments in technology infrastructure. These evaluation tools include the following metrics: internal rate of return (IRR), benefit–cost (B/C) ratio; and net present value (NPV).

The IRR is the value of the discount rate, i, that equates the NPV of the stream of net benefits associated with a research project to zero. The time series runs from the beginning of the research project, $t = 0$, to a terminal point, $t = n$.

Mathematically,

$$\text{NPV} = \frac{(B_0 - C_0)}{(1+i)^0} + \cdots + \frac{(B_n - C_n)}{(1+i)^n} = 0 \qquad (10.5)$$

where $(B_t - C_t)$ represents the net benefits associated with the project in year t, and n represents the number of time periods—years in the case study evaluated in this chapter—being considered in the evaluation.

For unique solutions for i, from equation (10.5), the IRR can be compared to a value r that represents the opportunity cost of funds invested by the technology-based public institution. Thus, if the opportunity cost of funds is less than the IRR, the project was worthwhile from an *ex post* social perspective.

The ratio of B/C is the ratio of the present value of all measured benefits to the present value of all measured costs. Both benefits and costs are referenced to the initial time period, $t = 0$, when the project began as:

$$\frac{B}{C} = \frac{\sum_{t=0 \text{ to } t=n} \frac{B_t}{(1+r)^t}}{\sum_{t=0 \text{ to } t=n} \frac{C_t}{(1+r)^t}} \qquad (10.6)$$

A $B/C = 1$ is said to indicate a project that breaks-even. Any project with $B/C > 1$ is a relatively successful project as defined in terms of benefits exceeding costs.

Fundamental to implementing the ratio of B/C is a value for the discount rate, r. While the discount rate representing the opportunity cost for public funds could differ across a portfolio of public investments, the calculated metrics in this chapter follow the guidelines set forth by the Office of Management and Budget (1992), which stated that 'constant-dollar benefit–cost analyses of proposed investments and regulations should report NPV and other outcomes determined using a real discount rate of 7 percent'.

The information developed to determine the B/C ratio can be used to determine NPV as:

$$\text{NPV}_{\text{initial year}} = B - C \qquad (10.7)$$

where, as in the calculation of B/C, B refers to the present value of all measured benefits and C refers to the present value of all measured costs and where present value refers to the initial year or time period in which the project began, $t = 0$ in terms of the B/C formula in equation (10.6). Note that NPV allows, in principle, one means of ranking several projects *ex post*, providing investment sizes are similar.

To compare the NPV across different case studies with different starting dates, the NPV for each can be brought forward to the same year. The $\text{NPV}_{\text{initial year}}$ is brought forward under the assumption that the NPV for the project was invested at the 7 percent real rate of return that is recommended by the Office of Management and Budget as the opportunity cost of government

Table 10.2. Empirical studies of the social need for public investments in technology infrastructure

Author(s) (Year)	Infrastructure technology	Type of technology infrastructure	Conclusion
RTI (1999a, 1999b)	US automobile supply chain	Interoperability standards	Underinvestment in the United States
RTI (2000a, 2000b)	Measurement standards for electric utilities	Standards	Underinvestment in the United States
RTI (2002a, 2002b)	Software testing infrastructure	Measurement standards	Underinvestment in the United States
RTI (2004a)	Interoperability standards for capital facilities	Interoperability standards	Underinvestment in the United States
RTI (2004b)	Interoperability for supply chain integration	Interoperability standards	Underinvestment in the United States
RTI (2004c)	Calibration improvements	Calibration test methods	Underinvestment in the United States
RTI (2005a, 2005b)	Internet protocols	Economic impact from mandated interoperability standards	Underinvestment in the United States

funds. NPV_{2007} is then a project's NPV multiplied by 1.07 raised to the power of current year minus the year that the project was initiated, initial year, as:

$$NPV_{2007} = NPV \times (1.07)^{2007 - \text{initial year}} \tag{10.8}$$

There has been a second group of studies related to the social needs associated with technology infrastructure. Such planning studies have motivated public policies as well as helped to focus research dollars to the expected highest value. These studies are summarized in Table 10.2.

10.5. **Technology infrastructure: Public–private partnerships**

As discussed above, technology infrastructure can be defined in a narrow sense as an organizational form that leverages knowledge creation and knowledge flows. One such example is URPs, as discussed in Chapter 9; another such example is focused public–private partnerships such as RJVs as stimulated in the United States under the National Cooperative Research Act (NCRA) of 1984.[4]

Public, as the term public–private partnership is used herein, refers to any aspect of the innovation process that involves the use of public sector or government resources, be they federal, state, or local in origin. Private refers to any aspect of the innovation process that involves the use of private sector resources. And resources are broadly defined to include all resources—financial, infrastructural, and research resources, and the like—that affect the

Table 10.3. Taxonomy of public–private partnerships

Government involvement	Economic objective	
	Leverage public R&D	Leverage private R&D
Indirect	—	—
Direct		
Financial resources	—	—
Infrastructural resources	—	—
Research resources	—	—

general environment in which innovation occurs. Finally, the term partnership refers to any and all innovation-related relationships, including but not limited to formal and informal collaborations.

The framework that describes public–private partnerships as related to the NCRA, or to any such partnership, is illustrated in Table 10.3. The first column of the table describes the nature and scope of government's involvement in a public–private partnership. Government's involvement could be indirect or direct, and if direct there is an explicit allocation of resources, including financial, infrastructural, and research resources.

The second and third columns of the table relate to the economic objective of the public–private partnership. Of course, with any innovation-related activity there are spillovers of knowledge and thus the economic objective of the partnership are multidimensional. But, for illustrative purposes, a single overriding objective is assumed. Broadly, this objective is either to leverage public R&D activity or to leverage private R&D activity.

As background for understanding the technology infrastructure created through the NCRA, in November 1983, the US House of Representatives proposed the Research and Development Joint Ventures Act of 1983. It stated:

[In hearings] many distinguished scientific and industry panels have recommended the need for some relaxation of current antitrust laws to encourage the formation of R&D joint ventures. . . . The encouragement and fostering of joint research and development ventures are needed responses to the problem of declining U.S. productivity and international competitiveness.

In an April 1984 House report on competitive legislation, the Joint Research and Development Act of 1984, the supposed benefits of joint R&D were first articulated:

Joint research and development . . . can reduce duplication, promote the efficient use of scarce technical personnel, and help to achieve desirable economies of scale.

The NCRA of 1984 was passed on October 11, 1984:

. . . to promote research and development, encourage innovation, stimulate trade, and make necessary and appropriate modifications in the operation of the antitrust laws.

Table 10.4. Public–private partnerships: the National Cooperative Research Act of 1984

Government involvement	Economic objective	
	Leverage public R&D	Leverage private R&D
Indirect	—	NCRA of 1984
Direct		
Financial resources	—	—
Infrastructural resources	—	—
Research resources	—	—

The NCRA created a registration process, later expanded by the National Cooperative Research and Production Act (NCRPA) of 1993 and the Standards Development Organization Advancement Act (SDOAA) of 2004, under which RJVs and standards organizations can voluntarily disclose their research intentions to the US Department of Justice. All disclosures are made public in the *Federal Register*.

Table 10.4 shows that the NCRA and subsequent legislation represent a public–private partnership. It is a partnership with indirect government involvement and a partnership that leverages private R&D. Link (2006*b*) has applied the taxonomy in the table to a number of other US innovation initiatives with direct government involvement.

Figure 10.2 illustrates the social benefits associated with an RJV or cooperative research in general, and thus it is a useful device for validating the government role in this aspect of innovation. Underlying the figure is the assumption that R&D is an investment into the production of technical knowledge and, as is well known, technical knowledge has the characteristics of a public good.

To understand the figure, assume that an industry is composed of two firms, firm A and firm B. Both firms invest independently in basic research and the technical knowledge obtained from the basic research has the characteristic of a public good (see Chapter 4).

Firm A is assumed to have an initial endowment of resources (a *numéraire* good) denoted by Oa on the horizontal axis, and firm B's initial endowment is Ob. The initial endowment in each case can be thought of as the budgeted R&D that can either be allocated to the applied component of R&D (i.e. applied research and development)—a private good, or to the basic component of R&D (i.e. basic research)—a public good, or any linear combination of the two. The specific transformation curves between the two components are noted as aa' and bb' for firms A and B, respectively. The slope of these transformation curves represents the marginal private cost of producing a unit of technical knowledge in terms of the applied component. The X, Y, and Z curves are isoprofit curves. The ray OO' represents the locus of optimal investment choices for the two firms acting independently.

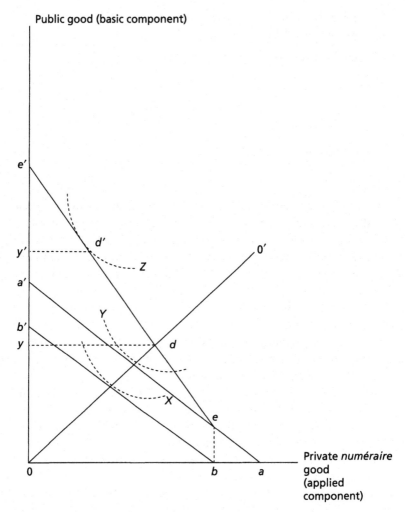

Figure 10.2. A public good model of R&D spending
Sources: Based on Link and Bauer (1989) and Bozeman, Link, and Zardkoohi (1986).

To compare the provision of the public good when investments are made both independently and through cooperation, each firm's investment choices are considered under the two alternatives. If each firm invests its entire endowment of the *numéraire* good on the public good, the total amount of the public good provided will be Oe' ($Oe' = Oa' + Ob'$), and each firm assuming that the public good diffuses perfectly. Point e', however, does not represent the locus of optimal investment choices. Each firm maximizes its profit along OO'. Because each firm independently moves to the optimal investment locus and because both firms must by definition eventually use identical amounts of the public good, it necessarily follows that both firms must simultaneously reach an identical and unique allocation on OO'.

One allocation that both firms can obtain simultaneously is point e'. There are, of course, an infinite number of such allocations that both firms can obtain simultaneously. These possible allocation points are defined by taking the feasible allocations on the horizontal axis that both firms can reach, and then locating the corresponding amount of the public good obtained by the firms. Firm B cannot obtain endowments exceeding Ob; at point b, firm B spends zero on the public good whereas firm A spends ba amount and provides be amount. Both firms thus reach the point e allocation simultaneously. All of the allocations that can be achieved by both firms simultaneously are defined by ee'. Point d represents the intersection of ee' and OO' and it is the equilibrium allocation obtained by both firms simultaneously given independent adjustments. At point d, both firms end up receiving the identical amount of the public good as well as the private good, although the initial endowments were different.

The allocation at point d is, however, not an economically efficient one because the slope of ee' is different from that of aa' or bb'. Both firms are better off by moving to d', and this point can be reached through cooperation in R&D. Cooperation in R&D, through a RJV, will increase the amount of technical knowledge from Oy (reached at point d) to Oy' (reached at point d'). And the model in Figure 10.2 predicts clearly that firms that engage in an RJV will have an incentive on their own for directing their own R&D spending toward basic research as opposed to applied research or development.

From a policy perspective, the literature has raised a number of questions about RJVs, in particular, or SRPs, in general. These questions include, Have research partnerships improved economic efficiency? Have research partnerships increased competition in the marketplace? And, Have research partnerships increased consumer surplus through improved products or faster introduction of products? While we have discussed aspects of collaborative research in previous chapters, we have not discussed that organizational form from a policy perspective. Table 10.5 summarizes the empirical and theoretical literature related to these questions by methodological approach. Thus, in the last column of the table the literature is segmented into what we call the transaction costs literature, the strategic management literature, and the IO literature.

Regarding whether research partnerships have improved efficiency, the evidence is overwhelmingly positive. Research partnerships lower transaction costs, reduce duplicative R&D expenditures, increase R&D that has a spillover benefit, yield economies of scale and scope, and they reduce technical risk.

Regarding whether research partnerships increase competition in the marketplace, the evidence is mixed. Some have argued that research partnerships increase market output and lower prices through production cost reductions, while others contend that they facilitate collusion in product markets.

Table 10.5. Recent studies of the effects of research partnerships on economic performance

Policy question	Finding	Author
Have research partnerships improved efficiency?	Yes—Can lower transactions costs	*Transactions cost:* Kogut (1988) Williamson (1996a, 1996b)
		Strategic management: Jarillo (1988) Mowery et al. (1998) Gomez-Casseres (1996)
	Yes—Reduces unnecessary duplicative R&D expenditures Via knowledge sharing in endogenous research partnerships	*IO:* Combs (1993) Katz (1986) Kamien, Mueller, and Zang (1992) Kamien and Zang (1993)
		Strategic Management: Pralahad and Hamel (1990)
	Yes—Can increase R&D expenditures if significant spillover effects	*IO:* Katz (1986) Motta (1992) D'Aspremont and Jacquemin (1988) DeBondt and Veugelers (1991) DeBondt et al. (1992) Kamien et al. (1992) Suzumura (1992) Simpson and Vonortas (1994) Vonortas (1994) Brod and Shivakumar (1997)
	Yes—Yields economies of scale, scope, or learning	*IO:* Combs (1993) Petit and Tolwinski (1996)
		Strategic management: Porter (1986) Harrigan (1985) Jarillo (1988) Pralahad and Hamel (1990)
	Yes—Reduces risk	*Strategic management:* Harrigan (1985) Kogut (1988) Sanchez (1993) Dixit and Pindyck (1995) Trigeorgis (1996)
Have research partnerships increased competition in the marketplace?	Yes—May decrease concentration	*IO:* Motta (1992) Combs (1993)
	Yes—Increases market output and lowers price (via production cost reductions) if significant spillover effects	*IO:* Katz (1986) D'Aspremont and Jacquemin (1988) DeBondt and Veugelers (1991) DeBondt et al. (1992) Kamien, et al. (1992) Suzumura (1992) Simpson and Vonortas (1994) Vonortas (1994) Brod and Shivakumar (1997)

(cont.)

Table 10.5. (*Continued*)

Policy question	Finding	Author
	No—Market power	
	Facilitates collusion in product market	*IO*: Martin (1994) Rosenkranz (1995)
	First mover advantage or unique aggregation of resources	*Strategic management*: Porter (1986) Harrigan (1985) Jarillo (1988) Mowery et al. (1998) Hamel and Pralahad (1989) Teece (1986)
Have research partnerships increased consumer surplus through improved products or faster introduction?	Yes But watch out for high pricing due to market power	*IO*: Poyago-Theotoky (1997) *Strategic management*: Harrigan (1985) Mowery et al. (1998) Pralahad and Hamel (1990) Hamel and Pralahad (1989)

Finally, there is limited evidence that research partnerships increase consumer surplus through improved products and faster introduction of new products.

10.6. **Conclusions**

R&D is a key determinant of economic growth. The willingness of companies to invest in technology will depend on their estimates of the private returns to R&D, or the benefits that accrue to them as a result of engaging in R&D. Given the public good nature of knowledge and difficulties in protecting intellectual property, firms typically cannot appropriate all of the benefits associated with innovation. Another barrier to investment in technology is that there is often a high degree of level of technical and commercial uncertainty associated with certain types of innovative activity, especially basic research. The risky nature of such projects serves to reduce projected private rates of return to R&D, since managers are typically focused on risk-adjusted returns.

As discussed in Link and Scott (2001), the existence of such barriers implies that certain R&D projects may not be funded because the perceived risk-adjusted private rate of return does not exceed a certain hurdle rate of return. The authors note that if this hurdle rate is not exceeded, firms cannot justify investment in an R&D project. From a social perspective, that is unfortunate, since such investments may generate high social returns, or benefits that accrue to society at large from process innovations and the creation of new products and new industries (e.g. lower prices and/or enhanced product quality and variety). To economists, this divergence between the private and social returns to R&D signifies the existence of what Martin and Scott (2000) refer to as an 'innovation' market failure.

Thus, there is a strong consensus that, in the absence of government intervention, there will be underinvestment in R&D in free market economies. The degree of underinvestment is hypothesized to be especially high for basic research, since difficulties in appropriability and the level of risk (both technical and commercial) and uncertainty are presumed to be most severe for fundamental, as opposed to applied, research. The failure of market forces to generate optimal levels of R&D can be addressed through direct financial support from government agencies for R&D projects, relaxation of antitrust statutes to promote collaborative R&D, and other modifications in technology policy that stimulate the formation of research partnerships. The empirical evidence presented in this chapter seems to indicate that innovation market failures exist and that government initiatives can alleviate them.

☐ NOTES

1. This section draws from Link (2006) and Link and Scott (1998*a*, 2005*b*).
2. See Leyden and Link (1999) on the role of a federal laboratory as an honest broker.
3. See David (1987) for detailed development of the ideas of path dependency in the context of business strategies and public policy toward innovation and diffusion of new technologies.
4. This section draws from Link (1998*b*, 2006).

11 Innovation, entrepreneurship, and technological change: a research agenda

11.1. Introduction

Throughout this book, we have reviewed a wide variety of academic literatures on innovation, entrepreneurship, and technological change. We assert that collectively this scholarship has deepened our understanding of the phenomena to which this book is devoted. A deep and thorough understanding of innovation, entrepreneurship, and technological change is important not only for academic purposes but also because the subject has salient managerial and policy implications. These implications relate to the profitability and competitiveness of the firm as well as to the overall economic performance of industry and the national economy. Not surprisingly, there has also been a substantial increase in recent years in technology-based economic development activities at local, state, and regional levels in most if not all developed nations. Universities are increasingly being viewed by policymakers at all levels as engines of regional economic growth through their involvement and through their perceived potential involvement in the commercialization of academic intellectual property and subsequent transfer of that technology. The academic literatures on these issues are still embryonic, although an increasing number of scholars are increasingly attracted to these topics.

The purpose of this chapter is to identify a set of unresolved theoretical and empirical issues related to the topics herein. We provide specific recommendations for future selected research including, but not limited to, the need for specific data collection efforts. Certainly, we do not claim to identify the entire spectrum of future research, but our discussion in this final chapter points to some unresolved issues especially regarding data collection. Data issues are critically important because many of the economic sectors in which economic agents are engaged in innovate and entrepreneurial activities are themselves somewhat embryonic (e.g. sectors developing around new technological breakthroughs) and, therefore, are not well documented by federal statistical agencies.

11.2. Agents versus institutions

The research discussed and reviewed in the previous chapters cuts across a number of disciplines. Furthermore, within and across these disciplines authors have employed both quantitative and qualitative methods to address key research questions. As well, there is also considerable heterogeneity in their analyses in terms of the units of analysis. Many researchers have focused on institutions—firms, universities, research parks, incubators, industrial laboratories, university TTOs, IUCRCs, and ERCs—while other, albeit only a few in comparison, have focused on new organizational forms—RJVs, strategic alliances, and strategic networks. Still other scholars have analyzed agents engaged in entrepreneurship and innovation such as industry and academic scientists or entrepreneurs in firms or universities.

Indeed, there is a pronounced trend in the academic literatures toward a more disaggregated analysis (e.g. moving from organizations to agents as the unit of analysis) of innovation, entrepreneurship, and technological change. We applaud this trend because there are a number of important research questions that are better addressed at the agent level than at the institutional level. As one example, a key issue that has been raised by several critics of university technology transfer is how faculty involvement in technology transfer and entrepreneurship influence teaching, service, and thus the culture of open science that is believed to define the role of academic institutions (e.g. Nelson 2001). A related issue is how commercialization activity affects the career paths of scientists and engineers. It is clearly better to examine these and other such issues using data on individual agents rather than data on a more aggregated institutional level. Specifically, it would be useful to track teaching and service activities among individual academics involved in patenting, licensing, and start-up activity both before and after their involvement in technology commercialization. Researchers should also conduct qualitative studies to determine whether academics are asking different research questions before and after, as well as whether academics tend to be more secretive after they have participated in the technology transfer process.

More generally, there is a strong need for better data to facilitate research on entrepreneurial behavior and technological phenomena at all levels of aggregation. Such research is necessitated by the pervasive importance of knowledge and intellectual property throughout the economy, as well as by a substantial increase in public–private partnerships between government programs (e.g. the SBIR Program) and technology-based institutions (e.g. universities, incubators, and research parks) that are designed to enhance entrepreneurship and technological change. The fact is that a technologically progressive economy is one characterized by a complex web of agents and institutions engaged in innovation, entrepreneurship, and technological change.

11.3. Future research on research partnerships

Our review of the extant literature on research partnerships revealed that incomplete and imprecise data preclude an accurate assessment of both the net private and net social returns to such collaborative relationships. In order to address these data limitations, we propose that statistical agencies consider broadening their coverage of these relationships to include a wide range of research partnerships (e.g. RJVs, technology alliances, strategic networks, incubators, industrial laboratories, university TTOs, IUCRCs, and ERCs).

One theme of this book is the importance of evaluating the net social returns to innovation. Therefore, in addition to the public sector spearheading relevant data collection efforts, we also propose that these data collection efforts include metrics associated with the inputs, outputs, and outcomes of public–private partnerships in which an understanding of net social returns is fundamental to the accountability of the partnerships.

Greater attention should be paid to collecting information on the outputs and outcomes of R&D and innovation regardless of the sector of funding or sector of performance. Quantifying the evolution of ideas and innovations that stem from R&D and other inputs will lead to a broader understanding of the complex web of agents and institutions involved in technological change and then to more effective innovation and technology policy.

In a similar vein, it would also be useful to document failures as well as successes of research partnerships, and to compare such outcome behavior to firms not involved in research partnerships. It is important from a public accountability perspective to assess not only the net returns from the partnership's R&D, especially when public moneys are supporting the partnership, but also the net returns of the institutional arrangements themselves that facilitated the partnerships. If such information were collected over time, researchers could begin to evaluate whether certain partnership relationships, especially public–private partnerships, are effectively overcoming barriers that caused market failures. Recall that the fundamental rationale for government's role in innovation and R&D is market failure (Martin and Scott 2000).

Given that many governments have streamlined existing data collection and have curtailed new data collection efforts, a potentially cost-effective approach for statistical agencies could be to partner with universities or organizations to undertake this responsibility and to disseminate the results. The NSF has done this for the collection of RJV statistics through the CORE database. Other possible partnerships could include, for example, the AUTM, which conducts an annual benchmarking survey of university patenting, licensing, and start-up activity.

It is also important to avoid duplication of effort in the collection of information on embryonic industries or sectors. Statistical agencies could exploit the numerous proprietary databases of research partnerships such as files created by the Securities Data Company, Science Citation Index, Recombinant Capital, Corporate Technology Directory, and Venture Economics.

One way to increase the return from existing data collection efforts is to foster linkages among the extant databases. An example is the Center for Economic Studies at the US Census Bureau, where researchers have been analyzing linked datasets since the late 1980s, subject to clearance procedures that preserve confidentiality.

US agencies can also draw on the experiences of foreign statistical agencies that have administered what are arguably more comprehensive innovation surveys that capture substantial research partnership activity. For example, the countries of the EU have implemented the Community Innovation Survey (CIS), under the auspices of Eurostat, for almost a decade. Japan and Canada have also been fairly aggressive in this arena. Statistics Canada has recently launched a comprehensive survey of intellectual property commercialization in higher education.

With respect to public investment in R&D, assembling data would allow researchers to investigate many new questions such as about the complementarity between government programs (e.g. ATP and SBIR) in general, and the complementarity between public and private R&D in particular.

11.4. **Future research on university technology transfer**

Given that research on university technology transfer is relatively nascent, it should not be surprising that a significant portion of the academic literature discussed in this book has been descriptive and qualitative. Our review of the university technology transfer literatures also revealed that some theoretical frameworks have been applied to understanding this phenomenon. These frameworks include, for example, agency theory and the role of information asymmetry (Jensen and Thursby 2001; Thursby, Jensen, and Thursby 2003) and social network theory (Owen-Smith and Powell 2001). Additional theoretical research is needed on this broad topic, especially with regard to the development and testing of theories of strategic investment.

For example, the notion of path dependence could partially explain the persistent difference in commercialization success rate between experienced universities and those that are newer to the game. In contrast to other studies on innovative behavior that have been described by productivity frontiers, there does not appear to be evidence of a regression to the mean in technology transfer activities. One reason might be that researchers have not been able to measure outcomes over a sufficiently long time, but another reason might be that all that has been observed to date is the start-up phase of a new generation of intellectual property commercialization.

However, a more compelling rationale may be that over time, more experienced TTOs learn how to manage this process more effectively and, to the extent that such learning becomes embedded in an institutional context, can then distance themselves from those that are newer. Theories of organizational learning appear to be especially appropriate to explain the antecedents and consequences of such activity. In addition, because of the geographically localized nature of successful technology transfer, it appears that the situations into which such expertise can be successfully transplanted may be limited. Hence, the use of institutional theory and evolutionary economics perspectives to explain the persistence of differences in effectiveness across regions may be a fruitful direction in which to take the research related to regional development and university technology transfer.

At the level of the organization, the academic literatures are clear that the consistency and congruency of organization design, incentive systems, information process capacity, and organization-wide values matter a great deal in technology transfer success and resulting new venture creation. Employing theories from the organization sciences—the RBV of the firm, structural contingency theory, and social network theory—may provide excellent foundations for deriving more sophisticated insights from future research in light of the budding international nature of university technology transfer.

As previously noted, there is an emerging literature that attempts to model the relationships between the TTO, the university scientist, and the university's administration from an agency theory perspective. This is a highly useful direction to pursue, but it can be taken a step further. Assumptions relating to principal–agent decisions are based largely on Bayesian rationality. Based on recent research on prospect theory, the notion of prior losses or gains could be incorporated into the choice models (e.g. into the faculty member's decision to disclose or not to disclose an invention, into the university's decision to license or not license a technology or to launch or not to launch a new venture) to more accurately evaluate the opportunity costs faced by the scientists and transactions costs faced by the university and/or the commercial enterprise. The specificity with which future researchers are able to model theoretically the TTO relationships will facilitate identifying latent constructs that determine the institutional, organizational, and individual relationships to technology transfer effectiveness, and hence build more predictive normative models.

We conjecture that additional research is needed on organizational practices in university management of intellectual property. Existing qualitative evidence (e.g. Siegel, Waldman, and Link 2003; Siegel et al. 2004) appears to indicate that the most critical organizational factors are reward systems for faculty involvement in university technology transfer, compensation and staffing practices in the TTO, and actions taken by administrators to eliminate informational and cultural barriers between universities and firms. More specifically, it appears that the propensity of faculty members to disclose inventions, and thus, increase the supply of technologies available for commercialization, is related to promotion and tenure policies and the university's royalty and equity distribution formula. Compensation practices in the TTO could also be relevant because technology transfer activity will depend on the efforts of technology licensing officers to elicit invention disclosures and market them effectively to private companies. Thus, it would not be surprising, *ceteris paribus*, if licensing activity will be greater at universities that have implemented some form of incentive compensation plan for technology licensing officers.

A natural extension of the exploratory qualitative research on university technology transfer is to survey technology transfer stakeholders at each university in an attempt to measure key organizational factors. Some variables such as the university's royalty and equity distribution formula are easy to measure with a survey and may even be available on the World Wide Web. Other variables such as measures of the skills of TTO, personnel, tenure and promotion policies, and other policy variables will be more perceptual in nature.

In designing such surveys, researchers will need to be mindful of the considerable heterogeneity in stakeholders' perspectives on university technology transfer. For example, scientists, managers/entrepreneurs, and university administrators have different norms, standards, and values, as well as different objectives and constraints. Thus, surveying scientists, managers/entrepreneurs, and administrators separately to generate a more accurate and unbiased view of the organizational environment could be a useful strategy.

Another important avenue of yet unexplored research is the role of personal relationships and social networks in university technology transfer, especially the entrepreneurial dimension of such activities, which requires more teamwork and interaction with potential investors and external agents. What little research there is suggests that the formation of social networks is important to effective university technology transfer. These networks include academic and industry scientists, investors, university administrators, TTO directors, and managers/entrepreneurs (Liebeskind et al. 1996; Powell 1990). Social networks that allow knowledge transfer appear to work in both directions, but the evidence to date is sketchy. Data collection efforts through face-to-face interviews, while not readily accepted in some disciplines, such as economics, may be the most effective way to document networks. Zucker and Darby (1996), among others, found that scientists who interacted with industry conducted more pathbreaking research compared to those who did not.

Accounting for the organizational practices in university management of intellectual property will be useful in several research dimensions. First, given the embryonic nature of the TTO as an organizational form, there is a need to simply document the nature of these practices. Interviews by Siegel et al. (2004) revealed that many university administrators would like to benchmark their intellectual property management practices relative to peer institutions. Perhaps the most important benefit of collecting this information is that it can be used to determine the fraction of the variance in relative productivity that can be attributed to organizational factors.

We also need to learn about specific practices that can enhance university technology transfer performance. Such information, transformed systematically into data, could be used to assess the performance effects of the adoption of complementary organizational practices. Recent theoretical research (e.g. Athey and Stern 1998) and empirical studies (e.g. Bresnahan, Brynjolfsson, and Hitt 2002; Ichniowski, Shaw, and Prennushi 1997) have highlighted the importance of clusters of complementary organizational practices in enhancing productivity. Their work, which stressed interaction effects, underscores the need for a greater understanding of such behavior.

11.5. Future research on research parks and incubators

As noted in previous chapters, there is limited evidence on both the net private and net social returns to location on property-based institutions such as research parks and incubators. Three, among many, unanswered research questions are: Do the returns to location on a research park or in an incubator vary according to the type or location of the park (e.g. geographical distance to a university)? Do such returns depend on the type of entrepreneur who locates on a park? And, How does activity in a research park or incubator affect other dimensions of university technology transfer (e.g. licensing agreements and other university-based start-ups)?

It is conceivable that existing evidence, albeit pioneering, could be masking important differences in the returns to different types of research parks. In this regard, it might be useful to develop a more detailed taxonomy of research parks (Link and Link 2003). It might be important to distinguish between managed and nonmanaged parks. The former are facilities that have a dedicated managerial team and a fairly clear strategic focus. In some countries (e.g. the United Kingdom) many parks have been established in depressed regions, which do not have a culture conducive to the development of new-technology-based firms. Some owner-managers of firms in these regions have chosen to locate on a managed park in order to have access to critical resources and establish the legitimacy of their ventures. What little research there is indicates that business closure rates on nonmanaged parks are lower than those reported on managed parks (Westhead and Batstone 1999), implying that parks placing a greater emphasis on increasing the supply of technology-based entrepreneurs in such depressed environments will have higher levels of business turbulence.

Additional research should also be undertaken to determine whether a particular research park strategy (e.g. university led and funded, joint venture strategy, cooperative venture strategy) or management agreement (e.g. informal teams, single research park manager on site or on-site management company) is associated with a wider range of benefits. A research park location and a proactive gatekeeper may develop an environment that engenders trust between science park tenants, the nearby university, and other local firms not located on a science park. The effectiveness of intermediaries (Perry 1996), such as research park managers, in the commercialization process and the linking of research park firms with universities and institutions of higher learning (e.g. teaching hospitals and nonprofit research organizations), other tenants on the park, as well as firms located off-park, needs to be carefully studied.

Another potential source of heterogeneity in the net social returns to research parks, and many parks were founded and/or continue on the basis of public funding, involves the match between the attributes of the entrepreneur and the park. In this regard, it might be useful to construct a large-scale, stratified database of entrepreneurs who choose to locate their firms on a research park. A few studies suggest (e.g. Westhead 1995) that there are different types of entrepreneurs—portfolio and serial entrepreneurs (Westhead and Wright 1998) and surrogate entrepreneurs (Franklin, Wright, and Lockett 2001)—and one type over another or the interaction among types could have performance implications for the new-technology-based firms located on a research park.

The relationship between URPs and other aspects of UITT warrants further attention. For instance, researchers have yet to examine the relationship between activity on a university research park and the licensing activity of university-based technologies to park firms, university patenting to park firms, sponsored research from park firms, coauthoring between academic and park scientists, university-based start-ups in parks, and the hiring by park firms of university graduates. Such insights would contribute to the debate on effective mechanisms for transferring technology from universities to firms (Bray and Lee 2000; Siegel, Waldman, and Link 2003). In particular, it might offer insights into the most appropriate modes for enhancing the performance of university spinout companies (Franklin, Wright, and Lockett 2001).

As these research agendas are pursued others will certainly develop, and thus research on research will continue to evolve.

⬜ REFERENCES

Abramovitz, M. (1956). 'Resource and Output Trends in the United States since 1870', *American Economic Review*, 46: 5–23.

Adams, J. D. (1990). 'Fundamental Stocks of Knowledge and Productivity Growth', *Journal of Political Economy*, 98: 673–702.

——— Chiang, E. P., and Jensen, J. L. (2000). 'The Influence of Federal Laboratory R&D on Industrial Research', NBER Working Paper No. 7612.

——— ——— and Starkey, K. (2001). 'Industry–University Cooperative Research Centers', *Journal of Technology Transfer*, 26: 73–86.

Aghion, P. and Howitt, P. (1990). 'A Model of Growth through Creative Destruction', *Econometrica*, 60: 323–51.

——— ——— (1992). 'A Model of Growth Through Creative Destruction', *Econometrica*, 60: 323–51.

Agrawal, A. and Cockburn I. (2003). 'The Anchor Tenant Hypothesis: Exploring the Role of Large, Local R&D-Intensive Firms in Regional Innovation Systems', *International Journal of Industrial Organization*, 21: 1227–53.

Aigner, D. J., Lovell, C. A. K., and Schmidt, P. (1977). 'Formulation and Estimation of Stochastic Frontier Production Functions', *Journal of Econometrics*, 6: 21–37.

Amable, B. and Palombarini, S. (1998). *Technical Change and Incorporated R&D in the Service Sector*. Paris: OECD.

Anand, B. N. and Khanna, T. (2000). 'Do Firms Learn to Create Value? The Case of Alliances', *Strategic Management Journal*, 2: 295–315.

Anderson, S. P., DePalma, A., and Thisse, J.-F. (1992). *Discrete Choice Theory of Product Differentiation*. Cambridge: MIT Press.

Arrow, K. J. M. (2000). 'Increasing Returns: Historiographic Issues and Path Dependence', *European Journal of the History of Economic Thought*, 7: 171–80.

——— Chenery, M., Minhas, B., and Solow, R. (1961). 'Capital–Labor Substitution and Economic Efficiency', *Review of Economics and Statistics*, 43: 225–50.

Arthur, W. B. (1989). 'Competing Technologies, Increasing Returns, and Lock-in by Historical Small Events', *Economic Journal*, 99: 116–31.

Association of University Related Research Parks (AURRP) (1997). 'Worldwide Research & Science Park Directory 1998', Reston, VA: BPI Communications.

Association of University Technology Managers (AUTM) (2004). 'The AUTM Licensing Survey, Fiscal Year 2003', Norwalk, CT: AUTM.

Athey, S. and Stern, S. (1998). 'An Empirical Framework for Testing Theories About Complementarity in Organizational Design', NBER Working Paper No. 6600, June 1998.

Audretsch, D. B. (1998). 'Agglomeration and the Location of Innovative Activity', *Oxford Review of Economic Policy*, 14: 18–29.

——— (2000). 'Is University Entrepreneurship Different?', mimeograph, Indiana University.

——— (2001). 'The Role of Small Firms in U.S. Biotechnology Clusters', *Small Business Economics*, 17: 3–15.

_____ and Feldman, M. P. (1996). 'R&D Spillovers and the Geography of Innovation and Production', _American Economic Review_, 86: 630–40.

_____ _____ (1999). 'Innovation in Cities: Science-based Diversity, Specialization, and Localized Competition', _European Economic Review_, 43: 409–29.

_____ and Lehmann, E. E. (2005). 'University Spillovers and New Firm Location', _Research Policy_, 34: 1058–75.

_____ and Stephan, P. E. (1996). 'Company-Scientist Locational Links: the Case of Biotechnology', _American Economic Review_, 86: 641–52.

_____ Link, A. N., and Scott, J. T. (2002). 'Public/Private Technology Partnerships: Evaluating SBIR-Supported Research', _Research Policy_, 31: 145–58.

Autor, D. H., Katz, L. F., and Krueger, A. B. (1998). 'Computing Inequality: Have Computers Changed the Labor Market?', _Quarterly Journal of Economics_, 113: 1169–215.

Bain, J. S. (1959). _Industrial Organization_. Cambridge, MA: Harvard University Press.

Bakouros, Y. L., Mardas, D. C., and Varsakelis, N. C. (2002). 'Science Park, A High Tech Fantasy? An Analysis of the Science Parks of Greece', _Technovation_, 22: 123–8.

Baldwin, W. L. and Scott, J. T. (1987). _Market Structure and Technological Change_. London: Harwood Academic Publishers.

Barney, J. (1991). 'Firm Resources and Sustained Competitive Advantage', _Journal of Management_, 17: 99–120.

Barras, R. (1986). 'Towards a Theory of Innovation in Services', _Research Policy_, 15: 161–73.

Barro, R. and Sala-i-Martin, X. (1998). _Economic Growth_. New York: McGraw-Hill.

Bartel, A. P. and Lichtenberg, F. R. (1987). 'The Comparative Advantage of Educated Workers in Implementing New Technology', _Review of Economics and Statistics_, 69: 1–11.

_____ _____ (1990). 'The Impact of Age of Technology on Employee Wages', _Economics of Innovation and New Technology_, 1: 1–17.

_____ and Sicherman, N. (1999). 'Technological Change and Wages: An Interindustry Analysis', _Journal of Political Economy_, 107: 285–325.

Bartelsman, E. J., Caballero, R. J., and Lyons, R. K. (1994). 'Customer and Supplier-Driven Externalities,' _American Economic Review_, 84: 1075–84.

Battese, G. and Coelli, T. (1995). 'A Model for Technical Inefficiency Effects in a Stochastic Frontier Production Function for Panel Data', _Empirical Economics_, 20: 325–32.

Baudeau, N. (1910, originally 1767). _Premiere Introduction a la Philosophie Economique_, edited by A. Dubois. Paris: P. Geuthner.

Baum, J. A. C., Calabrese, T., and Silverman, B. S. (2000). 'Don't Go It Alone: Alliance Network Composition and Startup Performance in Canadian Biotechnology', _Strategic Management Journal_, 21: 267–94.

Baumol, W. J. (1967). 'Macroeconomics of Unbalanced Growth: The Anatomy of Urban Crisis', _American Economic Review_, 57: 415–26.

_____ (2006). 'Textbook Entrepreneurship: Comment on Johanssen', _Econ Journal Watch_, 3: 133–6.

_____ and Wolff, E. N. (1983). 'Feedback from Productivity Growth to R&D', _Scandinavian Journal of Economics_, 85: 147–57.

Beaudry, C. and Breschi, S. (2003). 'Are Firms in Clusters Really More Innovative?', _Economics of Innovation and New Technology_, 12: 325–42.

Bentham, J. (1787). *Defense of Usury*. London: Payne and Foss.

——(1952). *Jeremy Bentham's Economic Writings*, edited by W. Stark. London: Allen & Unwin.

—— (1962, originally 1838–43). *The Works of Jeremy Bentham*, edited by J. Bowring. New York: Russell & Russell.

Bercovitz, J. and Feldman, M. P. (2004). 'Academic Entrepreneurs: Social Learning and Participation in University Technology Transfer', mimeograph, University of Toronto.

—— —— Feller, I., and Burton, R. (2001). 'Organizational Structure as Determinants of Academic Patent and Licensing Behavior: An Exploratory Study of Duke, Johns Hopkins, and Pennsylvania State Universities', *Journal of Technology Transfer*, 26: 21–35.

Berman, E., Bound, J., and Griliches, Z. (1994). 'Changes in the Demand for Skilled Labor within U.S. Manufacturing Industries: Evidence from the Annual Survey of Manufacturing', *Quarterly Journal of Economics*, 109: 367–97.

—— —— and Machin, S. (1998). 'Implications of Skill Biased Technical Change: International Evidence', *Quarterly Journal of Economics*, 113: 1245–79.

Berndt, E. R., Morrison, C. J., and Rosenblum, L. S. (1992). 'High-Tech Capital Formation and Labor Composition in U.S. Manufacturing Industries', NBER Working Paper No. 4010.

Bernstein, J. I. and Nadiri, M. I. (1989a). 'Rates of Return on Physical and R&D Capital and Structure of the Production Process: Cross Section and Time Series Evidence', in Z. Griliches and B. Raj (eds.), *Advances in Econometrics and Modeling*. London: Kluwer.

—— —— (1989b). 'Research and Development and Intraindustry Spillovers: An Empirical Application of Dynamic Duality', *Review of Economic Studies*, 56: 249–69.

Berry, S. T. (1994). 'Estimating Discrete-Choice Models of Product Differentiation', *Rand Journal of Economics*, 25: 242–62.

Betts, J. (1997). 'The Skill Bias of Technological Change in Canadian Manufacturing Industries', *Review of Economics and Statistics*, 79: 146–50.

Bharadwaj, A. S., Bharadwaj, S. G., and Konsynski, B. R. (1999). 'Information Technology Effects on Firm Performance as Measured by Tobin's q', *Management Science*, 45: 1008–24.

Binswanger, H. P. (1974). 'The Measurement of Technical Change Biases with Many Factors of Production', *American Economic Review*, 64: 964–76.

—— and Ruttan, V. W. (1978). *Induced Innovation: Technology, Institutions and Development*. Baltimore, MD: Johns Hopkins University Press.

Blumenthal, D., Campbell, E. G., Anderson, M., Causino, N., and Louis, K. S. (1997). 'Withholding Research Results in Academic Life Science: Evidence From a National Survey of Faculty', *Journal of the American Medical Association*, 277: 1224–8.

Blundell, R., Griffith, R., and van Reenen, J. (1995). 'Dynamic Count Data Models of Technological Innovation', *Economic Journal*, 105: 333–44.

Bozeman, B. and Boardman, C. (2004). 'Research and Technology Collaboration and Linkages: The Case of the National Nanotechnology Initiative', Report to the Council of Science and Technology Advisors, Study of Federal Science and Technology Linkages, Ottawa, Canada.

—— and Link, A. N. (1983). *Investments in Technology: Corporate Strategies and Public Policy Alternatives*. New York: Praeger.

—— —— and Zardkoohi, A. (1986). 'An Economic Analysis of R&D Joint Ventures', *Managerial and Decision Economics*, 7: 263–6.

—— Harden, J., and Link, A. N. (2006). 'Barriers to the Diffusion of Nanotechnology', mimeograph.

Branstetter, L. and Sakakibara, M. (1998). 'Japanese Research Consortia: A Microeconometric Analysis of Industrial Policy', *Journal of Industrial Economics*, 46: 207–35.

Bray, M. J. and Lee, J. N. (2000). 'University Reviews from Technology Transfer: Licensing Fees vs. Equity Positions', *Journal of Business Venturing*, 15: 385–92.

Breschi, S. and Lissoin, F. (2001). 'Knowledge Spillovers and Local Innovation Systems: A Critical Survey', *Industrial and Corporate Change*, 10: 975–1005.

Bresnahan, T. F. and Trajtenberg, M. (1995). 'General Purpose Technologies', *Journal of Econometrics*, 65: 83–108.

——Brynjolfsson, E., and Hitt, L. M. (2001). 'Information Technology, Workplace Organization, and the Demand for Skilled Labor: Firm Level Evidence', *Quarterly Journal of Economics*, 117: 339–76.

——————(2002). 'Information Technology, Workplace Organization, and the Demand for Skilled Labor: Firm Level Evidence', *Quarterly Journal of Economics*, 117: 339–76.

Brod, A. C. and Shivakumar, R. (1997). 'R&D Cooperation and the Joint Explosion of R&D', *Canadian Journal of Economics*, 30: 673–84.

Brouwer, M. (2005). 'Entrepreneurship and University Licensing', *Journal of Technology Transfer*, 30: 263–70.

Brynjolfsson, E. and Hitt, L. M. (1996). 'Paradox Lost: Firm Level Evidence and Returns on Information Systems Spending', *Management Science*, 42: 541–58.

Bush, V. (1945). *Science—the Endless Frontier*. Washington, DC: U.S. Government Printing Office.

Caballero, R. J. and Jaffe, A. B. (1993). 'How High Are the Giants' Shoulders: An Empirical Assessment of Knowledge Spillovers and Creative Destruction in a Model of Economic Growth', in O. J. Blanchard and S. Fischer (eds.), *NBER Macroeconomic Annual 1993*. Cambridge: MIT Press.

——and Lyons, R. K. (1990). 'Internal versus External Economies in U.S. Manufacturing', *European Economic Review*, 34: 805–26.

————(1992). 'External Effects in U.S. Procyclical Productivity', *Journal of Monetary Economics*, 29: 209–25.

Cain, L. P. and Patterson, D. G. (1981). 'Factor Biases and Technical Change in Manufacturing: The American System, 1850–1919', *Journal of Economic History*, 41: 341–60.

Caloghirou, Y., Tsakanikas, A., and Vonortas, N. S. (2001). 'University–Industry Cooperation in the Context of the European Framework Programmes', *Journal of Technology Transfer*, 26: 153–61.

Campbell, A. F. (2005). 'The Evolving Concept of Value add in University Commercialisation', *Journal of Commercial Biotechnology*, 11: 337–45.

Cantillon, R. (1931, originally 1755). *Essai Sur la Nature du Commerce en General*, edited and translated by H. Higgs. London: Macmillan.

Carayannis, E. G., Alexander, J., and Geraghty, J. (2001). 'Service Sector Productivity: B2B Electronic Commerce as a Strategic Driver', *Journal of Technology Transfer*, 26: 337–50.

Carlin, E. A. (1956). 'Schumpeter's Constructed Type—The Entrepreneur', *Kyklos*, 9: 27–43.

Carlsson, B. and Fridh, A. (2002). 'Technology Transfer in United States Universities: A Survey and Statistical Analysis', *Journal of Evolutionary Economics*, 12: 199–232.

Castells, M. and Hall, P. (1994). *Technopoles of the World*. London: Oxford University Press.

Chan, S. H., Martin, J. D., and Kensinger, J. W. (1990). 'Corporate Research and Development Expenditures and Share Value?', *Journal of Financial Economics*, 26: 255–76.

——— Kensinger, J. W., Keown, A., and Martin, J. D. (1997). 'Do Strategic Alliances Create Value?', *Journal of Financial Economics*, 46: 199–222.

Chapple, W., Lockett, A., Siegel, D. S., and Wright, M. (2005). 'Assessing the Relative Performance of University Technology Transfer Offices in the U.K.: Parametric and Non-Parametric Evidence', *Research Policy*, 34: 369–84.

Charles River Associates (1981). 'Productivity Impacts of NBS R&D: A Case Study of the NBS Semiconductor Technology Program', Program Office report, Gaithersburg, MD: National Bureau of Standards.

Chen, A. H. and Siems, T. F. (2001). 'B2B eMarketplace Announcement and Shareholder Wealth', *Economic and Financial Review*, 22: 1–5.

Chennells, L. and van Reenen, J. (1995). 'Wages and Technology in British Plants: Do Workers Get a Fair Share of the Plunder?', paper presented at the National Academy of Sciences Conference on Science, Technology, and Economic Growth, May 1995.

Choi, C. (2003). 'Analysis: Nano Bill Not Just a Grand Gesture; It Promises Real Results', *Small Times Media*, (http://www.smalltimes.com/document_display.cfm?document_id=7049).

Chordà, I. M. (1996). 'Towards the Maturity State: An Insight into the Performance of French Technopoles', *Technovation*, 16: 143–52.

Clark, K. B. and Griliches, Z. (1984). 'Productivity Growth and R&D at the Business Level: Results from the PIMS Data Base', in Z. Griliches (ed.), *R&D, Patents, and Productivity*. Chicago, IL: University of Chicago Press.

Clarke, B. R. (1998). *Creating Entrepreneurial Universities; Organizational Pathways of Transformation*. New York: IAU Press.

Clarysse, B., Wright, M., Lockett, A., van de Elde, E., and Vohora, A. (2005). 'Spinning Out New Ventures: A Typology of Incubation Strategies From European Research Institutions', *Journal of Business Venturing*, 20: 183–216.

Clemons, E. K. and Hitt L. M. (2001). 'Financial Services: Transparency, Differential Pricing, and Disintermediation', in R. Litan and A. Rivlin (eds.), *The Economic Payoff from the Internet Revolution*. Washington: The Brookings Institution, 87–128.

Cockburn, I. and Henderson, R. (1998). 'Absorptive Capacity, Coauthoring Behavior, and the Organization of Research in Drug Discovery', *Journal of Industrial Economics*, 46: 157–82.

——— ——— and Stern, S. (2000). 'Untangling the Origins of Competitive Advantage', *Strategic Management Journal*, 21: 1123–45.

Coe, D. T. and Helpman, E. (1993). 'International R&D Spillovers', *European Economic Review*, 39: 859–87.

Cohen, W. M. and Leventhal, D. A. (1989). 'Innovation and Learning: The Two Faces of R&D', *Economic Journal*, 99: 569–96.

——— Nelson, R. R., and Walsh, J. P. (2002). 'Who Is Selling the Ivory Tower? Sources of Growth in University Licensing', *Management Science*, 48: 90–104.

Cooke, P. (2001). 'Biotechnology Clusters in the U.K.: Lessons from Localization in the Commercialization of Science', *Small Business Economics*, 17: 43–59.

Combs, K. (1993). 'The Role of Information Sharing in Cooperative Research and Development', *International Journal of Industrial Organization*, 11: 535–51.

Coursey, B. and Link, A. N. (1998). 'Evaluating Technology-Based Public Institutions: The Case of Radiopharmaceutical Standards Research at the National Institute of Standards and Technology', *Research Evaluation*, 7: 147–58.

Crepon, B., Duguet, E., and Mairesse, J. (1998). 'Research, Innovation, and Productivity: An Econometric Analysis at the Firm Level', *Economics of Innovation and New Technology*, 2: 115–58.

Crow, M. and Bozeman, B. (1998). *Limited by Design: R&D Laboratories in the U.S. National Innovation System*. New York: Columbia University Press.

D'Aspremont, C. and Jacquemin, A. (1988). 'Cooperative and Non-Cooperative R&D in Duopoly with Spillovers', *American Economic Review*, 78: 1133–7.

Danilov, V. J. (1971). 'The Research Park Shake-Out', *Industrial Research*, 13: 1–4.

Danzon, P. M. and Furukawa, M. F. (2001). 'Health Care: Competition and Productivity', in R. Litan and A. Rivlin (eds.), *The Economic Payoff from the Internet Revolution*. Washington: The Brookings Institution, 189–234.

David, P. A. (1985). 'Clio and the Economics of QWERTY', *American Economic Review*, 75: 332–7.

—— (1990). 'The Dynamo and the Computer: An Historical Perspective on the Modern Productivity Paradox', *American Economic Review*, 80: 355–61.

—— Hall, B. H., and Toole, A. (2000). 'Is Public R&D a Complement or a Substitute for Private R&D: A Review of the Literature', *Research Policy*, 29: 497–529.

Davis, S. J. and Haltiwanger, J. (1991). 'Wage Dispersion Between and Within U.S. Manufacturing Plants, 1963–1986', *Brookings Papers on Economic Activity: Microeconomics*, 1: 115–200.

Debackere, K. and Veugelers, R. (2005). 'The Role of Academic Technology Transfer Organizations in Improving Industry Science Links', *Research Policy*, 34: 321–42.

DeBondt, R. and Veugelers, R. (1991). 'Strategic Investment with Spillovers', *European Journal of Political Economy*, 7: 345–66.

—— Slaets, P., and Cassiman, B. (1992). 'The Degree of Spillovers and the Number of Rivals for Maximum Effective R&D', *International Journal of Industrial Organization*, 10: 35–54.

DeGroof, J. J. and Roberts, E. B. (2004). 'Overcoming Weak Entrepreneurial Infrastructure for Academic Spin-Off Ventures', *Journal of Technology Transfer*, 29: 327–57.

DeLong, J. B. and Summers, L. H. (1991). 'Equipment Investment and Economic Growth', *Quarterly Journal of Economics*, 102: 445–502.

—— —— (1992). 'Equipment Investment and Economic Growth: How Robust Is the Nexus?', *Brookings Papers on Economic Activity* (Fall): 157–99.

Demsetz, H. (1973). 'Industry Structure, Market Rivalry, and Public Policy', *Journal of Law and Economics*, 16: 1–9.

DiGregorio, D. and Shane, S. (2003). 'Why Do Some Universities Generate More Start-ups than Others?', *Research Policy*, 32: 209–27.

DiNardo, J. E. and Pischke, J. S. (1997). 'The Returns to Computer Use Revisited: Have Pencils Changed the Wage Structure Too?', *Quarterly Journal of Economics*, 112: 291–303.

Dixit, A. K. and Pindyck, R. S. (1995). 'The Options Approach to Capital Investment', *Harvard Business Review*, 73: 105–15.

Domar, E. D. (1947). 'Expansion and Employment', *American Economic Review*, 37: 43–55.

—— (1961). 'On Measurement of Technological Change', *Economic Journal*, 71: 709–29.

Doms, M., Dunne, T., and Troske, K. R. (1997). 'Workers, Wages and Technology', *Quarterly Journal of Economics*, 112: 253–90.

Dos Santos, B. L., Peffers, K., and Mauer, C. (1993). 'The Impact of Information Technology Investment Announcements on the Market Value of Firm', *Information Systems Research*, 4: 1–23.

Dunne, T. and Schmitz, J. A. (1995). 'Wages, Employer Size–Wage Premia and Employment Structure: Their Relationship to Advanced Technology Usage in U.S. Manufacturing Establishments', *Economica*, 62: 89–107.

——— Haltiwanger, J., and Troske, K. R. (1996). 'Technology and Jobs: Secular Change and Cyclical Dynamics', NBER Working Paper No. 5656.

——— Foster, L., Haltiwanger, J., and Troske, K. R. (2000). 'Wages and Productivity Dispersion in U.S. Manufacturing: The Role of Computer Investment', NBER Working Paper No. 7465, January.

Eisenhardt, K. M. and Martin, J. A. (2000). 'Dynamic Capabilities: What Are They?', *Strategic Management Journal*, 11: 1105–21.

Ensley, M. D. and Hmieleski, K. M. (2005). 'A Comparative Study of New Venture Top Management Team Composition, Dynamics and Performance Between University-Based and Independent Start-ups', *Research Policy*, 34: 1091–105.

Entorf, H. and Kramarz, F. (1995). 'The Impact of New Technologies on Wages and Skills: Lessons from Matching Data on Employees and on Their Firms', paper presented at the National Academy of Sciences Conference on Science, Technology, and Economic Growth, May 1995.

Fabricant, S. (1954). *Economic Progress and Economic Change*. New York: National Bureau of Economic Research.

Feldman, M. P., Feller, I., Bercovitz, J., and Burton, R. (2002). 'Equity and the Technology Transfer Strategies of American Research Universities', *Management Science*, 48: 105–21.

Ferguson, R. and Olofsson, C. (2004). 'Science Parks and the Development of NTBFs: Location, Survival and Growth', *Journal of Technology Transfer*, 29: 5–17.

Fine, C. H. and Raff, D. (2001). 'Internet-Driven Innovation and Economic Performance in the American Automobile Industry', in R. Litan and A. Rivlin (eds.), *The Economic Payoff from the Internet Revolution*. Washington: The Brookings Institution, 62–86.

Fountain, J. E. and Osorio-Urzua, C. A. (2001). 'Public Sector: Early Stage of a Deep Transformation', in R. Litan and A. Rivlin (eds.), *The Economic Payoff from the Internet Revolution*. Washington: The Brookings Institution, 235–68.

Franklin, S., Wright, M., and Lockett, A. (2001). 'Academic and Surrogate Entrepreneurs in University Spin-out Companies', *Journal of Technology Transfer*, 26: 127–41.

Friedman, J. and Silberman, J. (2003). 'University Technology Transfer: Do Incentives, Management, and Location Matter?', *Journal of Technology Transfer*, 28: 81–5.

Fukugawa, N. (2006). 'Science Parks in Japan and Their Value-Added Contributions to New Technology-based Firms', *International Journal of Industrial Organization*, 24: 381–400.

Gallaher, M. P., Link, A. N., and Petrusa, J. E. (2006). *Innovation in the U.S. Service Sector*. London: Routledge.

Gallouj, F. and Weinstein, O. (1997). 'Innovation in Services', *Research Policy*, 26: 537–56.

George, G., Zahra, S. A., and Wood, D. R. (2002). 'The Effects of Business–University Alliances on Innovative Output and Financial Performance: A Study of Publicly-Traded Biotechnology Firms', *Journal of Business Venturing*, 17: 577–609.

Gera, S., Wu, W., and Lee, F. (1999). 'Information Technology and Labour Productivity Growth: An Empirical Analysis for Canada and the United States', *Canadian Journal of Economics*, 32: 384–407.

Gibb, M. J. (1985). *Science Parks and Innovation Centres: Their Economic and Social Impact.* Amsterdam: Elsevier.

Gilbert, R. J. and Newberry, D. M. G. (1982). 'Preemptive Patenting and the Persistence of Monopoly', *American Economic Review*, 72: 514–26.

——— ——— (1984). 'Uncertain Innovation and the Persistence of Monopoly: Comment', *American Economic Review*, 74: 238–42.

Goldfarb, B. and Henrekson, M. (2003). 'Bottom-Up vs. Top-Down Towards the Commercialization of University Intellectual Property', *Research Policy*, 32: 639–58.

Gomez-Casseres, B. (1996). *The Alliance Revolution: The New Shape of Business Rivalry.* Cambridge, MA: Harvard University Press.

Gompers, P. and Lerner, J. (1999). *The Venture Capital Cycle.* Cambridge, MA: MIT Press.

Gong, B. and Sickles, R. (1993). 'Finite Sample Evidence on Performance of Stochastic Frontiers using Panel Data', *Journal of Econometrics*, 51: 259–84.

Goolsbee, A. (2001). 'Higher Education: Promises for Future Delivery', in R. Litan and A. Rivlin (eds.), *The Economic Payoff from the Internet Revolution.* Washington: The Brookings Institution, 269–84.

Grayson, L. (1993). *Science Parks: An Experiment in High Technology Transfer.* London: The British Library Board.

Gray, D. O., Lindblad, M., and Rudolph, J. (2001). 'University-Based Industrial Research Consortia: A Multivariate Analysis of Member Retention', *Journal of Technology Transfer*, 26: 247–54.

Greenan, N. and Mairesse, J. (1996). 'Computers and Productivity in France: Some Evidence', NBER Working Paper No. 5836.

Greenwood, J., Hercovitz, Z., and Krusell, P. (1997). 'Long Run Implications of Investment-Specific Technological Change', *American Economic Review*, 87: 342–62.

Grossman, G. and Helpman, E. (1991a). *Innovation and Growth in the Global Economy.* Cambridge, MA: MIT Press.

——— ——— (1991b). 'Quality Ladders in the Theory of Economic Growth', *Review of Economic Studies*, 58: 43–61.

Griliches, Z. (1969). 'Capital-Skill Complementarity', *Review of Economics and Statistics*, 51: 465–8.

——— (1970). 'Notes on the Role of Education in Production Functions and Growth Accounting', in *Education and Income*, Vol. 35, NBER Studies in Income and Wealth, edited by Lee Hansen. New York: Columbia University Press.

——— (1980a). 'R&D and the Productivity Slowdown', *American Economic Review*, 70: 343–8.

——— (1980b). 'Returns to Research and Development Expenditures in the Private Sector,' in J. W. Kendrick and B. N. Vaccara (eds.), *New Developments in Productivity Measurement and Analysis.* Chicago, IL: University of Chicago Press.

——— (1986). 'Productivity Growth, R&D, and Basic Research at the Firm Level in the 1970s', *American Economic Review*, 76: 141–54.

Griliches, Z. (1992). *Output Measurement in the Service Sector*. Chicago: University of Chicago Press.

—— (1994). 'Productivity, R&D and the Data Constraint', *American Economic Review*, 84: 1–23.

—— (1996). 'The Discovery of the Residual: A Historical Note', *Journal of Economic Literature*, 34: 1324–30.

—— (1998). *R&D and Productivity: The Econometric Evidence*. Chicago, IL: University of Chicago Press.

—— and Lichtenberg, F. R. (1984). 'R&D and Productivity Growth at the Industry Level: Is There Still a Relationship?', in Z. Griliches (ed.), *R&D, Patents, and Productivity*. Chicago, IL: University of Chicago Press.

—— and Mairesse J. (1983). 'Comparing Productivity Growth: An Exploration of French and U.S. Industrial and Firm Data', *European Economic Review*, 21: 89–119.

—— —— (1984). 'Productivity and R&D at the Firm Level', in Z. Griliches (ed.), *R&D, Patents, and Productivity*. Chicago, IL: University of Chicago Press.

—— —— (1986). 'R&D and Productivity Growth: Comparing Japanese and U.S. Manufacturing Firms', NBER Working Paper No. 1778.

—— and Regev, H. (1995). 'Firm Productivity in Israeli Industry 1979–1988', *Journal of Econometrics*, 65: 175–203.

Guy, I. (1996a). 'A Look at Aston Science Park', *Technovation*, 16: 217–18.

—— (1996b). 'New Ventures on an Ancient Campus', *Technovation*, 16: 269–70.

Hagedoorn, J. and Schakenraad, J. (1994). 'The Effect of Strategic Technology Alliances on Company Performance', *Strategic Management Journal*, 15: 291–309.

—— Link, A. N., and Vonortas, N. S. (2000). 'Research Partnerships', *Research Policy*, 29: 567–86.

Halevy, E. (1955). *The Growth of Philosophic Radicalism*, translated by M. Morris. Boston, MA: Beacon Press.

Hall, B. H. and Mairesse, J. (1995). 'Exploring the Relationship Between R&D and Productivity in French Manufacturing Firms', *Journal of Econometrics*, 65: 175–203.

—— and van Reenen, J. (2000). 'How Effective are Fiscal Incentives for R&D? A Review of the Evidence', *Research Policy*, 29: 449–69.

—— Link, A. N., and Scott, J. T. (2001). 'Barriers Inhibiting Industry from Partnering with Universities: Evidence from the Advanced Technology Program', *Journal of Technology Transfer*, 26: 87–98.

Hall, R. E. (1990). 'Invariance Properties of Solow's Productivity Residual', in Peter Diamond (ed.), *Growth/Productivity/Employment: Essays to Celebrate Bob Solow's Birthday*. Cambridge, MA: MIT Press.

—— and Jones, C. I. (1996). 'The Productivity of Nations', NBER Working Paper No. 5812.

Hamel, G. P. and Pralahad, C. K. (1989). 'Strategic Intent', *Harvard Business Review*, 67: 63–76.

Harrigan, K. R. (1985). *Strategy for Joint Ventures*. Lexington, MA: Lexington Books.

Harrod, R. F. (1946). 'An Essay in Dynamic Theory', *Economic Journal*, 49: 14–33.

Haskel, J. (1999). 'Small Firms, Contracting-Out, Computers and Wage Inequality: Evidence from U.K. Manufacturing', *Economica*, 66: 1–21.

Hébert, R. F. and Link, A. N. (1988). *The Entrepreneur: Mainstream Views and Radical Critiques*, 2nd edn. New York: Praeger.

—— —— (1989). 'In Search of the Meaning of Entrepreneurship', *Small Business Economics*, 1: 39–49.

——— ——— (2006). 'The Entrepreneur as Innovator', *Journal of Technology Transfer*, 31: 589–97.

——— ——— (2007). 'Historical Perspectives on the Entrepreneur', *Foundations and Trends in Entrepreneurship*, 4: 1–164.

Helpman, E. (1998). *General Purpose Technologies and Economic Growth*. Cambridge, MA: MIT Press.

Henderson, J. V. (1986). 'The Efficiency of Resource Usage and City Size', *Journal of Urban Economics*, 19: 47–70.

Henderson, R. and Cockburn, I. (1994). 'Measuring Competence? Exploring Firm Effects in Pharmaceutical Research', *Strategic Management Journal*, 15: 63–84.

Hercowitz, Z. (1998). 'The "Embodiment" Controversy: A Review Essay', *Journal of Monetary Economics*, 41: 217–24.

Hertzfeld, H. R., Link, A. N., and Vonortas, N. S. (2006). 'Intellectual Property Protection Mechanisms in Research Partnerships', *Research Policy*, 35: 825–38.

Hicks, J. R. (1932). *Theory of Wages*. London: Macmillan.

Hoselitz, B. F. (1960). 'The Early History of Entrepreneurial Theory', in J. J. Spengler and W. R. Allen (eds.), *Essays in Economic Thought: Aristotle to Marshall*. Chicago, IL: Rand McNally.

——— (2000). 'Understanding the New Service Economy', in B. Andersen (ed.), *Knowledge and Innovation in the New Service Economy*. Northampton, MA: Edward Elgar.

——— (2001). 'The Nature of Innovation Services', in *Innovation and Productivity in Services*. Paris: OECD.

Hitt, L. M. and Brynjolfsson, E. (1996). 'Productivity, Business Profitability and Consumer Surplus: Three Different Measures of Information Technology Value', *MIS Quarterly*, 20: 121–42.

Ichniowski, C., Shaw, K., and Prennushi, G. (1997). 'The Effects of Human Resource Management Practices on Productivity: A Study of Steel Finishing Lines', *American Economic Review*, 87: 291–313.

IDC Research (2002). *Internet Usage and Commerce in Western Europe: 2001–2006* (summary available at www.idc.com/get-doc.jhtml?containerId=fr2002_04_19_115126).

Im, K. S., Dow, K. E., and Grover, V. (2001). 'Research Report: A Reexamination of IT Investment and the Market Value of Firm—An Event Study Methodology', *Information Systems Research*, 12: 103–17.

Jaffe, A. B. (1998). 'The Importance of "Spillovers" in the Policy Mission of the Advanced Technology Program', *Journal of Technology Transfer*, 23: 11–19.

——— Trajtenberg, M., and Henderson, R. (1993). 'Geographic Localization of Knowledge Spillovers as Evidenced by Patent Citations', *Quarterly Journal of Economics*, 108: 577–98.

——— Fogarty, M. S., and Banks, B. A. (1998). 'Evidence from Patents and Patent Citations on the Impact of NASA and Other Federal Labs on Commercial Innovation', *Journal of Industrial Economics*, 46: 183–206.

Jankowski, J. E. (2001). 'Measurement and Growth of R&D within the Service Economy', *Journal of Technology Transfer*, 26: 323–36.

Janney, J. J. and Folta, T. B. (2003). 'Signaling Through Private Equity Placements and Its Impact on the Valuation of Biotechnology Firms', *Journal of Business Venturing*, 18: 361–80.

Jarillo, J. (1988). 'On Strategic Networks', *Strategic Management Journal*, 19: 31–41.

Jensen, R. and Thursby, M. C. (2001). 'Proofs and Prototypes for Sale: The Licensing of University Inventions', *American Economic Review*, 91: 240–59.

—— Thursby, J. G., and Thursby, M. C. (2003). 'The Disclosure and Licensing of University Inventions: The Best We Can Do With the S**t We Get to Work With', *International Journal of Industrial Organization*, 21: 1271–300.

Jones, C. I. (1995). 'R&D-Based Models of Economic Growth', *Journal of Political Economy*, 103: 759–84.

Jorgenson, D. W. (1996). 'Technology in Growth Theory', in J. C. Fuhrer and J. S. Little (eds.), *Technology and Growth*. Boston, MA: Federal Reserve Bank of Boston.

—— and Stiroh, K. (1995). 'Computers and Growth', *Economics of Innovation and New Technology*, 3: 295–316.

—— —— (2000). 'Raising the Speed Limit: U.S. Economic Growth in the Information Age', *Brookings Papers on Economics Activity*, 1: 125–211.

—— Ho, M. S., and Stiroh, K. J. (2002). 'Lessons for Europe from the U.S. Growth Resurgence', Paper presented at the Munich Economic Summit on 'Europe After Enlargement', June 7–8, 2002.

Jovanovic, B. and Rousseau, P. L. (2005). 'General Purpose Technologies', NBER Working Paper No. 11093.

Juhn, C., Murphy, K. M., and Pierce, B. (1993). 'Wage Inequality and the Rise in Returns to Skill', *Journal of Political Economy*, 101: 410–42.

Kamien, M. I. and Schwartz, N. L. (1969). 'Induced Factor Augmenting Technical Progress from a Microeconomic Viewpoint', *Econometrica*, 37: 668–84.

—— —— (1971). 'Expenditure Patterns for Risky R and D Projects', *Journal of Applied Probability*, 8: 60–73.

—— and Zang, I. (1993). 'Competing Research Joint Ventures', *Journal of Economics and Management Strategy*, 2: 24–40.

—— Mueller, E., and Zang, I. (1992). 'Research Joint Ventures and R&D', *American Economic Review*, 82: 1293–306.

Kanbur, S. M. (1980). 'A Note on Risk-Taking, Entrepreneurship, and Schumpeter', *History of Political Economy*, 12: 489–98.

Katz, L. F. and Murphy, K. (1992). 'Changes in Relative Wages, 1963–1987: Supply and Demand Factors', *Quarterly Journal of Economics*, 107: 35–78.

Katz, M. L. (1986). 'An Analysis of Cooperative Research and Development', *Rand Journal of Economics*, 17: 527–43.

Kendrick, J. W. (1956). 'Productivity Trends: Capital and Labor', *The Review of Economics and Statistics*, 38: 248–57.

Kirzner, I. M. (1979). *Perception, Opportunity, and Profit: Studies in the Theory of Entrepreneurship*. Chicago, IL: University of Chicago Press.

—— (1985). *Discovery and the Capitalist Process*. Chicago, IL: University of Chicago Press.

Klette, T. J. and Griliches, Z. (1997). 'Empirical Patterns and Firm Growth and R&D Investment: A Quality Ladder Model Interpretation', NBER Working Paper No. 5945.

—— and Moen, J. (1998). 'R&D Investment Responses to R&D Subsidies: A Theoretical Analysis and a Microeconometric Study', paper presented at the 1998 NBER Summer Institute.

————— (1999). 'From Growth Theory to Technology Policy—Coordination Problems in Theory and Practice', *Nordic Journal of Political Economy*, 25: 53–74.

Kogut, B. (1988). 'Joint Ventures: Theoretical and Empirical Perspectives', *Strategic Management Journal*, 9: 319–32.

Krueger, A. B. (1993). 'How Computers have Changed the Wage Structure: Evidence from Microdata', *Quarterly Journal of Economics*, 108: 33–61.

Krugman, P. (1991). *Geography and Trade*. Cambridge: MIT Press.

Lach, S. and Schankerman, M. (2004). 'Royalty Sharing and Technology Licensing in Universities', *Journal of the European Economic Association*, 2: 252–64.

Lal, K. (2002). 'E-business and Export Behaviour', WIDER Discussion Paper, 2002/68.

Lehman, D. (2003). 'Biotechnology: Industry of the Future', *Plants Sites & Parks*, March: 1–5.

Lehr, W. and Lichtenberg, F. R. (1999). 'Information and Its Impact on Productivity: Firm-Level Evidence from Government and Private Data Sources, 1977–1993', *Canadian Journal of Economics*, 32: 335–62.

Lehrer, M. and Asakawa, K. (2004). 'Rethinking the Public Sector: Idiosyncrasies of Biotechnology Commercialization as Motors of National R&D Reform in Germany and Japan', *Research Policy*, 33: 921–38.

Leitch, C. M. and Harrison, R. T. (2005). 'Maximising the Potential of University Spin-Outs: The Development of Second-Order Commercialisation Activities', *R&D Management*, 35: 257–72.

Lerner, J. (1999). 'The Government as Venture Capitalist: The Long-Run Impact of the SBIR Program', *Journal of Business*, 72: 285–318.

————— and Merges, R. P. (1998). 'The Control of Technology Alliances: An Empirical Analysis of the Biotechnology Industry', *Journal of Industrial Economics*, 46: 125–56.

Levy, F. and Murnane, R. J. (1997). *The New Basic Skills*. Cambridge, MA: MIT Press.

Leyden, D. P. and Link, A. N. (1991*a*). 'Governmental R&D and Industrial Innovative Activity', *Applied Economics*, 23: 1673–81.

————— ————— (1991*b*). 'Why Are Government and Private R&D Complements?', *Applied Economics*, 23: 1673–81.

————— ————— (1999). 'Federal Laboratories and Research Partners', *International Journal of Industrial Organization*, 17: 572–92.

————— ————— and Bozeman, B. (1989). 'The Effects of Governmental Financing on Firms' R&D Activities: A Theoretical and Empirical Investigation', *Technovation*, 9: 561–75.

————— ————— and Siegel, D. S. (2007). 'A Theoretical and Empirical Analysis of the Decision to Locate on a University Research Park', *IEEE Transactions on Engineering Management*, forthcoming.

Libaers, D., Meyer, M., and Guena, A. (2006). 'The Role of University Spinout Companies in an Emerging Technology: The Case of Nanotechnology', *Journal of Technology Transfer*, 31: 443–50.

Licht, G. and Moch, D. (1999). 'Innovation and Information Technology in Services', *Canadian Journal of Economics*, 32: 363–83.

Lichtenberg, F. R. (1984). 'The Relationship between Federal Contract and Company R&D', *American Economic Review Papers and Proceedings*, 74: 73–8.

————— (1987). 'The Effect of Government Funding on Private Industrial Research and Development: A Re-assessment', *Journal of Industrial Economics*, 36: 97–104.

Lichtenberg, F. R. (1988). 'The Private R&D Investment Response to Federal Design and Technical Competitions', *American Economic Review*, 78: 550–9.

——— (1995). 'The Output Contributions of Computer Equipment and Personnel: A Firm-Level Analysis', *Economics of Innovation and New Technology*, 3: 201–17.

——— and Siegel, D. S. (1991). 'The Impact of R&D Investment on Productivity—New Evidence Using Linked R&D-LRD Data', *Economic Inquiry*, 29: 203–28.

Liebeskind, J. P., Oliver, A. L., Zucker, L. G., and Brewer, M. B. (1996). 'Social Networks, Learning, and Flexibility: Sourcing Scientific Knowledge in New Biotechnology Firms', *Organization Science*, 7: 428–43.

Lindelof, P. and Lofsten, H. (2003). 'Science Park Location and New Technology-Based Firms in Sweden: Implications for Strategy and Performance', *Small Business Economics*, 20: 245–58.

——— ——— (2004). 'Proximity as a Resource Base for Competitive Advantage: University–Industry Links for Technology Transfer', *Journal of Technology Transfer*, 29: 311–26.

Link, A. N. (1978). 'Rates of Induced Technology from Investments in Research and Development', *Southern Economic Journal*, 45: 370–9.

——— (1980). 'Firm Size and Efficient Entrepreneurial Activity: A Reformulation of the Schumpeter Hypothesis', *Journal of Political Economy*, 88: 771–82.

——— (1981a). *Research and Development Activity in U.S. Manufacturing*. New York: Praeger.

——— (1981b). 'Basic Research and Productivity Increase in Manufacturing: Some Additional Evidence', *American Economic Review*, 71: 1111–12.

——— (1982a). 'A Disaggregated Analysis of Industrial R&D: Product versus Process Innovation', in D. Sahal (ed.), *The Transfer and Utilization of Technical Knowledge*. Lexington, MA: D.C. Heath.

——— (1982b). 'The Impact of Federal Research and Development Spending on Productivity', *IEEE Transactions on Engineering Management*, 29: 166–9.

——— (1982c). 'Productivity Growth, Environmental Regulations and the Composition of R&D', *Bell Journal of Economics*, 13: 548–54.

——— (1983). 'Inter-Firm Technology Flows and Productivity Growth', *Economics Letters*, 11: 179–84.

——— (1987). *Technological Change and Productivity Growth*. Char: Harwood.

——— (1995a). *A Generosity of Spirit: The Early History of the Research Triangle Park*. Research Triangle Park, NC: University of North Carolina Press for the Research Triangle Park Foundation.

——— (1995b). 'The Use of Literature-Based Innovation Output Indicators for Research Evaluation', *Small Business Economics*, 7: 451–5.

——— (1996a). *Evaluating Public Sector Research and Development*. New York: Praeger.

——— (1996b). 'On the Classification of Industrial R&D', *Research Policy*, 25: 397–401.

——— (1997). 'Economic Evaluation of Radiopharmaceutical Research at NIST', NIST Planning Report No. 97–2.

——— (1998a). 'Case Study of R&D Efficiency in ATP Joint Ventures', *Journal of Technology Transfer*, 23: 43–51.

——— (1998b). 'The U.S. Display Consortium: An Analysis of a Public/Private Partnership', *Industry and Innovation*, 5: 35–50.

_____(1999). 'Public/Private Partnerships in the United States', *Industry and Innovation*, 6: 191–217.

_____(2001). 'Enhanced R&D Efficiency in an ATP-funded Joint Venture', in C. Wessner (ed.), *The Advanced Technology Program: Assessing Outcomes*. Washington, DC: National Academy Press.

_____(2002). *From Seed to Harvest: The History of the Growth of the Research Triangle Park*. Research Triangle Park, NC: University of North Carolina Press for the Research Triangle Park Foundation.

_____(2005). 'Economic Factors Related to the Development and Commercialization of Biotechnologies', Technical Report No. 05-0204, University of Kansas Center for Applied Economics.

_____(2006). *Public/Private Partnerships: Innovation Strategies and Policy Alternatives*. New York: Springer.

_____and Bauer, L. L. (1989). *Cooperative Research in U.S. Manufacturing*. Lexington, MA: Lexington Books.

_____and Link, K. R. (2003). 'On the Growth of U.S. Science Parks', *Journal of Technology Transfer*, 28: 81–5.

_____and Rees, J. (1990). 'Firm Size, University-Based Research, and the Returns to R&D', *Small Business Economics*, 2: 25–31.

_____and Scott, J. T. (1998a). *Public Accountability: Evaluating Technology-Based Institutions*. Norwell, MA: Kluwer.

_____ _____(1998b). 'Evaluating Technology-Based Public Institutions: Lessons from the National Institute of Standards and Technology', in G. Papaconstantinou (ed.), *Policy Evaluation in Innovation and Technology*. Paris: OECD.

_____ _____(1998c). 'Assessing the Infrastructural Needs of a Technology-Based Service Sector: A New Approach to Technology Policy Planning', *STI Review*, 22: 171–204.

_____ _____(2001). 'Public/Private Partnerships: Stimulating Competition in a Dynamic Market', *International Journal of Industrial Organization*, 19: 763–94.

_____ _____(2002). 'Explaining Observed Licensing Agreements: Toward a Broader Understanding of Technology Flows', *Economics of Innovation and New Technology*, 11: 221–31.

_____ _____(2003a). 'U.S. Science Parks: The Diffusion of an Innovation and Its Effects on the Academic Mission of Universities', *International Journal of Industrial Organization*, 21: 1323–56.

_____ _____(2003b). 'The Growth of Research Triangle Park', *Small Business Economics*, 20: 167–75.

_____ _____(2005a). 'Opening the Ivory Tower's Door: An Analysis of the Determinants of the Formation of U.S. University Spin-Off Companies', *Research Policy*, 34: 1106–12.

_____ _____(2005b). *Evaluating Public Research Institutions: The U.S. Advanced Technology Program's Intramural Research Initiative*. London: Routledge.

_____ _____(2005c). 'Evaluating Public Sector R&D Programs: The Advanced Technology Program's Investment in Wavelength References for Optical Fiber Communications', *Journal of Technology Transfer*, 30: 241–51.

_____ _____(2005d). 'Universities as Research Partners in U.S. Research Joint Ventures', *Research Policy*, 34: 385–93.

_____ _____(2006a). 'An Economic Evaluation of the Baldrige National Quality Program', *Economics of Innovation and New Technology*, 15: 83–100.

Link, A. N. and Scott, J. T. (2006b). 'U.S. University Research Parks', *Journal of Productivity Analysis*, 25: 43–55.

_____ and Siegel, D. S. (2003). *Technological Change and Economic Performance*. London: Routledge.

_____ _____ (2005). 'Generating Science-Based Growth: An Econometric Analysis of the Impact of Organizational Incentives on University–Industry Technology Transfer', *European Journal of Finance*, 11: 169–82.

_____ Tassey, G., and Zmud, R. B. (1983). 'The Induce versus Purchase Decision: An Empirical Analysis of Industrial R&D', *Decision Sciences*, 14: 46–61.

_____ Teece, D., and Finan, W. F. (1996). 'Estimating the Benefits from Collaboration: The Case of SEMATECH', *Review of Industrial Organization*, 11: 737–51.

Litan, R. and Rivlin, A. (2001). *The Economic Payoff from the Internet Revolution*. Washington, DC: Brookings Institution.

Lockett, A. and Wright, M. (2005). 'Resources, Capabilities, Risk Capital and the Creation of University Spin-Out Companies: Technology Transfer and Universities' Spin-out Strategies', *Research Policy*, 34: 1043–57.

_____ _____ and Franklin, S. (2003). 'Technology Transfer and Universities' Spin-out Strategies', *Small Business Economics*, 20: 185–201.

Loof, H. and Heshmati, A. (2002). 'Knowledge Capital and Performance Heterogeneity: A Firm-Level Innovation Study', *International Journal of Industrial Organization*, 76: 61–85.

Louis, K. S., Blumenthal, D., Gluck, M. E., and Stoto, M. A. (1989). 'Entrepreneurs in Academe: An Exploration of Behaviors Among Life Scientists', *Administrative Science Quarterly*, 34: 110–31.

Lucas, R. E. (1986). 'Adaptive Behavior and Economic Theory', *The Journal of Business*, 59: S401–S426.

_____ (1988). 'On the Mechanics of Economic Development', *Journal of Monetary Economics*, 22: 3–42.

Luger, M. and Goldstein, H. (1991). *Technology in the Garden*. Chapel Hill, NC: University of North Carolina Press.

Lux Research. (http://www.luxresearchinc.com).

Lynch, L. M. and Osterman, P. (1989). 'Technological Innovation and Employment in Telecommunications', *Industrial Relations*, 28: 188–205.

Machin, S. (1996). 'Changes in the Relative Demand for Skills in the U.K. Labour Market', in A. Booth and D. Snower (eds.), *Acquiring Skills*. Cambridge: Cambridge University Press.

Machlup, F. (1980). *Knowledge and Knowledge Production*. Princeton, NJ: Princeton University Press.

Madhavan, R. and Prescott, J. E. (1995). 'Market Value of Joint Ventures: The Effects of Industry Information-Processing Load', *Academy of Management Journal*, 38: 900–15.

Mankiw, G., Romer, D., and Weil, D. N. (1992). 'A Contribution to the Empirics of Economic Growth', *Quarterly Journal of Economics*, 107: 407–37.

Mansfield, E. (1980). 'Basic Research and the Productivity Increase in Manufacturing', *American Economic Review*, 70: 863–73.

Markman, G., Gianiodis, P. T., and Phan, P. (2006). 'An Agency Theoretic Study of the Relationship Between Knowledge Agents and University Technology Transfer Offices', *Rensselaer Polytechnic Working Paper*, Troy, NY.

——— ——— ——— and Balkin, D. (2005*a*). 'Innovation Speed: Transferring University Technology to Market', *Research Policy*, 34: 1058–75.

——— Phan, P., Balkin, D., and Gianiodis, P. T. (2004). 'Entrepreneurship from the Ivory Tower: Do Incentive Systems Matter?', *Journal of Technology Transfer*, 29: 353–64.

——— ——— ——— ——— (2005*b*). 'Entrepreneurship and University-Based Technology Transfer', *Journal of Business Venturing*, 20: 241–63.

Marshall, A. (1920). *Principles of Economics*, 8th edn. London: Macmillan.

Marshall, E. (1985). 'Japan and the Economics of Invention', *Science*, April 12: 157–8.

Martin, S. (1994). 'R&D Joint Ventures and Tacit Product Market Collusion', *European Journal of Political Economy*, 11: 733–41.

——— and Scott, J. T. (2000). 'The Nature of Innovation Market Failure and the Design of Public Support for Private Innovation', *Research Policy*, 29: 437–48.

Mason, E. (1939). 'Price and Production Policies of Large-Scale Enterprise', *American Economic Review*, 29: 61–74.

McAfee, A. (2001). 'Manufacturing: Lowering Boundaries, Improving Productivity', in R. Litan and A. Rivlin (eds.), *The Economic Payoff from the Internet Revolution*. Washington: The Brookings Institution, 29–61.

McGuckin, P., Streitwieser, M., and Doms, M. (1998). 'The Effects of Technology Use on Productivity Growth,' *Economics of Innovation and New Technology*, 7: 1–27.

McGuckin, R. H. and Stiroh, K. J. (1999). 'Computers and Productivity: Are Aggregation Effects Important?', unpublished manuscript, November 1999.

McWilliams, A. and Siegel, D. S. (1997). 'Event Studies in Management Research: Theoretical and Empirical Issues', *Academy of Management Journal*, 40: 626–57.

Medda, G., Piga, C., and Siegel, D. S. (2003). 'On the Relationship between R&D and Productivity: A Treatment Effect Analysis', mimeograph.

Meeusen, W. and van den Broeck, J. (1977). 'Efficiency Estimation from Cobb–Douglas Production Functions with Composed Errors', *International Economic Review*, 18: 435–44.

Merges, R. and Nelson, R. R. (1990). 'On the Complex Economics of Patent Scope,' *Columbia Law Review*, 90: 839–916.

Merchant, H. and Schendel, D. (2000). 'How Do International Joint Ventures Create Shareholder Value?', *Strategic Management Journal*, 21: 723–37.

Meseri, O. and Maital, S. (2001). 'A Survey Analysis of University Technology Transfer in Israel: Evaluation of Projects and Determinants of Success', *Journal of Technology Transfer*, 26: 115–25.

Metcalfe, S. (1995). 'The Economic Foundations of Technology Policy: Equilibrium and Evolutionary Perspectives', in P. Stoneman (ed.), *Handbook of the Economics of Innovation and Technological Change*. Oxford: Blackwell Publishers.

Mills, F. C. (1952). *Productivity and Economic Progress*. National Bureau of Economic Research Occasional Paper 38.

Mincer, J. (1989). 'Human Capital Responses to Technological Change in the Labor Market', NBER Working Paper No. 3581.

Minasian, J. (1969). 'Research and Development, Production Functions, and Rates of Return', *American Economic Review*, 59: 80–5.

Mishel, L. and Bernstein, J. (1994). 'Is the Technology Black Box Empty?', mimeograph.

Monck, C. S. P., Porter, R. B., Quintas, P., Storey, D. J., and Wynarczyk, P. (1988). *Science Parks and the Growth of High Technology Firms*. London: Croom Helm.

Moray, N. and Clarysse, B. (2005). 'Institutional Change and Resource Endowments to Science-based Entrepreneurial Firms', *Research Policy*, 34: 1010–27.

Moroney, J. R. (1972). *The Structure of Production in American Manufacturing*. Chapel Hill, NC: University of North Carolina Press.

Morrison, C. J. (1997). 'Assessing the Productivity of Information Technology Equipment in U.S. Manufacturing Industries', *The Review of Economics and Statistics*, 79(3): 471–81.

—— and Siegel, D. (1997). 'External Capital Factors and Increasing Returns in U.S. Manufacturing', *The Review of Economics and Statistics*, 79: 647–54.

Motta, M. (1992). 'Cooperative R&D and Vertical Product Differentiation', *International Journal of Industrial Organization*, 10: 643–61.

Mowery, D. C. and Simcoe, T. (2002). 'Is the Internet a U.S. Invention? An Economic and Technological History of Computer Networking', *Research Policy*, 31: 1369–87.

—— and Ziedonis, A. A. (2000). 'Numbers, Quality and Entry: How Has the Bayh–Dole Act Affected U.S. University Patenting and Licensing,' in A. Jaffe, J. Lerner, and S. Stern (eds.), *Innovation Policy and the Economy*. Cambridge, MA: MIT Press.

—— Oxley, J. E., and Silverman, B. S. (1998). 'Technolgical Overlap and Interfirm Cooperation for the Resource-Based View of the Firm', *Research Policy*, 27: 507–23.

—— Nelson, R. R., Sampat, B., and Ziedonis, A. A. (2001). 'The Growth of Patenting and Licensing by U.S. Universities: An Assessment of the Effects of the Bayh–Dole Act of 1980', *Research Policy*, 30: 99–119.

Murphy, K. M. and Welch, F. (1992). 'The Structure of Wages', *Quarterly Journal of Economics*, 107: 215–26.

Mustar, P., Renault, M., Colombo, M. G., Piva, E., Fontes, M., Lockett, A., Wright, M., Clarysse, B., and Moray, N. (2006). 'Conceptualising the Heterogeneity of Research-Based Spin-Offs: A Multi-Dimensional Taxonomy', *Research Policy*, 35: 289–303.

Nagarajan, A., Canessa, E., Mitchell, W., and White, C. C. (2001). 'Trucking Industry: Challenges to Keep Pace', in R. Litan and A. Rivlin (eds.), *The Economic Payoff from the Internet Revolution*. Washington: The Brookings Institution.

National Institute of Standards and Technology (NIST) (2005). 'Measuring Service-Sector Research and Development', NIST Planning Report 05-1.

National Nanotechnology Initiative. (http://www.nano.gov).

National Research Council (NRC) (2002). *Small Wonders, Endless Frontiers: A Review of the National Nanotechnology Initiative*. Washington, DC: National Academy Press.

National Science Board (2002). *Science and Engineering Indicators—2002*. Arlington, VA: National Science Foundation.

—— (2006). *Science & Engineering Indicators—2006*. Arlington, VA: National Science Foundation.

Nelson, R. R. (1981). 'Research on Productivity Growth and Productivity Differences: Dead Ends and New Departures', *Journal of Economic Literature*, 19: 1029–64.

—— (1993). *National Innovation Systems: A Comparative Analysis*. Oxford: Oxford University Press.

—— (1997). 'How New Is New Growth Theory?', *Challenge*, 40: 29–58.

_____ (2001). 'Observations on the Post Bayh-Dole Rise of Patenting at American Universities', _Journal of Technology Transfer_, 26: 13–19.

_____ and Phelps, E. S. (1966). 'Investment in Humans, Technological Diffusion, and Economic Growth,' _American Economic Review_, 56: 69–75.

_____ and Winter, S. G. (1982). _An Evolutionary Theory of Economic Change_. Cambridge, MA: Harvard University Press.

Nerkar, A. and Shane, S. (2003). 'When Do Startups that Exploit Academic Knowledge Survive?', _International Journal of Industrial Organization_, 21: 1391–410.

Nicolaou, N. and Birley, S. (2003). 'Social Networks in Organizational Emergence: The University Spinout Phenomenon', _Management Science_, 49: 1702–25.

Nightingale, P. (1998). 'A Cognitive Model of Innovation', _Research Policy_, 27: 689–709.

Nordhaws, W. D. (2002). 'Productivity Growth and the New Economy', _Brooking Papers on Economic Activity 2002_, 2: 211–44.

Odagiri, H. (1983). 'R&D Expenditures, Royalty Payments, and Sales Growth in Japanese Manufacturing Corporations', _Journal of Industrial Economics_, 22: 61–71.

Oliner, S. and Sichel, D. (1994). 'Computers and Output Growth Revisited: How Big is the Puzzle?', _Brookings Papers on Economic Activity: Macroeconomics_, 2: 273–317.

Organisation for Economic Co-operation and Development (2001a). _Innovation and Productivity in Services_. Paris: OECD.

_____ (2001b). _Research and Development Expenditures in Industry 1987–1999_. Paris: OECD.

Oliver, A. L. (2001). 'Strategic Alliances and the Learning Life-Cycle of Biotechnology Firms', _Organization Studies_, 22: 467–89.

_____ (2004). 'Biotechnology Entrepreneurial Scientists and their Collaborations', _Research Policy_, 33: 583–97.

Orsenigo, L. (1989). _The Emergence of Biotechnology: Institutions and Markets in Industrial Innovation_. New York: St. Martin's Press.

_____ (2001). 'The (Failed) Development of a Biotechnology Cluster: The Case of Lombardy', _Small Business Economics_, 17: 77–92.

O'Shea, R., Allen, T., and Chevalier, A. (2005). 'Entrepreneurial Orientation, Technology Transfer, and Spin-Off Performance of U.S. Universities', _Research Policy_, 34: 994–1009.

Owen-Smith, J. and Powell, W. W. (2001). 'To Patent or Not: Faculty Decisions and Institutional Success at Technology Transfer', _Journal of Technology Transfer_, 26: 99–114.

_____ _____ (2003). 'The Expanding Role of University Patenting in the Life Sciences: Assessing the Importance of Experience and Connectivity', _Research Policy_, 32: 1695–711.

Park, K. S. (1996). 'Economic Growth and Multiskilled Workers in Manufacturing', _Journal of Labor Economics_, 12: 254–85.

Parsons, D. J., Gottlieb, C. C., and Denny, M. (1993). 'Productivity and Computers in Canadian Banking', _Journal of Productivity Analysis_, 4: 91–110.

Paugh, J. and Lafrance, J. C. (1997). 'Meeting the Challenge: U.S. Industry Faces the 21st Century, the U.S. Biotechnology Industry', Washington, DC: U.S. Department of Commerce, Office of Technology Policy.

Paul, C. J. M. and Siegel, D. S. (1999). 'Scale Economies and Industry Agglomeration Externalities: A Dynamic Cost Function Approach', _American Economic Review_, 89: 272–90.

Paul, C. J. M. and Siegel, D. S. (2001). 'The Impacts of Technology, Trade, and Outsourcing on Employment and Labor Composition', *Scandinavian Journal of Economics*, 103: 241–64.

Pavitt, K. (1984). 'Sectoral Patterns of Technical Change: Towards a Taxonomy and a Theory', *Research Policy*, 134: 343–73.

Penrose, E. T. (1959). *The Theory of the Growth of the Firm*. New York: John Wiley & Sons.

Perry, M. (1996). 'Network Intermediaries and Their Effectiveness', *International Small Business Journal*, 14: 72–80.

Petit, M. L. and Tolwinski, B. (1996). 'Technology Sharing Cartels and Industrial Structure', *International Journal of Industrial Organization*, 15: 77–101.

Phan, P., Siegel, D. S., and Wright, M. (2005). 'Science Parks and Incubators: Observations, Synthesis and Future Research', *Journal of Business Venturing*, 20: 165–82.

Phillimore, J. (1999). 'Beyond the Linear View of Innovation in Science Park Evaluation: An Analysis of Western Australian Technology Park', *Technovation*, 19: 673–80.

Pilat, D. (2001). 'Innovation and Productivity in Services: State of the Art', in *Innovation and Productivity in Services*. France: Organisation for Economic Co-operation and Development.

Porter, M. E. (1980). *Competitive Strategy: Techniques for Analyzing Industries and Competitors*. New York: Free Press.

——— (1985). *Competitive Advantage: Creating and Sustaining Superior Performance*. New York: Free Press.

——— (1986). 'Changing Patterns of International Competition', *California Management Review*, XXVII: 9–40.

——— (1998). 'Clusters and the New Economics of Competition,' *Harvard Business Review*, 77: 77–91.

——— (2001a). 'Clusters and Competitiveness: Findings from the Cluster Mapping Project', paper presented at the Corporate Strategies for the Digital Economy conference.

——— (2001b). *Clusters of Innovation: Regional Foundations of U.S. Competitiveness*. Washington, DC: Council on Competitiveness.

Powell, W. W. (1990). 'Neither Market Nor Hierarchy: Network Forms of Organization', in B. M. Staw and L. Cummings (eds.), *Research in Organizational Behavior*. Greenwich, CT, London: JAI Press, pp. 295–336.

——— Koput, K. W., and Smith-Doerr, L. (1996). 'Inter-Organizational Collaboration and the Locus of Innovation: Networks of Learning in Biotechnology', *Administrative Science Quarterly*, 41: 116–45.

——— ——— Bowie, J. I., and Smith-Doerr, L. (2002). 'The Spatial Clustering of Science and Capital: Accounting for Biotech Firm–Venture Capital Relationships', *Regional Studies*, 36: 291–305.

Powers, J. B. and McDougall, P. (2005a). 'University Start-Up Formation and Technology Licensing with Firms that Go Public: A Resource-Based View of Academic Entrepreneurship', *Journal of Business Venturing*, 20: 291–311.

——— ——— (2005b). 'Policy Orientation Effects on Performance with Licensing to Start-Ups and Small Companies', *Research Policy*, 34: 1028–42.

Poyago-Theotoky, J. (1997). 'Research Joint Ventures and Product Innovation: Some Welfare Aspects', *Economics of Innovation and New Technology*, 5: 51–73.

Pralahad, C. K. and Hamel, G. (1990). 'The Core Competence of the Corporation', *Harvard Business Review*, 68: 79–81.

President's Council of Advisors on Science and Technology (PCAST) (2005). *The National Nanotechnology Initiative at Five Years: Assessments and Recommendations of the National Nanotechnology Advisory Panel.* Washington, DC: Executive Office of the President.

Prevezer, M. (1998). 'Clustering in Biotechnology in the USA', in G. M. P. Swann, M. Prevezer, and D. Stout (eds.), *The Dynamics of Industrial Clustering.* Oxford: Oxford University Press.

_____ (2001). 'Ingredients in the Early Development of the U.S. Biotechnology Industry', *Small Business Economics*, 17: 17–29.

Regev, H. (1995). 'Innovation, Skilled Labor, Technology and Performance in Israeli Industrial Firms', *Economics of Innovation and New Technology*, 5: 301–24.

Reilly, K. T. (1995). 'Human Capital and Information', *Journal of Human Resources*, 30: 1–18.

Reinganum, J. (1985). 'Innovation and Industry Evolution', *Quarterly Journal of Economics*, 100: 81–98.

Renault, C. S. (2006). 'Academic Capitalism and University Incentives for Faculty Entrepreneurship', *Journal of Technology Transfer*, 31: 227–39.

Research Triangle Institute (RTI) (1999a). 'Benefit Analysis of IGBT Power Device Simulation Modeling', NIST Planning Report No. 99-3.

_____ (1999b). 'Interoperability Cost Analysis of the U.S. Automobile Supply Chain', NIST Planning Report No. 99-1.

_____ (2000a). 'Changing Measurement and Standards Needs in a Deregulated Electrical Utility Industry', NIST Planning Report No. 00-2.

_____ (2000b). 'Economic Impact of Standard Reference Materials for Sulfer in Fossil Fuels', NIST Planning Report No. 00-1.

_____ (2002a). 'The Economic Impact of the Gas-Mixture NIST-Traceable Reference Materials Program', NIST Planning Report No. 02-04.

_____ (2002b). 'The Economic Impact of Role-Based Access Control', NIST Planning Report No. 02-1.

_____ (2002c). 'The Economic Impacts of Inadequate Infrastructure for Software Testing', NIST Planning Report No. 02-3.

_____ (2004a). 'Cost Analysis of Inadequate Interoperability in the U.S. Capital Facilities Industry', NIST Report No. GCR 04-867.

_____ (2004b). 'Economic Impact of Inadequate Infrastructure for Supply Chain Integration', NIST Planning Report No. 04-2.

_____ (2004c). 'The Impact of Calibration Error in Medical Decision Making', NIST Planning Report No. 04-1.

_____ (2005a). 'Economic Impact Assessment of the International Standard for the Exchange of Product Model Data (STEP) in Transportation Equipment Industries', NIST Planning Report No. 02-5.

_____ (2005b). 'IPv6 Economic Impact Assessment', NIST Planning Report 05-2.

Reuer, J. J. (2000). 'Parent Firm Performance Across International Joint Venture Life-Cycle Stages', *Journal of International Business Studies*, 31: 1–21.

Roberts, E. (1991). *Entrepreneurs in High Technology, Lessons from MIT and Beyond.* Oxford: Oxford University Press.

_____ and Malone, D. E. (1996). 'Policies and Structures for Spinning Off New Companies from Research and Development Organizations', *R&D Management*, 26: 17–48.

Romer, P. M. (1986). 'Increasing Returns and Long Run Growth', *Journal of Political Economy*, 94: 1002–37.

—— (1990). 'Endogenous Technological Change', *Journal of Political Economy*, 98: S71–S102.

Rosenberg, N. and Trajtenberg, M. (2001). 'A General Purpose Technology at Work: The Corliss Steam Engine in the Late 19th Century U.S.', NBER Working Paper No. 8485.

Rosenkranz, S. (1995). 'Innovation and Cooperation under Vertical Product Differentiation', *International Journal of Industrial Organization*, 13: 1–22.

Rothaermel, F. and Thursby, M. C. (2005). 'Incubator Firm Failure or Graduation? Their Role of University Linkages', *Research Policy*, 34: 1076–90.

Sakakibara, M. (1997*a*). 'Heterogeneity of Firm Capabilities and Co-operative Research and Development: An Empirical Examination', *Strategic Management Journal*, 18: 143–64.

—— (1997*b*.) 'Evaluating Government Sponsored R&D Consortia in Japan: Who Benefits and How?', *Research Policy*, 26: 447–73.

Sanchez, R. A. (1993). 'Strategic Flexibility, Firm Organization, and Managerial work in Dynamic Markets: A Strategic-Options Perspective', in P. Shrivastava, A. Huff, and J. E. Dutton (eds.), *Advances in Strategic Management*. Greenwich, CT: JAI Press.

Santoro, M. and Gopalakrishnan, S. (2001). 'Relationship Dynamics between University Research Centers and Industrial Firms: Their Impact on Technology Transfer Activities', *Journal of Technology Transfer*, 26: 163–71.

Savary, L. (1723). *Dictionnaire Universel de Commerce*. Paris.

Saxenian, A. L. (1994). *Regional Advantage*. Cambridge, MA: Harvard University Press.

Schankerman, M. (1981). 'The Effects of Double-Counting and Expensing on the Measured Returns to R&D', *Review of Economics and Statistics*, 63: 454–8.

Scherer, F. M. (1965). 'Invention and Innovation in the Watt–Boulton Steam-Engine Venture', *Technology and Culture*, 6: 165–87.

—— (1982). 'Inter-Industry Technology Flows and Productivity Growth', *Review of Economics and Statistics*, 6: 627–34.

—— (1983). 'R&D and Declining Productivity Growth', *American Economic Review*, 73: 215–18.

Schmookler, J. (1952). 'The Changing Efficiency of the American Economy, 1869–1938', *Review of Economics and Statistics*, 34: 214–31.

Schultz, T. W. (1953). *The Economic Organization of Agriculture*. New York, McGraw-Hill.

Schumpeter, J. A. (1928). 'The Instability of Capitalism', *Economic Journal*, 38: 361–86.

—— (1934). *The Theory of Economic Development*, translated by R. Opie from the 2nd German edition [1926]. Cambridge, MA: Harvard University Press.

—— (1939). *Business Cycles*. New York: McGraw-Hill.

—— (1950). *Capitalism, Socialism and Democracy*, 3rd edn. New York: Harper & Row.

Scott, J. T. (1996). 'Environmental Research Joint Ventures among Manufacturers', *Review of Industrial Organization*, 11: 655–79.

Shane, S. (2003). *A General Theory of Entrepreneurship: The Individual–Opportunity Nexus*. Cheltenham, UK: Edward Elgar.

—— and Stuart, T. (2002). 'Organizational Endowments and the Performance of University Start-Ups', *Management Science*, 48: 154–71.

Sharp, M. (1991). 'The Science of Nations: European Multinationals and American Biotechnology', *Biotechnology*, 1: 132–62.

Shleifer, A. (2000). *Inefficient Markets*. New York: Oxford University Press.

Siegel, D. S. (1994). 'Errors in Output Deflators Revisited: Unit Values and the PPI', *Economic Inquiry*, 32: 11–32.

—— (1997). 'The Impact of Investments in Computers on Manufacturing Productivity Growth: A Multiple-Indicators, Multiple-Causes Approach', *Review of Economics and Statistics*, 79: 68–78.

—— (1999). *Skill-Biased Technological Change: Evidence from a Firm-Level Survey*. Kalamazoo, MI: W.E. Upjohn Institute Press.

—— and Griliches, Z. (1992). 'Purchased Services, Outsourcing, Computers, and Productivity in Manufacturing', in Z. Griliches (ed.), *Output Measurement in the Service Sector* (pp. 429–58). Chicago: University of Chicago Press.

—— Waldman, D., and Youngdahl, W. E. (1997). 'The Adoption of Advanced Manufacturing Technologies: Human Resource Management Implications', *IEEE Transactions on Engineering Management*, 44: 288–98.

—— —— and Link, A. N. (2003). 'Assessing the Impact of Organizational Practices on the Productivity of University Technology Transfer Offices: An Exploratory Study', *Research Policy*, 32: 27–48.

—— Westhead, P., and Wright, M. (2003*a*). 'Assessing the Impact of Science Parks on the Research Productivity of Firms: Exploratory Evidence from the United Kingdom', *International Journal of Industrial Organization*, 21: 1357–69.

—— —— —— (2003*b*). 'Science Parks and the Performance of New Technology-Based Firms: A Review of Recent U.K. Evidence and an Agenda for Future Research', *Small Business Economics*, 20: 177–84.

—— Waldman, D., Atwater, L., and Link, A. N. (2003). 'Commercial Knowledge Transfers from Universities to Firms: Improving the Effectiveness of University–Industry Collaboration', *Journal of High Technology Management Research*, 14: 111–33.

—— —— —— —— (2004). 'Toward a Model of the Effective Transfer of Scientific Knowledge from Academicians to Practitioners: Qualitative Evidence from the Commercialization of University Technologies', *Journal of Engineering and Technology Management*, 21: 115–42.

Simpson, R. D. and Vonortas, N. S. (1994). 'Cournot Equilibrium with Imperfectly Appropriable R&D', *Journal of Industrial Economics*, 42: 79–92.

Sirilli, G. and Evangelista, R. (1998). 'Technological Innovation in Services and Manufacturing: Results from Italian Surveys', *Research Policy*, 27: 881–99.

Small Business Administration (2002). 'The Influence of R&D Expenditures on New Firm Formation and Economic Growth', Maplewood, NJ: BJK Associates.

Soete, L. and Miozzo, M. (1989). 'Trade and Development in Services: A Technological Perspective', Maastricht: MERIT Working Paper No. 89-031.

Sofouli, E. and Vonortas, N. S. (2007). 'S&T Parks and Business Incubators in Middle-Sized Countries: The Case of Greece', *Journal of Technology Transfer*, 32: forthcoming.

Solow, R. M. (1956). 'A Contribution to the Theory of Economic Growth', *Quarterly Journal of Economics*, 70: 65–94.

—— (1957). 'Technical Change and the Aggregate Production Function', *Review of Economics and Statistics*, 39: 312–20.

Solow, R. M. (1960). 'Investment in Technical Progress', in K. J. Arrow (ed.), *Mathematical Methods in the Social Sciences, 1959*. Stanford, CA: Stanford University Press.

Stiroh, K. J. (1998). 'Computers, Productivity, and Input Substitution', *Economic Inquiry*, 36: 175–91.

—— (2001). 'What Drives Productivity Growth?', *FRBNY Economic Policy Review*, 16: 37–59.

Stolarick, K. M. (1999). 'IT Spending and Firm Productivity: Additional Evidence from the Manufacturing Sector', mimeograph.

Stoneman, P. (1983). *The Economic Analysis of Technological Change*. Oxford: Oxford University Press.

Subramani, M. R. and Walden, E. A. (2001). 'The Impact of E-Commerce Announcements on the Market Value of Firms', *Information Systems Research*, 12: 135–54.

Summers, R. and Heston, A. (1988). 'A New Set of International Comparisons of Real Product and Price Levels Estimates for 130 Countries, 1950–1985', *Review of Income and Wealth*, 34: 1–25.

Sundaram, A. K., John, T. A., and John, K. (1996). 'An Empirical Analysis of Strategic Competition: The Case of R&D Competition', *Journal of Financial Economics*, 40: 459–86.

Sundbo, J. (1997). 'Management of Innovation in Services', *The Services Industries Journal*, 17: 432–56.

Suzumura, K. (1992). 'Cooperative and Non-Cooperative R&D in Oligopoly with Spillovers', *American Economic Review*, 82: 1307–20.

Swan, T. W. (1956). 'Economic Growth and Capital Accumulation', *Economic Record*, 32: 334–61.

Swann, G. M. P. (1998). 'Towards a Model of Clustering in High-Technology Industries', in G. M. P. Swann, M. Prevezer, and D. Stout (eds.), *The Dynamics of Industrial Clustering*. Oxford: Oxford University Press.

—— Prevezer, M., and Stout, D. (1998). *The Dynamics of Industrial Clustering*. Oxford: Oxford University Press.

TASC (1997). 'Economic Assessment of the NIST Thermocouple Calibration Program', NIST Planning Report No. 97-1.

—— (1998a). 'Economic Assessment of the NIST Alternative Refrigerants Research Program', NIST Planning Report No. 98-1.

—— (1998b). 'Economic Assessment of the NIST Ceramic Phase Diagram Program', NIST Planning Report No. 98-3.

—— (2000a). 'The Economic Impacts of the NIST Cholesterol Standards Program', NIST Planning Report No. 00-4.

—— (2000b). 'Economic Impact Assessment: NIST-EEEL Laser and Fiberoptic Power and Energy Calibration Services', NIST Planning Report No. 00-3.

—— (2001a). 'The Economic Impacts of NIST's Data Encryption Standard (DES) Program', NIST Planning Report No. 01-2.

—— (2001b). 'Economic Impact Assessment of the NIST's Josephson Volt Standard Program', NIST Planning Report No. 01-2.

Tassey, G. (1982). 'Infrastructure Technologies and the Role of Government', *Technological Forecasting and Social Change*, 21: 163–80.

—— (1997). *The Economics of R&D Policy*, Westport, CT: Quorum.

_____ (2005). 'Underinvestment in Public Good Technology', _Journal of Technology Transfer_, 30: 89–113.

Teece, D. J. (1986). 'Profiting from Technological Innovation: Implication for Integration, Collaboration, Licensing and Public Policy', _Research Policy_, 15: 285–305.

_____ Pisano, G., and Shuen, A. (1997). 'Dynamic Capabilities and Strategic Management', _Strategic Management Journal_, 18: 509–33.

Terleckyj, N. E. (1974). _Effects of R&D on the Productivity Growth of Industries: An Exploratory Study_. Washington, DC: National Planning Association.

_____ (1982). 'R&D and the U.S. Industrial Productivity in the 1970s', in D. Sahal (ed.), _The Transfer and Utilization of Technical Knowledge_. Lexington, MA: D.C. Heath.

Thünen, J. H. von (1850). _The Isolated State_. London: Oxford.

_____ (1960). _The Isolated State in Relation to Agriculture and Political Economy_, vol. 2, translated by B. W. Dempsey, in _The Frontier Wage_. Chicago, IL: Loyola University Press.

Thursby, J. G. and Thursby, M. C. (2002). 'Who Is Selling the Ivory Tower? Sources of Growth in University Licensing', _Management Science_, 48: 90–104.

_____ _____ (2004). 'Are Faculty Critical? Their Role in University Licensing', _Contemporary Economic Policy_, 22: 162–78.

_____ _____ (2005). 'Gender Patterns of Research and Licensing Activity of Science and Engineering Faculty', _Journal of Technology Transfer_, 30: 343–53.

_____ and Kemp, S. (2002). 'Growth and Productive Efficiency of University Intellectual Property Licencing', _Research Policy_, 31: 109–24.

_____ Jensen, R., and Thursby, M. C. (2000). 'Objectives, Characteristics, and Outcomes from University Licensing: A Survey of Major Universities', _Journal of Technology Transfer_, 26: 59–72.

_____ _____ _____ (2001). 'Objectives, Characteristics and Outcomes of University Licensing: A Survey of Major U.S. Universities', _Journal of Technology Transfer_, 26: 59–72.

Toole, A. A. (2003). 'Understanding Entrepreneurship in the U.S. Biotechnology Industry', in D. M. Hart (ed.), _The Emergence of Entrepreneurship Policy: Governance, Start-Ups, and Growth in the U.S. Knowledge Economy_. Cambridge: Cambridge University Press.

Trigeorgis, L. (1996). _Real Options—Managerial Flexibility and Strategy in Resource Allocation_. Cambridge, MA: MIT Press.

Troske, K. (1994). 'Evidence on the Employer Size–Wage Premium from Worker-Establishment Matched Data', U.S. Census Bureau for Economic Studies Working Paper 94–10.

Tushman, M. and Anderson, P. (1986). 'Technological Discontinuities and Organizational Environments', _Administrative Science Quarterly_, 31: 439–65.

UNCTAD (2002). _E-commerce and Development Report 2002_. New York and Geneva, Switzerland: The United Nations.

Usher, A. P. (1954). _A History of Mechanical Inventions_. Cambridge, MA: Harvard University Press.

U.S. Department of Commerce (2003). 'A Survey of the Use of Biotechnology in U.S. Industry', Washington, DC: U.S. Department of Commerce, Technology Administration.

van Reenen, J. (1996). 'The Creation and Capture of Rents: Wages and Innovation in a Panel of U.K. Companies', _Quarterly Journal of Economics_, 111: 195–226.

Vedovello, C. (1997). 'Science Parks and University–Industry Interaction: Geographical Proximity between the Agents as a Driving Force', *Technovation*, 17: 491–502.

Vohora, A., Wright, M., and Lockett, A. (2004). 'Critical Junctures in the Development of University High-Tech Spin-Out Companies', *Research Policy*, 33: 147–75.

von Hippel, E. (1988). *The Sources of Innovation*. New York: Oxford University Press.

Vonortas, N. S. (1994). 'Interfirm Cooperation with Imperfectly Appropriable Research', *International Journal of Industrial Organization*, 12: 413–35.

—— (1999). 'Business Diversification through Research Joint Ventures: The Advanced Technology Program', final report to the Advanced Technology Program, Gaithersburg, MD: NIST.

Wallsten, S. (2000). 'The Effects of Government–Industry R&D Programs on Private R&D: The Case of the Small Business Innovation Research Program', *Rand Journal of Economics*, 31: 82–100.

Weber, M. (1930, originally 1904–05). *The Protestant Ethic and the Spirit of Capitalism*, translated by T. Parsons. New York: Scribner's.

Weisenfeld, U., Reeves, J. C., and Hunck-Meiswinkel, A. (2001). 'Technology Management and Collaboration Profile: Virtual Companies and Industrial Platforms in the High-Tech Biotechnology Industries', *R&D Management*, 31: 91–100.

Welch, F. (1970). 'Education in Production', *Journal of Political Economy*, 78: 35–59.

Wernerfelt, B. (1984). 'A Resource Based View of the Firm', *Strategic Management Journal*, 5: 171–80.

Westhead, P. (1995). 'Survival and Employment Growth Contrasts Between Types of Owner-Managed High-Technology Firms', *Entrepreneurship Theory and Practice*, 20: 5–27.

—— (1997). 'R&D "Inputs" and "Outputs" of Technology-based Firms Located on and off Science Parks', *R&D Management*, 27: 45–61.

—— and Wright, M. (1998). 'Novice, Portfolio and Serial Founders: Are They Different?', *Journal of Business Venturing*, 13: 173–204.

—— and Batstone, S. (1999). 'Perceived Benefits of a Managed Science Park Location for Independent Technology-Based Firms', *Entrepreneurship and Regional Development*, 11: 129–54.

—— and Cowling, M. (1995). 'Employment Change in Independent Owner-Managed High-Technology Firms in Great Britain', *Small Business Economics*, 7: 111–40.

—— and Storey, D. J. (1994). *An Assessment of Firms Located On and Off Science Parks in the United Kingdom*. London: HMSO.

—— —— and Cowling, M. (1995). 'An Exploratory Analysis of the Factors Associated with the Survival of Independent High-Technology Firms in Great Britain', in F. Chittenden, M. Robertson, and I. Marshall (eds.), *Small Firms: Partnerships for Growth*. London: Paul Chapman, pp. 63–99.

Williamson, O. E. (1996a). 'Economics and Organization: A Primer', *California Management Review*, 38: 131–46.

—— (1996b). *The Mechanics of Governance*. Oxford: Oxford University Press.

Wolff, E. N. (1999). 'Specialization and Productivity Performance in Low-, Medium-, and High-Tech Manufacturing Industries', in A. Heston and R. E. Lipsey (eds.), *International and Interarea Comparisons of Prices, Income, and Output*, Studies of Income and Wealth Vol. 61. Chicago University Press (NBER), pp. 419–52.

Wright, M., Lockett, A., Clarysse, B., and Binks, M. (2006). 'University Spin-Out Companies and Venture Capital', *Research Policy*, 35: 481–501.

Zeller, C. (2001). 'Clustering Biotech: A Recipe for Success? Spatial Patterns of Growth of Biotechnology in Munich, Rhineland and Hamburg', *Small Business, Economics*, 17: 123–41.

Zrinyi, J. (1962). 'Entrepreneurial Behavior in Economic Theory: An Historical and Analytical Approach', Ph.D. dissertation, Georgetown University.

Zucker, L. G. and Darby, M. R. (1997). 'Present at the Biotechnological Revolution: Transformation of Technological Identity for a Large Number of Incumbent Pharmaceutical Firms', *Research Policy*, 26: 429–46.

_____ _____ (2001). 'Capturing Technological Opportunity Via Japan's Star Scientists: Evidence from Japanese Firms' Biotech Patents and Products', *Journal of Technology Transfer*, 26: 37–58.

_____ _____ (2007). 'Evolution of Nanotechnology from Science to Firm', *Journal of Technology Transfer*, 31: forthcoming.

_____ _____ and Armstrong, J. S. (1998). 'Geographically Localized Knowledge: Spillovers or Markets?', *Economic Inquiry*, 36: 65–86.

_____ _____ _____ (2000). 'University Science, Venture Capital, and the Performance of U.S. Biotechnology Firms', mimeograph, UCLA.

_____ _____ _____ (2002). 'Commercializing Knowledge: University Science, Knowledge Capture, and Firm Performance in Biotechnology', *Management Science*, 48: 138–53.

_____ _____ and Brewer, M. B. (1998). 'Intellectual Human Capital and the Birth of U.S. Biotechnology Enterprises', *American Economic Review*, 88: 290–306.

☐ INDEX

abnormal stock return 57
Abramovitz, M. 75, 76
absorptive capacity 127
Adams, J. D. 55
adjustment costs 61
aerospace industry 89
agents 3, 172–3
  critical 12
agglomeration 10, 82
Aghion, P. 79
agriculture 15–16, 34
AIDS 133
Aigner, D. J. 134, 135
Alexander, J. 62
Allen, T. 115
allocation of resources 130, 164
America Online 98
American National Standard Code for
  Electricity Metering 159
Ameritech 99
Anand, B. N. 55
Anderson Consulting 98
Anderson, P. 126
Anderson, S. P. 80
Andreessen, Marc 100
antitrust policies/laws 100, 164
applied research 40, 47
appropriability:
  imperfect 81
  limited 100, 151
  returns to investment 154
appropriable assets 44
aptitudes 25
arbitrage 15
Arizona 110
arm's-length markets 9
Armstrong, J. S. 119
ARPANET 98, 99
Arrow, K. 81, 151
ASM (Annual Survey of Manufacturers) 68
Athey, S. 177
Audretsch, D. B. 5, 10, 55, 118, 119, 128
AURIL (Association for University Research
  Industry Links) 108
AURP (Association of University Research
  Parks) 140, 141, 143
Australia 143

AUTM (Association of University Technology
  Managers) 55, 108, 109, 110, 120, 121,
  174
automobile industry 89

B2B (business-to-business) commerce 62,
  63, 100
Bain, J. S. 43
Bakouros, Y. L. 143
Bangalore 142
Barney, J. 43
Barras, R. 87
Barro, R. 80
Bartel, A. P. 64, 65–7
Bartelsman, E. J. 82
basic research 40, 47, 100, 110
  linked to improvements in productivity
   growth 138
  productivity premium associated with 51
Battese, G. 134–5
Baudeau, Abbé Nicholas 15–16, 20
Bauer, L. L. 50, 55
Baumol, W. J. 51, 86
Bayesian rationality 129, 175
Bayh-Dole Act (US 1980) 108, 109, 118, 143
BCFs (biotechnology commercializing
  firms) 7, 8, 9
Beaudry, C. 10
benefit-cost ratio 161, 162
Bentham, Jeremy 16–18, 20
Beranek 98
Bercovitz, J. 112, 120, 126, 130
Berman, E. 65, 67
Berndt, E. R. 60, 65
Bernstein, J. I. 50, 65
Berry, S. T. 80
beta interferon 8
Betts, J. 67
Binswanger, H. P. 33, 34
Biogen 8, 9
bioscience 7–10
biotechnology clusters 9–10
Birley, S. 120, 126
BLS (US Bureau of Labor Statistics) 46
blue-collar labor 67
Blumenthal, D. 120, 133
Blundell, R. 115

Boardman, C. 103, 104
Bolt 98
Boston 143
Bound, J. 65, 67
Boyer, Herbert 8
Bozeman, B. 3, 7, 37, 50, 103, 104
Breschi, S. 10
Bresnahan, T. F. 62, 70, 71, 97–8, 177
Bristol-Myers Squibb 133
browsers 99–100
Brynjolfsson, E. 60, 62, 70, 71, 177
Burnham Institute 10
Bush, George W. 101
Bush, Vannevar 37–40
business cycle fluctuations 78
buyers and sellers 43

Caballero, R. J. 80, 82
Cain, L. P. 33, 34
California 7, 142, 143
    see also University of California
Cambridge (MA) 9, 10
Canada 37, 174
    low returns to IT investment by banks 60
    manufacturing industries 67
    R&D performed in industry 37
    workers with access to computers 67
Cantillon, Richard 14–16, 20, 26
capacity utilization 33
capital 28–9, 50, 80
    computer 60, 62
    demand for 70
    diminishing returns to 78, 79
    external 83
    fixities in 83
    growth of 76
    noncomputer 62
    percentage change in 31
    shares of income distributed to 30, 32
    technical 31, 35, 81, 150
capital asset pricing model 56
capital augmentation 35
capital-to-labor ratio 29
capitalism 20, 22
Carayannis, E. 62
Castells, M. 143
cellular biology 5
Census of Manufacturers 68
CFCs (chlorofluorocarbons) 161
Chandler, A. D. 112
Chapple, W. 121, 128, 130, 136
charismatic leaders 21
Charles River Associates 45

chemicals industry 62
Chennells, L. 69
Chiang, E. P. 55
Chicago School 43–4
China 142
choice models 130
Chordà, I. M. 143
circular flow 22–3, 24
circularity 17
CIS (EU Community Innovation
    Survey) 174
Cisco Systems 62, 64, 98
Clarke, B. R. 110–11
Clarysse, B. 115–16
classification schemes 28–30
Clemons, R. 63
Clinton administration 103
Cobb-Douglas production function 30, 31,
    33, 34, 35, 45, 50, 57, 61, 82, 83, 136
    three factor 62
Cockburn, I. 44, 55
Coelli, T. 134–5
Cohen, S. 8
collaboration 88
    firms with universities 94
    scientific 44
    star university scientists and biotechnology
        firms 119
collective action groups 88
college degrees 70
commercialization 114, 115, 178
    accelerating 109
    advanced 117
    biotechnology 4–10
    faculty participation in 110
    intellectual property 2, 174, 175
    most popular mechanism for 121
    nanotechnology 104
    potential precursor to 120
    R&D results 155
    speedy 116
    success of technical universities in
        facilitating 128
    university technology transfer
        mechanisms 108
compatibility 157
competition 22
    imperfect 33, 81
    obsolete 93
    perfect 30, 32, 77, 78
    Schumpeterian 79
competitive advantage 41, 43, 44, 127
competitive planning 93

competitiveness 36, 152
  international 164
Compustat 46
computers 69, 84
  effects of 70
  external investments in 61
  global network of 97
  inflation-adjusted prices 100
  investment in 60
  technology used to link 98
  training courses 64
  workers who use on the job 67
consumption 97
consumption goods 23
contract management 17, 18
control 16
Cornell Business & Technology Park 142
Corporate Technology Directory 55, 174
cost function 50–1, 61, 65
  dynamic framework 82
cost savings 62, 63
counterfactual evaluation method 158
CPS (Current Population Survey) 68
creative destruction 15, 79
creativity 27
credibility 127
Crepon, B. 51
Crick, F. 8
Crow, M. 37

Daimler-Benz 63
Danilov, V. J. 142
Danish service firms 88
Danzon, P. 63
Darby, M. R. 10, 119, 177
DARPA (Defense Advanced Research Projects
  Agency) 98
Datastream 46
David, P. A. 50
DBFs (dedicated biotechnology firms) 7, 8, 9
  clustering of 10
  San Diego's first 10
DEA (data envelopment analysis) 128, 134,
  135
Debackere, K. 127
Decennial Census (1990) 68
decentralization 62, 70
decision-making 134
  decentralized 71
DeGroof, J. J. 111
DeLong, J. B. 80, 82
demand 10, 70
  entrepreneurship and 14, 20–5

demographic data 68
Demsetz, H. 43
Denny, M. 60
DePalma, A. 80
depreciation 79
development 40, 47
Dictionnaire Universel de Commerce
  (Savary) 14
diffusion process 28
digital packet-switching 98
DigitalThink 64
DiGregorio, D. 115, 120
DIP (distributed innovation process) 88
disclosures 114, 116, 120, 121, 130, 131,
  132
  made public in Federal Register 165
  poor-quality 117
discount rate 156, 161, 162
discrete choice models 80
disembodied shift factor 76
disequilibrating process 21, 22, 93
distribution 22–3
Divisia index 32
DMUs (decision-making units) 134
DNA 5, 8
DoD (US Department of Defense) 98,
  99
Domar, E. D. 33, 77
Doms, M. 61, 69
downsizing 68
Duguet, E. 51
Duke University 112, 120
Dunne, T. 68, 69
dynamic capabilities 43, 44

e-commerce 62, 63
  global 100
econometric issues 65
economic change 22
economic development regional 139
  Schumpeter's theory 22, 25
economic growth 4, 8, 11, 74–85
  one of the major drivers of 101
  regional 2, 138, 139
  services driven 88
  technology-based 149
  transfer of new technologies into products
    for 104
economic liberalism 16
economies of scope 167
education 70, 76, 82
  broad-based 71
  higher 63, 174

efficiency 17, 63
  absolute 128
  DMU 134
  market 16
  R&D 44, 56
efficient markets hypothesis 56
Eisenhardt, K. M. 44
electric energy 159
Eli Lilly 9, 10
e-mail 99
embodiment hypothesis 80
Ensley, M. 117
Entorf, H. 69
entrepreneurship 14–26, 79, 91, 93, 95, 119,
    149–70, 171–9
  academic 120
  commitment 127
  defined 3
  external environment for 116
  infrastructure for 111
  positively correlated to gray market
    activities 126
  science-based 115
  surrogate 121, 126
entry barriers 43
environmental changes 43
equilibrium 22, 23
  highly stylized model 79
equity investment 116
Ernst & Young 7
EU (European Union) 41, 174
Eurostat 174
Evangelista, R. 87, 89
event studies 56–7
exchange 23
experience effects 81
experimentation:
  controlled and random 27
  expenditures 32
externalities 61, 74, 78, 81, 151
  agglomeration 82, 83
  network 98–9
  R&D investments generate 82

Fabricant, S. 76
factor markets 30, 50, 77, 78
factor substitution 23
factor-to-factor ratio 30
factors of production 21, 29, 45
  new combinations of 22
FDA (US Food and Drug Administration) 9
Feldman, M. P. 120
Ferguson, R. 147

financial market failure 151
Fine, C. 63
Fishman, Lillian 10
Fishman, William H. 10
fixed costs 16
flexible work practices 71
Fountain, T. 63
France 16, 47, 61, 67, 69
  research parks 143
Franklin, S. 55, 111, 121
Frascati Manual, The 41
Friedman, J. 114, 121
Fukugawa, N. 147
Furukawa, T. 63

Gallaher, M. P. 90, 91, 93, 96
Gallouj, F. 87–8, 89
GDP (gross domestic product) 128
Genentech 8, 9
Genentech-Eli Lilly 9
general knowledge 44
Generalized Leontief functional form 61
genetic material 5
geometric index 32
Georgia Institute of Technology 127
  Advanced Technology Development
    Center 117
Geraghty, J. 62
Germany 20, 37, 118, 143
  technical universities 128
Gianiodis, P. T. 113, 114, 116, 126
Gibb, M. J. 143
Gilbert, R. J. 80
Gilbert, Walter 8
Gluck, M. E. 120
Goldstein, H. 143
Gompertz pattern 146
Goolsbee, A. 63
Gotlieb, C. 60
government 80, 81
  R&D funded by 45
  roles of 81, 150–8
government laboratories 104
GPTs (general purpose technologies) 11–12,
    61, 62, 84, 97–107
gray market activity 113, 114, 126
Grayson, L. 143
Greece 143
Greenan, N. 61
Greenwood, M. 80
Griffith, R. 115
Griliches, Z. 45, 47, 50, 60, 64, 65, 77, 79, 80,
    83, 84, 86, 138

Grossman, G. 79–80
Guy, I. 143

H-form (holding company form) 112
Hagedoorn, J. 52
Halevy, E. 17
Hall, B. H. 50
Hall, P. 143
Haltiwanger 69
Harrod, R. 77
Harvard School 43
Harvard University 9
health 63
Hébert, R. F. 3, 14
Helpman, E. 79–80
Henderson, R. 44, 55
Hercovitz, Z. 80
Hertzfeld, H. 55
Heshmati, A. 51
Heston, R. 80
Hicks, J. R. 33
hierarchies 9
historicists 20, 21
Hitt, L. M. 60, 62, 63, 70, 71, 177
Hmieleski, K. 117
homeworking 71–2
Hong Kong 142
Howitt, P. 79
HTML/HTTP document format/retrieval
    protocol 99, 100
human capital 80, 118
    importance as spillover mechanism 82
Humulin 9
Hybritech 10

IAB (Internet Activities Board) 99, 100
IASP (International Association of Science
    Parks) 139
IBM 88
ICCB (Internet Configuration Control
    Board) 99, 100
Ichniowski 177
ICT (information and communication
    technology) 63
IDC 100
idyllic state 22
IMEC 115
incentive systems 114–15
incubators 108, 109, 116, 117, 126, 127, 138,
    150, 177–9
India 142
industrial organization 43
inexcludability 90

inflation 46, 100
information 27, 93
    ability to collect and process 16
    asymmetry 174
    communication across networked
        computers 98
    cost of transmission 100
    embedded 28
    imperfect 151
    sharing 151, 156
    speed of delivery 100
    see also IT
infrastructure 80, 102, 104
    entrepreneurship 111
    network 99
    see also technology infrastructure
innovation 171–9
    fundamental concepts of 27–35
    government's role in 150–8
    importance of knowledge as a source of
        78
    manufacturing sector firms 90–2
    process 3, 47
    product 3, 28, 30, 47, 119
    service sector 86–96
    wage implications of 67
innovation complementarities 98
inspiration 27
institutional factors 81
institutions 3, 20
    agents versus 172–3
    bridging 98, 100
    critical 12
    efficiency in providing technology
        150
    interconnected 37
    property-based 138, 177
    self-governance 99
    technology-based 173
intangibles 88, 90
Intel 64
intellectual capital 93, 94
intellectual property 100, 139
    commercialization of 2, 174, 175
    expenditure on protection 116
    imperfect protection of 81
    policies 110
    restrictions over 113
    university administrators would like to
        benchmark 177
    university ownership and management
        of 109
intellectual property rights 156

intelligence 16
Internet 12, 61, 62, 63, 74, 84, 97–100
  economic benefits from 62
interoperability 88, 157
IPOs (initial public offerings) 116
IRR (internal rate of return) 161–2
ISOC (Internet Society) 99, 100
ISPs (Internet Service Providers) 98, 100
Israel 68
IT (information technology) 46, 83, 88, 96
  and firm performance 57–64
  productivity and 60–1
  rapid diffusion of 74
  R&D and worker performance 64–72
  specialized 45
Italy 50, 51, 143
IWGN (Interagency Working Group on
  Nanotechnology) 102, 103

Jaffe, A. B. 80, 153
Japan 37, 47, 63, 119, 174
  science parks 142, 147
Jensen, R. 114
job creation 68, 146
Johns Hopkins University 112, 120
Joint Research and Development Act (US
  1984) 164
joint ventures 118, 164
  see also RJVs
Jones, C. I. 80
Jorgenson, D. W. 60, 79, 83

Kamien, M. I. 35
key scientists 9
Khanna, T. 55
KIBSs (knowledge-intensive business
  services) 88
Kleiner Perkins 8
Klette, T. J. 79, 80
Knight, F. H. 19
know-how 81
  commercial 121
  scientific and technological 127
knowledge 86, 92, 93
  ability to collect and process 16
  codified 9
  commercialization of 128
  creation of 151
  general 44
  growth in the stock of 76
  importance as a source of innovation 78
  leadership and 25
  new and unapplied 7

scientific 24, 27, 40, 90
technical/technological 45, 90, 161, 165,
  167
technology as the physical representation
  of 27
transfer of 127
see also tacit knowledge
knowledge-based firms 128, 139
Koput, K. W. 44
Kornberg, A. 8
Kramarz, F. 69
Krueger, A. B. 67
Krusell, P. 80
Kuznets, S. 77

labor 28–9, 50, 62, 80
  clerical 63
  computer 60
  fixities in 83
  growth of 76
  outsourcing to developing countries 71
  percentage change in 31
  shares of income distributed to 30, 32
labor augmentation 35
labor composition:
  changes/shifts in 65, 68, 69, 70
  overall impact of trade on 70
labor demand curves 67–8
labor markets 68
  important IT-induced changes in 71
  improved outcomes for women 71
labor mobility 81, 82
Lach, S. 114, 131
Lafrance, J. C. 5
landowners 15
LANs (local-area networks) 99
leaders 25
learning by doing 81
Lehman, D. 7
Lehman, E. E. 118, 128
Lerner, J. 55
Leyden, D. P. 50, 146
licensing 108, 110, 112, 114, 128
  poor central administration support
    for 116
  revenue subject to increasing returns
    121
  royalty fees 120
  university revenues from 109
Lichtenberg, F. R. 45, 46, 47, 50, 60, 61, 64,
  65–7
life insurance 18
Lindelof, P. 142, 147

Link, A. N. 3, 7, 14, 33, 35, 40, 44, 46, 47, 50, 52, 55, 74, 90, 91, 93, 96, 110, 113, 114, 117, 118, 121, 127, 128, 138, 141, 142, 143, 146, 151, 153, 158, 159, 161, 165, 176
Litan, R. 62, 98
location 118
Lockett, A. 55, 111, 113, 116, 121, 127
Lofsten, H. 142, 147
Loof, H. 51
Louis, K. S. 120
Lovell, C. A. K. 134, 135
LRD (Longitudinal Research Database) 68
Lucas, R. E. 79, 82
Luger, M. 143
Lynch, L. M. 67–8
Lyons, R. K. 82

M-form (multidivisional form) 112
McAfee, P. 62
Macau 142
McDougall, P. 116
McGuckin, P. 61
Machin, S. 67, 69
Machlup, F. 27
macroeconomics 79
McWilliams, A. 56
Mairesse, J. 47, 51, 61
Maital, S. 55
Malaysia 142
Malone, D. E. 111, 120
management 24, 70–1
  decentralized 127
  difference between entrepreneurship and 19
  more efficient 62
  static 25
  supply chain 63
Mankiw, G. 80
Mansfield, E. 47, 138
manufacturing industry 60, 61, 67, 86, 93
  innovation in 90–2
  R&D 94
Mardas, D. C. 143
marginal costs 32, 78, 154
market development 92
market failure 151, 154, 155
market imperfections 100
market opportunities 100
market power 151
  exploiting 43
Markman, G. 112, 113, 114, 115, 116, 126, 130, 132

Martin, J. A. 44
Martin, S. 98, 151
Maryland 7
Mason, E. 43
Massachusetts 7
  see also Boston; Cambridge; MIT
means of production 23
'measure of ignorance' 76
measurement errors 46, 61
Medda, G. 47, 50, 51
Meeusen, W. 134
Merges, R. P. 55, 126
MERIT-CATI (Maastricht Economic Research Institute on Innovation and Technology-Cooperative Agreements & Technology Indicators) 55
Meseri, O. 55
Metcalfe, S. 37
MFS Bell 99
Microsoft Internet Explorer 100
Minasian, J. 47
Miozzo, M. 87
Mishel, L. 65
MIT (Massachusetts Institute of Technology) 9, 98, 111, 126
molecular biology 5
molecular electronics 101
Montreal Protocol (1987) 161
Moray, N. 115–16
Moroney, J. R. 33, 34
Morrison, C. J. 60, 65, 82
Morrison, C. 50, 66, 69
mortality 18
Mosaic 99–100
Motorola 64
Mowery, D. C. 84, 97, 98, 99, 126
multimedia documents 99
multinational companies 71
multi-skilled workers 67
multi-tasking 71
Mustar, P. 111–12, 113, 120, 126, 130
MX-form (matrix form) 112

Nadiri, M. I. 50
Nagarajan, R. 63
nanoelectronics 115
nanotechnology 12, 84, 97, 101–5
Nanotechnology Research and Development Act (US 2003) 101, 102–3, 104
National Bureau of Economic Research 77
National Center for Supercomputing Applications 99–100
National Income and Product Accounts 77

national innovation system 37
National Nanotechnology Initiative Strategic Plan (2004) 104, 105
National Research Council 101
NCRA (National Cooperation Research Act, US 1984) 108, 143, 163–5
  NCRA-RJV (Research Joint Venture) 55
NCRPA (National Cooperative Research and Production Act, US 1993) 165
Nelson, R. R. 37, 64, 75, 78, 126, 133
neoclassical economics 30, 77, 79, 80
Nerkar, A. 126
Netherlands 143
Netscape 100
network effects 81
networks:
  bilateral and multilateral 88
  computer 98, 99
  corporate 99
  first killer application for 99
  high-speed communication 100
  information 87
  strategic 172
  see also social networks
new growth theory 79–81, 81–2
New York 142
New York University 131
Newberry, D. M. G. 80
Newman (BBN) 98
NGOs (nongovernmental organizations) 133
Nicolaou, N. 120, 126
NIST (US National Institute of Standards and Technology) 151–2, 158, 159, 161
  ATP (Advanced Technology Program) 55, 108, 174
NLS (National Longitudinal Survey) 68
NNI (National Nanotechnology Initiative) 101–2, 103, 104–5
nonparametric methods 128, 134
Nordhaus, W. 86
norms:
  institutional 110
  local group 120
  social 111
North Carolina 7, 110
  Biotechnology Center 5
  Research Triangle Park 142, 143
Novartis 133
NPV (net present value) 161–3
NSF (US National Science Foundation) 40, 41, 98, 99, 100, 142

CORE (COoperative REsearch)
  data-set 55, 128, 174
  Research Centers 108
NSFNET 99
NSTC (National Science and Technology Council) 102, 104
  NSET (Nanoscale Science, Engineering, and Technology) subcommittee 103

obligational contracts 157
Odagiri, H. 47
OECD (Organization for Economic Co-operation and Development) 40
Office of Management and Budget 162, 163
Office of Standard Weights and Measures 152
oil price shocks 78
old growth theory 77–9
Oliner, S. 60
Olofsson, C. 147
Omnibus Trade and Competitiveness Act (US 1988) 152
Onesource 46
online purchasing 100
opportunistic behavior 151, 156, 157
opportunity costs 115, 130, 162
opportunity recognition 127
Oracle 98
Organic Act (US 1901) 152
organizational change 62, 71
  relationship between technical and 70
organizational forms 112
O'Shea, R. 115
Osorio-Urzua, J. 63
Osterman, P. 67–8
OSTP (White House Office of Science and Technology Policy) 102, 103
output 29, 46, 76
  mismeasurement of 33
  observable market 56
  source of growth per unit of labor 76
outsourcing 62, 69, 70, 95
  high-skilled labor to developing countries 71
ozone layer damage 161

Pacific Bell 99
Panopticon 17
paradigm activities 12
parametric approaches 128
Paris 15
Park, K. S. 67
Parsons, D. J. 60

patents 55, 81, 133, 146, 147
  broad scope 126
  citations 114
  linking to new-firm creation 126
  number granted 119
  service sector 90
path dependency 43, 115, 157, 175
Patterson, D. G. 33, 34
Paugh, J. 5
Paul, C. J. M. 50, 66, 69, 71, 82
Pavitt, K. 87
PCAST (President's Council of Advisers on Science and Technology) 103, 104–5
Penn State University 112
Pennsylvania 7
Penrose, E. T. 43
perception of opportunity 93, 94
perceptiveness 27
performance:
  enhancing 74
  financial 55
  firm 28–9, 52–64
  understanding 76
  worker 64–72
personal computers 99
petroleum industry 62
Petrusa, J. E. 90, 91, 93, 96
Phan, P. 113, 114, 116, 126, 142
pharmaceutical companies/industry 8, 9, 63
Phelps, E. S. 64
Phillimore, J. 143
Physiocrats 15, 16
Piga, C. 47, 50, 51
Pisano, G. 43
Porter, M. E. 9, 10, 43, 44
Powell, W. W. 44
Powers, J. B. 116
predatory behavior 43
Prennushi, G. 177
Prevezer, M. 6–7
price discrimination 81
price indexes 46
price takers 30
prices 22
  adjusted for improvements in quality 46
  computer 100
  output 78
  relative 77
principal-agent decisions 175
PRIs (Public Research Institutes) 115–16
prisons 17–18
private hurdle rate 154–5, 158, 169

problem-solving skills 71
Prodigy 98
producer behavior markets 77
product differentiation 80
product enhancement 30
product life cycle 89
production 15–16, 22–33, 97
  creation of new methods of 21
  effect/impact of technological change on 28, 31
  marginal cost of 78
production functions 24, 28, 29, 44, 46, 80, 121, 150
  aggregate 30, 32, 76, 77, 79
  estimated at industry level 60
  invariant 23
  see also Cobb-Douglas
productivity 18
  ability to elicit maximum 21
  enhancing 177
  gains in 63, 80
  global slowdown of 51
  Internet-related 62, 63
  IT and 60–1
  marginal 46
  measurement of 128, 134–7
  multi-skilled workers in manufacturing 67
  relative 177
  research 119, 147
productivity growth 67, 81, 86
  computers' impact on 84
  determinants of 76
  impact of computers on 61
  IT uncorrelated with 60
  R&D and 47, 50, 51, 52
  residually measured 34
  services important role in 88
  slowdown 78
  Solow's study of 76
  see also TFP
profit maximization 30, 51
profitability 147
  accounting 55
  potential future 56
profits 18, 20, 154
  excess 43
property rights 151
prospect theory 129, 175
Protestant ethic 22
provosts 146
PSID (Panel Study of Income Dynamics) 68
public goods 149, 150, 151, 153, 165, 166–7, 169

public policy 31–2, 47, 52, 143, 151
public policy appropriate, design of 151
  primary objective of 74
public sector infratechnologies 158–63
public-private partnerships 100, 138, 150,
  163–9, 173

quality 62
  costless improvements in 46
quality assurance 152

R&D (research and development) 28, 79, 86,
  93
  applied 153, 165, 167
  automated 5
  collecting information on outputs and
    outcomes of 173
  complementarity between public and
    private 174
  corporate, parks failed due to restraints
    on 142
  dimensions of 36–40
  economics of 11, 74–85
  encouragement and fostering of joint
    ventures 164
  expenditures positive 146
  firm performance and 41–52
  firms have little incentive to invest in
    78
  high technical risk associated with 151
  impact of investments on productivity
    growth 31
  in house 94
  information technology and worker
    performance 64–72
  initiatives to foster cooperation 98
  measuring the productivity of 89
  productivity gains to labor from 80
  regions with higher levels of 128
  returns to 31, 32, 36, 44, 47, 50, 51, 52
  strong focus on 104
  underinvestment in 154, 155, 158, 170
  world-class 104
R&D expenditures 31, 40, 142–3
  duplicative 167
  nanotechnology-related 101
  self-financed 35
R&E (US Research and Experimentation) tax
  credit 32, 41, 143
radicalness 126
rates of return 57
  excess 45
  expected private 155

marginal private 154
net private 158–9
to R&D 51
see also IRR
rationalization 22
RBSOs (research-based spin-offs) 111,
  113
RBV (resource based view) 43, 44, 52, 113,
  126, 127, 129, 175
Real National Accounts 80
Recombinant Capital 55, 174
Rees, J. 44, 50
REFPROP (refrigerant properties)
  program 161
Regev, H. 68
regression market index model 57
regulatory policies 100
Reilly, K. T. 67
Reinganum, J. 80
religious imperatives 22
rents 15–16
reputations 111
research 76
  collaborative 50, 108
  contract 50
  cooperative partnerships 143
  defense 98
  multidisciplinary 156
  unique facilities not generally available
    156
Research and Development Joint Ventures
  Act (US 1983) 164
research institutes/centers 7, 99, 150
research laboratories 37, 102
  federal 98
research parks 12, 98, 138–48, 177–9
  managed and nonmanaged 178
research partnerships 173–4
  and firm performance 52–7
residuals 31, 33
resources and capabilities 43–4, 113, 127
returns to scale 33
  constant 32, 76, 77, 78
  decreasing 128
  increasing 78, 81
reverse product cycle 87
rewards 115
risks 20, 100
  market 15, 16, 92, 94, 95, 151, 155
  systematic 57
  technical 94, 95, 151, 155, 167
  uninsurable 19
Rivlin, A. 62, 98

RJVs (research joint ventures) 50, 52, 128, 163, 165, 167, 172, 173, 174
   subsidies for 108
Roberts, E. 111, 120
Roco, Mihail 102–3
Romer, D. 80
Romer, P. M. 79, 81
Roosevelt, F. D. 37
Rosenberg, N. 98
Rosenblum, L. S. 60, 65
Rothaermel, F. 117, 127
Route 128 phenomenon 143
royalty payments 120, 127
   distribution formula 115, 176
   flows 116
   revenues 114
Russian Federation 37
Ruttan, V. W. 33, 34

Sala-i-Martin, X. 80
Salk Institute 10
San Diego biotechnology area 10
San Francisco 8, 9, 10
Sargent, T. 79
savings rate 78
Saxenian, A. L. 143
SBIR (US Small Business Innovation Research) program 55, 104, 173, 174
SBTC (skill-biased technological change) 64, 65
scale economies 82, 167
   biased estimates of 83
Schankerman, M. 45, 114, 131
Scherer, F. M. 28, 45, 47
Schering-Plough 8, 9
Schmidt, P. 134, 135
Schmitz, J. 68, 69
Schmoller, Gustav 20–1
Schumpeter, J. A. 11, 14, 15, 20, 22–5, 26, 28, 79, 91, 149
Schwartz, N. L. 35
science 7, 90, 92
   bridging the intellectual gap between technology and 9
Science and Engineering Indicators, 2002 (National Science Board) 142
Science Citation Index 55, 174
science parks 138, 139–40, 142, 146, 147, 150
   support for 108
   see also research parks

Scott, J. T. 55, 74, 98, 117, 128, 141, 142, 143, 146, 151, 153, 158, 161
S-C-P (structure-conduct-performance) paradigm 43
Scripps Research Institute 10
SDOAA (Standards Development Organization Advancement Act, US 2004) 165
Securities Data Company 55, 174
selectivity 116
self-interest 18
semi-skilled workers 69
service sector innovation 86–96
servicization 89
SFE (stochastic frontier estimation) 121, 128, 134–5
Shane, S. 115, 120, 126
Sharpe, Phillip 8
Shaw, K. 177
Shleifer, A. 56
Shuen, A. 43
Sichel, D. 60
Siegel, D. S. 33, 46, 47, 50, 51, 52, 56, 60, 61, 62, 68, 69, 70, 71, 74, 82, 110, 112, 113, 114, 118, 121, 127, 132, 138, 142, 146, 147, 176, 177
Siemens 88
Silberman, J. 114, 121
Silicon Valley 8, 143
Simcoe, T. 84, 97, 98, 99
simultaneity 65
Singapore 142
Sirilli, G. 87, 89
skilled workers 64, 65, 67, 69
Smith, Adam 16, 77
Smith-Doerr, L. 44
SMT (US Survey of Manufacturing Technology) 68–9
social change 22
social costs 156, 158
social network theory 175
social networks 120, 126, 176–7
sociology 22
Soete, L. 87
Sofouli, E. 143
software 97, 98
Solow, R. M. 30, 32, 76, 77, 78–9, 80
Solow residual 31, 33
Sombart, Werner 21
South Africa 133
South Korea 37, 67, 142
spillover evaluation method 158

spillover gap 154
spillovers 10, 74, 81–4, 97–107, 117, 118, 156, 167
  geographically localized 119
  regional 128
  success of technical universities in facilitating 128
spin-offs 9, 98, 112, 118, 146
  research-based 111, 113
spinouts 116, 120, 126
  reasons for and consequences of 127
Sprint 99
SPRU (Science Policy Research Unit) 69
SRPs (strategic research partnerships) 52–6, 57
standards 100
  and protocols 98
Stanford Research Park 142
Stanford University 98, 120, 126
star scientists 119
Starkey, K. 55
start-ups 111, 121
  entrepreneurial 113
  formation of 112, 113, 115
  fostering the creation of 138
  key determinants of 120
  networks that help generate 126
  university-based 108
  young high-technology 118
stationary state situation 21
Statistics Canada 174
steady-state growth 78
Stephan, P. E. 10
Stern, S. 44, 177
Stiroh, K. 60, 83
stock price effect 56
Stolarick, K. M. 61
Stoneman, P. 33
Storey, D. J. 146, 147
Stoto, M. A. 120
strategic alliances 10, 172
strategic innovation paradigm 88
strategic planning 91, 92, 93, 95
Streitwieser, M. 61
structural contingency theory 175
STTR (Small Business Technology Transfer) program 104
stylized facts 56
subsidies:
  RJV 108
  targeted 98
substitution patterns 82

Summers, L. H. 80, 82
Sun Microsystems 98
Sundbo, J. 88
supply 10, 20
  entrepreneurship and 14–16
supply chains 63
  virtual 62
sustainability 127
Swan, T. 77
Swann, G. M. P. 10
Swanson, Robert 8
Sweden 51, 142, 147
synergies 142
systems integration 94, 95

tacit knowledge 9, 10
Taiwan 142
Tassey, G. 45, 50, 90, 91, 153
tax credit 32, 41, 143
TCP/IP (transmission control protocol/Internet protocol) 98–9, 100
technical progress 60, 76
technical universities 128
technological change 7, 28, 64, 71, 80, 171–9
  capital-saving 29
  costless improvements in quality due to 46
  described 3, 4
  disembodied 32, 33
  endogenous 81
  exogenous 81
  Harrod neutral 33
  Hicks neutral 32, 33, 34
  impact on production 31
  innovation as a source for 78
  labor-saving 29
  method for assessing the rate of 76
  models of 30–1
  neutral 29
  nonneutrality of 65, 67
  organizational changes accompanying 62
  phases in the process of 28
  proxies for 64, 65
  rapid 44
  services important role in 88
  Solow neutral 33
  treated as endogenous factor of growth 79
  underlying force for productivity growth 76
  wage and employment shifts linked to 67
technological gatekeepers 44
technological lock-in 157

technological spillovers 81–4
  and general purpose technologies 97–107
technology 7, 27
  advanced manufacturing 68
  bridging the intellectual gap between
    science and 9
  chemical and computer 5
  described 3–4
  development of 90–1
  enabling 97
  established 43
  generic 91, 92, 100
  impact on shifts in labor composition 70
  licensing 55, 95, 121
  marginal productivity of investments in 46
  proprietary 91
  purchasing 95
  sharing 158
  specialized 87
technology infrastructure 91, 92, 94, 149–51,
    158–69
  high costs of creating 100
  key 99
technology parks 117
technology transfer 12, 105, 108–37, 141,
    174–7
  commercialization of intellectual property
    through 2
  faculty involvement in 172, 176
  property-based institutions that
    facilitate 138
  successful 157, 175
  see also TTOs; UITT
Teece, D. J. 43, 157
telecommunications industry 67–8
  incumbent firms 100
Terleckyj, N. E. 47, 50
TFP (total factor productivity) growth 31,
    33, 45, 46, 50, 55, 61, 73
  residually measured 77
Thailand 142
thick market effects 82
Thisse, J.-F. 80
Thünen, J. H. von 18–20
Thursby, J. G. 114, 121
Thursby, M. C. 114, 117, 121, 127
TMTs (top management teams) 117
Toole, A. A. 5, 6, 50
trade secrets 90
Trajtenberg, M. 97–8
transactions costs 130
  savings on 62
transparency 63

transportation costs 15
Troske, K. R. 68, 69
trucking industry 63
trust management 17–18
TTOs (technology transfer offices) 52, 109,
    112–14, 115, 116, 118, 121, 126, 127–8,
    129–30, 131, 132, 172, 173, 175–7
Tufts University School of Medicine 10
turnover 22
Tushman, M. 126

U-Form (unitary form) 112
UCSD (University of California at San
    Diego) 10
UITT (university-industry technology
    transfer) 52, 55, 178
UKSPA (United Kingdom Science Park
    Association) 139, 141, 142
uncertainty 155, 159
UNCTAD (UN Conference on Trade and
    Development) 100
underinvestment 150, 151, 154, 155, 156,
    158, 170
UNESCO (UN Educational, Scientific and
    Cultural Organization) 140, 141
UNICO (University Companies
    Association) 108
United Kingdom 67, 68, 69, 108
  relative performance in technology transfer
    across universities 128
  resources and capabilities of TTOs 113
  science/research parks 142, 143, 146
  venture capital in university spin-offs 111
United States 4, 67, 68, 108, 127, 159, 161
  creation and location of new biotechnology
    firms 119
  economic growth 76
  national innovation system 37, 98
  R&D 37, 40, 57
  research parks 138, 141, 142, 143, 146
  research universities 109
  service sector 86
  see also under entries prefixed 'US'
universities 7, 8, 9, 12, 98, 99, 108–37
  collaboration with 94
  engines of regional economic growth 2
  see also research parks; technology transfer;
    UITT
University of California:
  Berkeley 126, 133
  San Francisco 9
  see also UCSD
University of Illinois 100

University of North Carolina at Chapel
    Hill 131
unskilled workers 69
US Census Bureau 68, 105
    Center for Economic Studies 174
US Department of Commerce 5, 6
    see also NIST
US Department of Justice 165
US Department of the Treasury 152
US House of Representatives 164
US National Institutes of Health 120
Usher, A. P. 28
usury 16–17
utility 15

value added 92, 147
Van den Broeck, J. 134
Van Reenen, J. 68, 69, 115
Varsakelis, N. C. 143
Vedovello, C. 143
venture capital 111
Venture Economics 55, 174
vertical integration 9
    quasi 63
Veugelers, R. 127
Vienna Circle 22
Vienna Convention (1985) 161
Vohora, A. 127
Vonortas, N. S. 52, 55, 143

wage differentials 68
wage premiums 67, 71
    highest 69
    technological 69
wages 18, 68
    gender gap in 71

positive correlation between technology
    usage and 69
relative 65
Waldman, D. 52, 70, 110, 113, 114, 118, 121,
    176
Wallsten, S. 55
Watson, J. 8
Watt-Boulton venture 28
weavers 21–2
Weber, Max 21–2
WECD (Worker-Establishment Characteristic
    Database) 68, 69
Weil, D. N. 80
Weinstein, O. 88, 89
Welch, F. 64
Wernerfelt, B. 43
Westhead, P. 146, 147, 178
white-collar workers 68
Williamson, O. 112
Windows 100
WIRS (Workplace Industrial Relations Survey
    1984) 69
Wol, E. N. 51
women 71–2
World Wide Web 97, 99, 100
    distinct periods in creation of 98
    speedy access to 100
Wright, M. 55, 111, 113, 116, 121, 127, 142,
    147, 178

Yale University 133
Youngdahl, W. E. 70

Zerit 133
Zmud, R. B. 50, 91
Zucker, L. G. 10, 119, 177

Printed and bound by CPI Group (UK) Ltd, Croydon, CR0 4YY

Printed in the United States
By Bookmasters